To Jean & Tom

With my very sincere good wishes

Ray Stubbs

BOURNEMOUTH

APRIL 1995.

Prisoner of Nippon

Courtesy of Lieut J. Wallace Kemp, RN

July 1940

September 1940

November 1945

Ray Stubbs

Prisoner of Nippon

Ray S Stubbs

A Square One Publication

First published in 1995 by
Square One Publications,
The Tudor House
Upton upon Severn, Worcs WR8 0HT

British Library Cataloguing in Publication Data

Stubbs, Raymond S.
  Prisoner of Nippon
  I. Title
  940.547252092

  ISBN 1 872017 88 6

*Typeset in Times 11 on 12 pt by Avon Dataset Ltd, Waterloo Road,
Bidford-on-Avon, B50 4JH
Printed by Antony Rowe Ltd of Chippenham, England*

Chapters and Appendices

List of Appendices

Illustrations

Acknowledgements

I have been so grateful for good friends, both as a Prisoner of War, and since. I was one of the lucky ones who thereby found the will to live, and later, the nourishment to challenge and overcome the memory of that nightmare existence.

This book is founded on my personal recollections and could not have been undertaken without the considerable help and assistance rendered by many people.

Neither would it be complete without the many illustrations and contributions from so many who shared those violent years in the Far East. I am greatly indebted to all who have assisted my memory and shared my commentary.

It is not possible to mention them all by name, but I would like to record and thank Captain Philip Reid RN (Retd), OBE, ex-Telegraphist Johnnie MacMillan, Ex-Chief Petty Officer Charlie Rogers, Lieut Frank Brewer, CMG, OBE, and other inmates of the POW camps in Palembang for stirring their memories, Lieut-Cdr J. C. W. Kemp, Private Peter Bivand, and Ronald Searle for their excellent drawings, Sir Sam Falle, KCMG, KCVO, DSC for so kindly writing the Foreword, ex-Telegraphist Robert Steel (dec) and other old shipmates on HMS Encounter, for their assistance. I also am indebted to Terence Kelly and Geoffrey Brooke for allowing me to reproduce some of their photographs.

The archives of the Public Record Office, the Admiralty, the Commonwealth War Graves Commission, and the British Red Cross Society have all made a significant contribution.

The constructive criticism of the Newbury Town Saturday Afternoon Writers' Group has encouraged and helped to no small degree.

Above all, the home comforts provided by my dear wife have rendered the whole effort possible. She provided care and understanding, love and comfort, in place of hatred and bare existence. Meeting her was the luckiest stroke of all.

Foreword by
Sir Sam Falle, KCMG, KCVO, DSC

It is with great pleasure that I write a few words to introduce Ray Stubbs' fascinating book. I feel myself greatly honoured to be asked to do this because Ray and I were shipmates in *HMS Encounter* in the early 1940s, and we both later fell into the hands of the Japanese. *Encounter* is not the main subject of Ray's book and he had left her before she met her fate in the Battle of the Java Sea, which resulted in my becoming also a "Prisoner of Nippon".

Nevertheless, *Encounter* deserves a mention, because that is where Ray's and my respective adventures started, and because that little ship, a 1934 1300-ton destroyer and her ship's company symbolise so much that is remarkable in the British people. We were 170 men, from all walks of life, aged between 18 and 40, cooped up in this little tin can that rolled 30 degrees either way and stood on its head when it pitched; immeasurable discomfort, constant danger,and endless monotony. Add to that the ever-present worry about families in Britain during the bombing. In spite of all this those 170 men displayed courage, endurance, comradeship and, above all, humour that had to be experienced to be believed.

Ray Stubbs was not long turned 20 when he joined *Encounter* as a Coder. The Coder was an important member of the Signals department and the name describes the job. I remember him clearly as a tall young man, always smartly turned out. Ray survived the tough experience of life on the lower deck with courage and good humour, making friends along the way. I have no direct knowledge of his life in Sumatra because we were not then together, but I do know what it was like to be a POW. It was grim, humiliating, and at times terrifying. We were usually hungry and often sick, but the worst ordeal was the uncertainty. The Japanese did not recognise the Geneva convention and regarded POWs as less than human, to be used as forced labour, or disposed of at will. A Japanese preferred death to surrender and would not allow himself to be taken prisoner, or so the legend goes. There was something in it. This meant that we never knew when our captors would decide to kill us. Furthermore, they tended to beat us up when the spirit moved them, and attempted escape was dealt with by beheading.

Ray endured all that and has since had a happy and successful life, shared with a fine wife and family. I commend this book unreservedly as a tribute especially to the author himself, but also to the men of Britain, who ensured our ultimate victory.

Sam Falle

Sam Falle was Second Lieutenant on HMS Encounter.
After leaving the Royal Navy, he served as Ambassador in Kuwait, and Sweden, and as High Commissioner in Singapore and Nigeria.

Introduction

The third day of September, 1939, was an unforgettable day, in many lives, the whole world over.

The Civil Defence Control Room at the rear of the Town Hall, in Old Street, Shoreditch, was hushed. The clock on the wall showed the hour of eleven. We listened intently to the radio.

"This morning," said the Prime Minister, "the British Ambassador in Berlin, handed the German Government a final note, stating that, unless we heard from them by 11 o'clock, that they were prepared, at once, to withdraw their troops from Poland, a state of war would exist between us. I have to tell you now that no such undertaking has been received, and that consequently, this country is at war with Germany."

The strident clang of the telephone in front of me broke the silence inside. Outside, beyond the sandbags, and plywood window covers, the intermittent wail of the air raid sirens was fading in the bright September sunlight.

In this autumn of unpreparedness, what was to happen to us all? Perhaps it was as well we didn't know.

The 'phoney war' dragged on through winter into spring.

It was early summer when the buff envelope dropped on the mat at our house in North London. I was to report for a medical examination at the Territorial Drill Hall at Mill Hill.

A1, and selected for the Royal Navy, which pleased me intensely, I left home on 10th July 1940, with my Dad, and the current girl-friend, to make my way to King's Cross. My mother stayed at home, struggling with her innermost thoughts.

Butlin's Holiday Camp at Skegness, now functioning under its new title, HMS Royal Arthur, was the transition from civilian to service life. The wheels were set in motion.

Chief Petty Officer 'Daisy' Bell had the daunting task of converting this motley crowd of 'Hostility Only' labels into disciplined ratings.

We made new acquaintances, we were kitted up, we drilled, we learned of our new assignment as Coders, a fresh grade of rating to assist in the communications branch.

And so, exactly 3 months later, after brief spells at HMS Wellesley (Liverpool) and HMS Pembroke (Chatham), I found myself, still wet behind the ears, en route to Liverpool again, to join one of His Majesty's destroyers.

There was no chance to say any 'goodbyes'. One weekend leave, and one short spell of embarkation leave, in the middle of London's blitz, and carrying an arm numbed with inoculations, was the sum total of furlough. I wasn't unduly worried. I was off to see the world, and likely, I would be home again soon.

SS Aguila led the convoy down the Mersey. As the Liver building faded from view, her 3,000 tons shivered now and then as the grey sea thudded into her plates. This strange and exciting experience of life at sea was opening its first chapter.

Duties as lookout helped to pass the interminable 14 days of this 7 knot convoy to Gibraltar. Sometimes rolling in the heavy swell, sometimes bucking and tossing as we ran headlong into Biscay's restless waves, I felt the first qualms of 'mal de mer'.

One unfortunate never completed the journey. Bound in a hammock shroud, the corpse was dispatched down a chute, with due ceremony, into the deep.

"Unlucky ship," commented an older member of the crew.

"Bad omen," seemed to be the general consensus.

Whatever the truth of that forecast, the convoy sailed into Gibraltar without any untoward incident, and certainly no losses. But within a year, Aguila was lost in another Gibraltar-bound convoy, with the loss of 65 of her crew, 5 gunners, the Commodore and his staff, and 89 passengers, including the first draft of WRNS overseas.

The lights of Gib twinkled around, competing with Algeciras, and La Linea, on the Spanish shore. Especially prominent were the rows of lit portholes of HMS Renown, and HMS Ark Royal, scintillating on the water at the other side of the harbour. After the strict blackout imposed in the United Kingdom, we were amazed to see the blaze of identification.

Next day, I was transferred, on board a small naval pinnace, to the destroyer HMS Encounter. I was led off through the seamen's messdeck, into the bows.

"That's your mess down there," said the Cox'n, pointing to a hole in the deck, about the size of a dustbin lid.

"Down there?" I echoed, almost unbelievingly.

Down there was the watchkeeper's mess, telegraphers, signalmen, quartermasters, and a few others. It was to be my home for 14 months.

"Just in time for a cuppa, grab a mug, how many sugars?"

"I'm Sid, Sid Lillywhite, everyone calls me Lil," said one.

Introductions flowed. The mess was dim, though lit from both sides by rows of portholes. A long mess table reached along each side, flanked by wooden lockers. This claustrophobic space was the temporary dwelling of 18 ratings. No wonder that at one time they drew a 'hard-lying allowance'.

At the end of the break, I was invited onto the deck above, to find my working quarters, the wireless office. Inside the iron door, I found this small room, the hub of the ship's communications.

The sound of voices inside translated itself into four people. There was Lil, Robert (Jock) Steel, a very dark, swarthy Scot from Glasgow, another fellow with a huge frame, and grinning, boyish face, one of his white, front, teeth, broken at an angle. These three were all in overalls, busy polishing the wireless sets, which seemed to take up all the available space, except for the necessary circulating area by the door.

In the corner, sat the fourth member, in a white shirt, and navy blue trousers.

"Right," said the latter, "pleased to meet you," putting down a screwdriver, and extending his hand to shake mine. "I'm Mike Hunt, and I'm the Petty Officer in charge in here. I believe that you've met Lil and Jock already. This is Peter, better known as 'Horse' – you can see why."

The grin widened, and a great fist applied undue pressure to the bones of my fingers.

These then were to be the principal players, and this the stage, where the drama, the boredom, the hopes and fears of us all were to be enacted over the ensuing months.

A strange mixture – the Petty Officer and Peter Denham, our Leading Telegraphist, both Regulars, Lil, a Fleet Reservist, and Jock and myself, both being Hostility Only ratings.

So it was that that night, HMS Encounter set off to sea, with the latest member of her crew.

There was little sleep for me that night, as I chafed in the confines of my hammock, moving restlessly as Encounter pitched and rolled on her patrol of the Straits of Gibraltar.

But as day succeeded day, the very oddness of our existence became routine, absolute strangers became companions, and the daily round became the norm.

I became used to the order of 'Canteen Messing', when the rota few had the duty of preparing food for all the mess. Timing by 'bells' was as natural after a time as the Greenwich time signal, and naval language, some proper, and some foul, interpolated itself into common usage.

Sometimes though the matters of food and time were thrust aside, as 'Action Stations' reminded us forcefully, of our small part in the world-wide hostilities into which we had been plunged.

From Gibraltar to Alexandria, from the Azores to Crete, from the Bay of Biscay to Simonstown, we ploughed the seas. Sometimes calm, sometimes not, we experienced the placid and the cruel.

3

21st Birthday – Durban – 23rd March, 1941.

Swimming party at Malta, May 1941
('Jock' Steel – left at rear. Self – right at front)

Encounter hockey team
(Lt. Sam Falle – second from left, back row, 'Horse' Denham – third from
left, back row, P.O. Mike Hunt – third from right, front row)

5

Alexandria to Singapore

Occasionally we patrolled alone. Sometimes, we escorted the slow-moving convoys of assorted merchantmen, or screened the cruisers and battleships on exercise, or in earnest.

On occasion, we were in company with the famous. HMS Renown, HMS Warspite, HMS Ark Royal (we could have told Lord Haw-Haw where she was), HMS Ajax, Kelly, Sheffield, and so many others.

At other times, we spent days silently quartering the seas with Electra, Velox, Wishart, Faulknor, Duncan, Firedrake, Hotspur, Isis, Javelin, Jupiter – too many names to remember.

Some actions have become part of the annals of history. Encounter's Battle Honours include the Battle of the Atlantic, Spartivento and the bombardment of Genoa, Libya and the Malta convoys. But much of the time was taken up with mundane and routine patrols and convoys, when boredom crept in, and the highlight was the return to harbour, and the possibility of mail from home.

The ship's pets provided some amusement. There was 'Smuts' a small black kitten given to us by friends in Simonstown, and 'Jenny' a monkey rescued from the Atlantic together with the survivors of SS British Zeal. We also had a small white hound, who always knew when we were casting off, and made her escape to the shore. The famous Great Dane, 'Just Nuisance' known throughout the Cape Peninsula and beyond, favoured us with his visits.

Ashore, we enjoyed very briefly the kindness and hospitality of folks in Capetown, Durban, and Alexandria, among others. We also experienced the siege of Malta, and the frequent visitations of both German and Italian Air Forces.

It was while we were at the George Cross Island that we received almost mortal blows, and sustained extreme damage, fortunately with negligible human injuries.

Encounter took part in the great retreat through the Greek Islands, and helped to sustain Tobruk, during the time of its long siege.

But ceaseless sea time, abundant wear and tear, and incipient damage, coupled with forebodings in the Far East, determined the powers-that-be to send us off to the Far East citadel of Singapore – or so we thought.

"Are you interested in becoming a leading rank?"

Petty Officer Hunt was poring through some official papers, and threw the question at me without looking up.

"It will mean a short course ashore, and then probably a transfer. I will recommend you, if you like."

"Yes, thanks, I'll have a go – a bit more pay, if I'm lucky."

"OK, I'll have a word with the First Lieutenant – there's a course some time at the end of November. Try and get you on it, but we'll have to have someone else to take your place on Encounter."

But the tides of war were not influenced by the aspirations of a solitary Coder, or a few bob a day. On 24th November, Encounter sailed to join the Eastern Fleet, and Alexandria was left many thousands of miles behind.

We sailed southwards through Suez, this time accompanied by HMS Jupiter, and some days later, entered harbour in Colombo. The two small ships were dwarfed by the huge advertisement for tea – I think it was Mazawatee – which we could see well before we made landfall.

First morning in harbour, First Lieutenant's requestmen were piped to fall in, and I had been duly warned to fall in with them. So, in clean, laundered whites, I hastened aft to join the small queue.

The coxswain trotted out the few repetitious phrases.

"Coder Stubbs – Attention, two steps forward – march, halt, off cap."

There was the First Lieutenant at his table, a small pile of papers at his side, glancing down at the one he held in his hand.

"Request to attend Leading Coders' course at Alexandria."

He spoke as he ran his eyes down the sheet. "Too late for that now. Maybe when we get to Singapore, there will be another opportunity. Request dismissed."

"On cap, about turn, two steps forward – march. Dismiss."

So back to the mess. Routine satisfied. Ambition unsatisfied.

The next day we sailed eastwards, and made rendezvous with the battleship HMS Prince of Wales, and the battle cruiser, HMS Repulse, to accompany them to Malaya.

Since we were heading further into tropical territory, I was one of those selected for more inoculations. What they were, I don't know, but have since thought how fortunate I was in view of subsequent developments, to have had up-to-date injections against the infections of the jungle. They knocked me sideways for a couple of days, and I was confined to my hammock for a short spell.

When I did get up, my arm throbbed, my head reeled, and despite the damp heat, I shivered. I felt that I must get up on deck and get some air.

Astern, I could see the huge bulks of the two capital ships. Perhaps it was the hallucinating effects of the jabs, for despite their size, and a

Smuts, the kitten – Malta 1941.
A gift from the kind people of Simonstown.

Jenny, the monkey – Gibraltar 1941.
Rescued from mid-Atlantic with
survivors of British Zeal.

Just Nuisance, 'A.B.' Simonstown,
1941. See App. IX.

*HMS Isis
Half-Leader
13th Destroyer
Flotilla*

*HMS Malaya in the
'Mare Nostrum'
after bombarding
Genoa and Pisa,
February 1941*

*HMS Fury
in rough seas*

HMS Ark Royal off the coast of Spain, 1941

HMS Formidable and HMS Warspite Suda Bay, Crete, April, 1941

HMS Glenroy, Evacuation of Lemnos, Greece, April, 1941.

The above and other photographs, taken from HMS Encounter and "buried" in Palembang, Sumatra, 1942–1945.

relatively calm sea, these two vessels appeared to fade, and then reappear, to be lost to sight, and then be seen again, in startling clarity. We weren't to know then, how soon they would be lost forever.

Later, the night sky was racked by constant flashes of distant tropical lightning. The golden orb, at the top of the mast, traced its path through the overcast, clouded night, reflecting the brilliance of this nocturnal phenomena.

The morning revealed the verdant coast line of northern Sumatra, and then as we edged southwards, and further east into the Malacca Strait, the shore of Malaya became visible.

It was the afternoon of 3rd December, when our quartet of four ships entered the Johore Straits, between Malaya and Singapore Island. The green banks were lined with cheering crowds. This show of strength, in the light of gathering fears about the security of Singapore and the Malay Peninsular, produced a dramatic relief.

The wash of the ships caused huge waves along the banks, and the small, moored boats seemed to tip their masts and prows in recognition.

Sid Lillywhite, as always my guide, stood at my side, as I drank in the scene.

"We should have a good time here. There's a magnificent Naval Base. Cost millions to build. There's a huge floating dock, a graving dock, workshops, foundry, everything. It's got all kinds of recreational facilities – almost like a town in itself."

As soon as a berth was possible, Encounter proceeded into dry dock. To the north were the hills and forests of Johore. To the south lay the base, and linking the two, the long, low stretch of the Causeway, over 1000 yards long, carrying a metalled roadway and a railway track.

The luxuriant green of the sports pitches in the naval base contrasted with the white buildings, and we soon took advantage of the relaxing facilities offered – the sports, the canteen, the cinema.

Being in dock, the ship was stripped of ammunition, and anything explosive, but we stayed on board.

And so it happened that we had a rude awakening on the night of 7th December, when the Japanese struck without warning. There was no blackout of the ships, or shore base.

By the time that anti-aircraft batteries were in action, and the searchlights were sweeping the sky, the attacking aircraft had caused considerable damage in Singapore Town, and were withdrawing.

The news bulletins soon revealed the gravity of these overnight developments. We were, even then, optimistic enough to look on the bright side.

"So the Yanks are in the war at last," said Mike Hunt, as we talked in

11

the office. "That should swing the pendulum a bit."

The next day, we saw Prince of Wales and Repulse set sail with an escort of four destroyers. There were two 'E' class, like ourselves, Express and Electra, and two ancient craft from the First World War, Vampire and Tenedos.

I was in the base cinema on the afternoon of 10th December, when the news came through that both major ships had been lost. Stunned silence greeted this announcement when it was flashed up on the screen. Singapore's defence was reduced to a handful of old and damaged destroyers. It was a shattering blow to local morale.

We filed back to Encounter, the full realisation of this disaster not yet fully appreciated.

In the mess there were glum faces. We now knew that both Allied navies, had, in the space of a few days, been virtually eliminated in this area of the war.

Sid Lillywhite took my arm and sat down on the lockers, motioning me to do the same.

"I don't know what it is all about, but while you were ashore, the coxswain was looking for you. May be something about the Leading Coders' course."

I had the feeling that Sid did know what it was all about.

"You wanted me, Coxswain?" I enquired as I pushed open his door.

"Ah, Stubbs, yes. You may be in luck with your Course. Anyway, there is a personal transfer for you to HMS Sultan."

"Sultan, what's she?"

"HMS Sultan. That's the shore signal station. You will be going to the Extended Defence Office, at Fortcanning, just outside Singapore City, later in the month. That's where they control all the shipping movements. Liaison with the Army and Air Force – that kind of thing. It's part of Rear Admiral Malaya's set up."

"I suppose there will be a replacement for me, will there?"

"I hope so. That's why you've got to wait until towards the end of December. Anyway, I wish you well. I'll let you know more, as soon as I hear anything."

The next few days were days of intense activity. The repair work was completed on HMS Encounter, and we left dry dock to sail on patrol, covering the various approaches to Singapore. All seemed quiet enough, and the only incidents were to intercept a number of small junks, and fishing vessels. It was my first direct contact with the inscrutable Orientals.

Destroyer HMS Encounter – Johore Straits, December, 1941.

HMS Repulse at sunset.

13

Such challenges that were given were met with a kind of bland silence. It was quite impossible to detect whether even the most basic English words were understood. Eventual searches were carried out, while the crews of Chinese, Malays, maybe, even Japanese (to my untrained eye, they all looked the same), stood watching, passive, unhelpful.

On one of our patrols, we went as far south as Java, and put into Tanjong Priok, the port of Batavia, as it then was, the capital of this island.

My final patrol finished, we returned to, and anchored in the Johore Straits. Past the rows of native fishing nets, strung along posts, running into the swampy foreshore, and past the small bamboo huts, that formed their kampongs, until we were in sight of the long straight Causeway.

The next day, I was to leave what had been my home for well over a year. The good friends, with whom I had spent 24 hours of the day, 7 days of the week, and all those others, who had been shipmates, and were to be, as 'Daisy' Bell had forecast at HMS Royal Arthur, in Skegness, 'ships that pass in the night'.

Sid Lillywhite, Jock Steel, Horse Denham, and myself had a 'last fling' – if that is the right word for it – in the canteen. In fact, it was more like a wake. The atmosphere was overburdened by the losses now known of the crews of Prince of Wales, and Repulse. On that dreadful December morning, nearly 900 officers and men had lost their lives, including Admiral Sir Tom Phillips, C-in-C, Eastern Fleet, and Captain John Leach, of the Prince of Wales.

The only event that disturbed the quiet was the arrival of some of the crew of four old American destroyers, who pointedly remarked that now the Yanks were in the war, we should be alright. They would show us the way to do it. Uncle Sam would help out. This after we had been battling, virtually alone, for over two years.

These, and similar remarks, did not go down exceptionally well with some of the UK naval contingents, and it needed the naval police to sort out the mêlée that resulted.

Early the next morning, I had to muster all my kit, complete with overnight bag, kit bag, and a leather case, holding my most personal belongings. As I sat in the wireless office, awaiting my call, Horse, referring to the standard form of alterations to the code books, casually remarked.

"Delete 'Encounter', insert 'Sultan'."

Another phase had ended.

I was later bundled onto a lorry, and as the vehicle slowly moved away, I could see Jock Steel at the handrail, his arm raised in a brief farewell.

My trip traversed Singapore Island. Out of the naval base, down through swampy, low ground, up past neat rows of rubber trees, in a tidy plantation. The driver continuously tooted his horn as he overtook Chinese pedestrians, clad largely in dark, loose fitting, pyjama like, clothes, or skirted squads of Malay work people, very largely women, with big straw hats on their heads, and equally large, straw baskets, in which, like armies of ants, they carried the stones, or spoil, to and from where they were repairing the roads, under the keen eye of their white-shirted overseer, or mandoer.

Soon the lush vegetation gave way to a succession of small native houses, and then the more ordered, and impressive structures of Singapore town itself.

The lorry trundled up the hill, stopping outside a range of two-storey living quarters, and with my kit, I was helped down, and left in the roadway, at an open shuttered door.

Hardly had my transport come to a standstill, before a figure, smart in white shirt, shorts and stockings, was at the entrance.

"Here, let me give you a hand with your stuff," he said. "I take it that you're the new Coder. That's good, completes our complement. They've cleared a space upstairs for you."

Upstairs, I found a series of large, airy bedrooms, and my individual bed was one of three, in what was quite a pleasant room at the rear, also containing a range of small wardrobes, or lockers, and a few other bits of occasional furniture.

'Pots', as he was known, pointed to the bed, by a shuttered window, the drawn back mosquito net revealing the startling whiteness of the sheet and pillow case.

"I'm Petty Officer Telegraphist Ainsworth – we shall see a lot of each other, no doubt, but you will be with Leading Telegraphist Jock Stewart – he's in the Battle Box at the present time."

"Battle Box?" I queried "What's that?"

"Oh, sorry, we get so used to that term. It's the underground HQ."

It was a new world, with new colleagues, and as I was soon to find, a very different existence to life on Encounter.

I was called within a few minutes to join my messmates from HMS Sultan, at midday meal. Many, including Pots, were survivors from the two doomed capital ships, Repulse and Prince of Wales, and they had now been found temporary billets in the shore signal station.

"Hope you like chicken," said my companion to my left. "You'll get plenty of it here. That, or pork – you'll soon be clucking, or snorting, like the rest of us."

"Well, that will be a change," I answered, "I can't remember having either on the ship."

With that, the swing door opened, and in walked a diminutive Chinaman, balancing three dinner plates, up each arm, steaming with hot food. It was my introduction to the cushioned life of having Chinese 'boys' to cook, to clean, to launder, and generally release us from any domestic chores.

The meal eventually finished, the tables were cleared, while we sat chatting.

"Like to have a look round, for a wee while," came a Scottish voice. "We'll go outside, and you can find your bearings."

With a number of my new messmates, I strolled to a point high above Keppel Harbour, from where we could see in the distance, a number of ships at anchor, some of the larger buildings in the Town, and across the sea, the green dotted islands.

Down the hill, we passed the entrance to the Battle Box.

"That's where you will spend your duty hours," said the soft, Scottish voice. "I suppose you haven't yet got your pass. You'll get a special one here, because without it, you won't get past the Sikh guards."

To the right was the entrance to a small, enclosed, open air swimming pool, where apparently, Other Ranks were allowed to use the facilities, on certain hours on certain days.

There were Army quarters, too, and I could see a line of soldiers queueing up with their mess tins – obviously not in the same class as our favoured living.

That night, I lay on my white, crisp sheets, the slight movement of air from the open shutter just providing a faint freshness. After the strait-jacket of a hammock, with 18 men crammed in a small mess, the constant movement and vibration of the ship, and the dripping of the illfitting portholes, it was absolute bliss.

The only sound to break the night silence was the chirping of insects, and instead of the incessant smell of warm fuel oil, there was the faintest perfume of some nearby tropical plant.

The next morning at 8 am I had to report to the Extended Defence Office, and commence my new duties. I had had my photograph taken for my pass – what a horrible thing it was. Pots took me there. We turned down the steps to the 'Battle Box', tunnelled into the hill side. We descended about ten steps, and then up five or six; This was apparently some kind of defence against blast, and also, flooding. It also provided a convenient position for the Sikh sentry to mount his guard. As our heads appeared over the peak of the barrier, I could see the turbanned figure, lying against the incline, rifle and bayonet straight out in front. There was a curt challenge.

"Halt, and present pass."

The bayonet touched my chest, as I fished for the document.

Once the sentry was satisfied, we passed on through a concreted passageway, and came eventually to our duty station. This was a medium sized room, in which were a number of wireless transmitters and receivers, and benches with telephones. The walls were covered with all kinds of charts, a large notice board, and various of the current wartime posters, warning of secrecy, 'The enemy is listening' etc. Off this room were several doors, to those parts reserved for the Officer of the Watch, and certainly others, of higher station. There was a slight hum from the air conditioning, supplemented by a whirring fan.

"This is Lieut. Christie."

Pots introduced me to an officer, bent over some plans, illuminated by an angle poise light, and we briefly shook hands.

This was quite different from Encounter. I think I only saw the officers, apart from Surgeon Lieut. Syred, the Cypher Officer, with whom I sometimes worked, when they came on their regular Rounds of Inspection, or when I was paraded as a Requestman, or a Defaulter. This was probably due to the very different task, and ratio of officers and ratings in the two establishments.

Being on land, a lot of our local messages came in by telephone, every one scrambled, to prevent any casual, or planned, eavesdropping. However, many more coded messages were routed via this HQ, and it was quite exceptional to sit and twiddle our thumbs during the hours on duty.

Lieut. Christie asked me something about Encounter, and whether I had family back in the UK, then handed me back to Pots to detail my duties.

Apparently XDO was responsible for the shipping movements in the seas immediately around Singapore, and we were in radio and telephone communication with the naval vessels, and shore defences, to maintain liaison, and conduct the convoys in and out.

Pots had a kind of family tree, which detailed the names of the officers and ratings to each of the four watches.

"We have four Lieutenants, working round the clock, and the Officer in Charge is Captain Mulok," he explained, as he pointed to this chart. "We don't see a lot of the Captain out here. He's quite a character. Bark's worse than his bite. He was a subbie on Scott's Antarctic expedition, you know."

I think I settled down fairly quickly in my new 'ship'. Being very near to Singapore Town, we could take great advantage of all our off duty hours.

I remember visiting the Great World, that supreme Oriental entertainment centre, where we could enjoy the centuries-old dances of the many Eastern cultures, find a quiet bar for a drink, or a coffee, or watch the Malaysian taxi dancers, as they plied for hire.

Of course, Other Ranks were not permitted to enter the portals of the famous Raffles Hotel, but we were left in no doubt of the opulent living of the resident whites, who in our terms were lumped together in the all embracing description of 'rubber planters'.

We did have the modern, air-conditioned, Cathay cinema, and could enjoy up-to-the-minute films, in very comfortable surroundings.

It was interesting to see the mixture of Europeans, Asiatics, and those in between, the Eurasians. We spent many hours in the street markets, intrigued by the cosmopolitan fusion of the population. We were fascinated to see the Chinese manipulating their chopsticks, at the open air eating stalls, and to see the Indian night watchmen, taking their rest, and apparently out to the wide on their charpoys, amid the bustle and noise of the streets.

One of my new friends was Johnnie MacMillan, a Scot from Argyllshire. He was a Glaswegian Master of Arts, and before coming into the Royal Navy, had just ventured into the teaching profession. He was a fortunate survivor of HMS Prince of Wales.

"Look," he said, as we walked along, "they're still using counting beads, like my infant bairns at school." He pointed to a Chinaman busy calculating a bill on his abacus. We were amazed how these elementary tools produced a rapid and accurate answer in their expert and swift fingers.

Our wanderings took us down past the Cathedral of St Andrew, and the impressive Supreme Court Buildings. We strolled along the water front, and up by the Singapore River, ever amazed at the teeming life on the moored sampans. We cheerfully negotiated the pitfalls of the deep open drains, and sometimes, the smells which assailed our noses. They seldom mention those in the geography books!

In the streets, away from HMS Sultan, the bustling life of Singapore seemed unchanged. Christmas, and the coming New Year loomed larger than the war still many miles away up in Malaya. Neither of these important Festivals in our Calendar made much impact on our routine, and my only recollection was of a better than usual menu on these two occasions.

I had letters from Horse, and Jock Steel. Jock had written at 1.30 am during the middle watch, and headed his letter with a drawn coat of arms, depicting in the four quarters, a bunch of bananas, a pair of headphones, a wine goblet, and a beer mug, with the motto 'In vino Veritas'.

"Xmas was just the usual half-hearted sort of affair," he wrote, "though we did manage to spend it in harbour. The turkey was well and truly stuffed, and those who were capable had it for dinner; the others, who fell by the wayside, had theirs for supper. A couple of days later, we did push off, and consequently, the Day of Days, Hogmanay, Der Tag, or simply to you, New Year, was spent at sea, much to my Scottish disgust.

"It makes my poor old heart bleed to hear of you wallowing night and day in an ocean of clean sheets. That long enamelled thing, I believe you called it a bath, strikes a familiar chord, but it is now some two years or more since civvy street.

"This sardine can (Tyneside edition) is beginning to get a trifle bouncy, and there is a twerp, rather persistent, keeps stamping on a morse key, and making funny noises in my ear, so with a 'di-di-di-da' here's to the next time, JOCK." The 'next time' proved to be in 1946.

Horse must have followed him on watch, for he wrote to say that he had "Just relieved the modern Rip Van Winkle, off the middle watch. We duly drank to absent friends on Christmas Day, and just to liven things up, I did arrange a 'Red Warning'. The names, and references, to my ancestors, on the arrival of Jock and Sid, would quite easily compile a new type of dictionary. It seems that Jock objects to my getting warnings, while he is obtaining his beauty sleep. I suppose he really does need it.

"The thought of clean smelling white sheets makes me decidedly envious, etc. etc. All the best till we meet again. Signed 'Horse' (Naval Nag, Royal Navy)."

We never did meet again. Horse, probably the strongest, and fittest, of Encounter's crew, died in Maccassar, on 12th May, 1945. After over 3 years captivity, he succumbed to the inhuman treatment by the Japanese.

As January wore on, the Singapore Times gave news of some Allied successes, and General Wavell, who had followed us down from the Middle East, made some encouraging announcements.

However, the days were now punctuated with attacks by Jap aircraft. They flew in perfect formations of nines, or twenty-sevens, dropping their bombs, or their leaflets, with impunity, quite undisturbed by our lumbering Brewster Buffaloes, or the ineffective anti-aircraft fire.

"If only we had some Hurricanes out here." It was an oft repeated wish, but we knew deep down now that we were on the receiving end.

As day succeeded day, it was clear that the Nipponese advance southward down Malaya was coming threateningly near to Johore. The last main obstacle, the Straits which separated Singapore Island from the Malay Peninsular, were in sight of the invaders.

Friday, The Thirteenth

By early February, Lieutenant General Percival, GOC, Malaya, had found it necessary to inform the public that the Battle for Malaya had come to an end, and the Battle for Singapore had started. Within days, we knew that the northern defences of the Island itself had been breached.

The electric storms, which lit the night, were now in competition with the sounds and signs of the nearing battle front. The Chinese and Malayan refugees were streaming south, creating severe traffic and administrative problems, and demoralised troops were heading for escape.

I looked from the bedroom window one morning to see our Chinese 'boys' sitting in huddled, and worried, conclave. They were in animated conversation, and their high pitched voices showed their concern, though not one of their words was understood. As they got up and dispersed, I watched one of them catch two chickens, which had been grubbing about in the yard. He wrung their necks, then threw them to the ground, where they ran several circuits of the enclosure, impelled by nervous energy, when the threads of life had all but gone. I wondered how long these boys' loyalty would overcome their natural fears of the invaders. As employees of the British Crown, their lives could equally casually be ended.

But, had we not been told of the impregnability of this Island fortress? Had we not been told of aircraft and troop reinforcements on the way?

Early on the morning of 5th February, in our protected position, in the battle box, we lived out the drama of what was to be the last convoy into Singapore. Movement in the seas around was now perilous in the extreme, but every effort was made to receive such outside succour, as was now being diverted from other theatres, and to evacuate the last wives and families of civilians and servicemen.

Into this cauldron sailed the Empress of Asia, and three other ships, hoping to make harbour during the dark of night. As the dramatic events of the dawn unfolded, we in Signals were but the backstage prompters. The Empress, loaded with units of the 18th British Division, was hit, and set on fire.

Orders and messages were flashing to and from the shore, and rescue boats managed to save the vast majority of the crew, and the troops being transported. The ship itself eventually sunk, with the loss of vital arms and equipment.

Hopes were fading fast. The airfields on Singapore Island had either been overrun, or were untenable, and Wavell ordered the withdrawal of the Air Force to bases in Sumatra. Churchill cabled –

"The battle must be fought to the bitter end, at all costs."

It must have been around this time that Johnnie MacMillan was admitted into the Alexandra Military Hospital but his illness was overshadowed by the anxiety felt all around.

I don't think any of us, even at this stage, were expressing pessimism, but as Mr Micawber might have said, we were strongly hoping for something to turn up! What could be done?

"There are several abandoned lorries in the town," stated Jock Stewart. "Could be useful to have one available, if we have to make a break for it."

We discussed this possibility, and Jock, being a driver, became the prime mover in this direction.

"If we are going to do this, we should have some emergency kits, that we can just throw into the back of the lorry, and away. Some changes of clothing, iron rations, matches, cash."

Individually, we made our own preparations for any future developments. It was a situation without precedent, but we figured that even if the Japs' advance was not stemmed, we could perhaps keep our options open.

Trying to visualise the future, I sorted out my possessions into the indispensable, the necessary, and a few irreplaceable personal items. These I packed into a small leather case – another souvenir from Alexandria. I had one change of clothing, and a spare pair of boots. There was soap and a towel, rolls of bandage, a box of matches, two candles, a penknife, a ball of string, and some chocolate. I found room for my photograph album, my fountain pen, a couple of pencils, and some paper. Pretty well everything else would have to be abandoned. We loaded some tins of corned beef, and packs of navy biscuits.

These preparations eventually proved sound.

Late on the afternoon of Friday, 13th February, the message came through. Jock Stewart was the bearer.

"This is it," he gasped, as he ran into the messroom. "All organised naval operations are at an end, and personnel have been given carte blanche to get down to the harbour, as quickly as we can. There are a number of small craft there. If we can get them to sea, we can scarper."

Before we could do this, we had to destroy anything of any possible use, and pursue a scorched earth policy.

As a Coder, my last task was to assist with the destruction of the codes, and confidential books. These had to be brought out from the Battle Box, and burned. I stoked the reluctant bonfire into flames. The pages smouldered, and curled. It seemed hours before the task was finally completed. Only a hill away, I could make out the movement of uniformed men. Were they the Japs, so close? If so, they could surely see me, by the light of the obstinate fire.

My job done at last, I hurled my case on the lorry, and with the engine already revving, I leapt aboard. Jock Stewart was at the wheel. At breakneck speed, we raced through the streets making for the fires and spiralling black funeral pyres, which pinpointed Keppel Harbour, the oil installations, and go-downs. The vanguard of the Jap troops couldn't be far away. Would we succeed in running the gauntlet?

As soon as we reached the waterside, we were halted by a Naval Petty Officer, directing personnel to the various craft available.

"One signalman, two seamen, and one stoker required here.

21

"One seaman, one sparker over there on that motor torpedo boat.

"Six hands – anybody – crew for a small water carrier.

"Two men to complete the complement of an air sea rescue launch.

"C'mon, look sharp. Four volunteers to . . ." The words were lost in the urgent clamour.

There were abandoned vehicles everywhere. There was the acrid stench of burning. The bombers came over again.

An army wife was bidding her tearful farewells to her husband. Stray troops wandered in the hope of a berth on anything that was moving. Anything that offered an escape out of this turmoil and conflagration.

"Here we are, Stubbie, this'll do us." Pots tugged my arm.

'This' was a little minesweeper, later identified as HMS Tapah.*

I was hustled on board, along with Pots and Jones. In just a few minutes, the deck seemed crammed with people. There was a tall naval lieutenant giving instructions.

"Right, that must be it. Sorry, no more. No, no more. OK Petty Officer, we'd better cast off, or we shall be inundated."

Tapah must have doubled, or even trebled her normal complement, including a few of the last service wives to quit Singapore.

In the darkness, orders were shouted, and we slid slowly, and silently away from the billowing smoke, and leaping flames.

"Phew, that was a close one," said Pots.

We learned that our course was to be southwards, via the Java Sea, towards the eventual haven of Australia.

In the fading light, we tried to make ourselves useful, and comfortable. Sitting, or standing, on the open deck, we peered astern, somewhat crestfallen, but breathing again, having escaped from certain capture.

After a very short time, Tapah slowed to a halt, and we were informed that our duty that night was to anchor and display guide lights at the entrance to the channel through the minefields, so that the many other minor vessels following could safely negotiate the passage en route for Java.

Those final few hours ashore had been frantic, and I was glad to find that there were several of my shipmates from Sultan now aboard Tapah with me. Jock Stewart had presumably been put on one of the other boats. I wondered what had happened to Johnnie MacMillan. We realised that all the food we had put on the lorry had either been left behind, or had been loaded elsewhere.

*(HMS Tapah. 208 tons gross. Built 1926. Straits Shipping Co. Ltd)

Yeoman Jones wanted a hand to fix the signal halliard.

'Anyone got a knife to strip the insulation off this flex?" he enquired. My penknife found an immediate use. As we worked we grumbled at the delay.

"Just our so-and-so luck. Could have put a good few miles under our belts by dawn. Instead of that, we're stuck here, while all the rest of the lucky blighters are on their way."

The job was finished, and a trio of small lights, just barely visible, offered a gleam of hope to the other craft.

Pots Ainsworth, Yeoman Jones and myself had found the small cubby hole which contained the wireless set. It wasn't working – but at the time that didn't bother us. There was not room for all of us even to sit, and so we propped ourselves against the bulkhead, watching, waiting.

Dawn was scarcely lightening the horizon, when the churning of the engines signalled progress. We headed straight for one of the many islands we could see – I think we passed Pulau Blakang Mati, and Pulau Bukum, so often names in signals – and this was a much smaller hump in the water. We ran straight in and beached.

A working party was detailed ashore to cut branches and foliage, and soon these were draped overall, in the attempt to camouflage our presence. It was clearly impracticable to attempt to sail on during daylight hours.

Every now and again, the drone of a plane could be heard, and everyone froze. Only the few pairs of binoculars moved to seek out the intruder, and attempt its identity.

In the confusion of the night of the 13th, there had been orders to head across to Sumatra, and some craft had turned north, up the Malacca Straits, towards Ceylon. For some reason, these earlier orders had been countermanded, and the vast majority of the evacuation vessels were now strung out to the southward.

The rapidly changing situation in the Dutch East Indies was not within our knowledge, but we still believed that if we could make our way down through the Sunda Straits, or the Bali Straits, our escape was assured.

I thought of the evening, only a few weeks earlier, when Encounter had visited Batavia, and swept nonchalantly past the menacing bulk of Krakatoa, at the southernmost tip of Sumatra.

Where was Encounter now?

We moved off again, tightly hugging the jungle shore, on our starboard side. At first light, we cruised close in to the coastline mangrove swamps, and dropped anchor, seeking what shelter there was.

Some bread was produced, and this, together with an assorted mixture of tinned food made a very scratch meal. In our haste to escape we had not thought of the necessity of crockery, or cutlery. I was fortunate to have been given an Army dixie. It later served me well as a plate, cooking pot, shaving mug, and even wash basin!

Despite some light hearted talk of Robinson Crusoe, and life on a desert island, it was becoming increasingly apparent that our deeper apprehensions were fast dispelling the optimism of our escape.

The discomfort of our cramped sleeping spaces, the sparse rations which were available, the realisation of our lack of useful utensils, and other personal items, resulted in an air of gloomy silence.

At daylight, preparations were made to slip anchor, and move further south. Alas, this was not to be. We were held fast by the tenacious mud of the swamps, and despite efforts to see-saw the hull from its bondage, by all rushing, in unison, from side to side, we had to await the next high tide before we could leave.

More frustrating hours were lost – but we were not to know then that these delays, probably meant the difference between life and death.

So we proceeded, close in to the coast of Sumatra, fingers tightly crossed as hour succeeded hour.

The hard deck became a welcome mattress, and sleep eventually overcame weariness.

The next night was uneventful, and we made reasonable, but slow progress.

As the solitary wireless set was out of action, we had no contact whatever with anyone, or anything, outside our horizons. We did not know that hardly more than 24 hours after we had left our mooring on the Saturday morning, Singapore had capitulated, and the Japs were now rapidly spreading their tentacles much further south, into the Dutch East Indies.

During the daylight hours of Tuesday, 17th February, we watched silently as a plane passed over now and then, high in the sky. If it had spotted us, it gave no indication, and certainly dropped no lower to investigate.

At one time, all eyes were fixed on a small outrigger that appeared round the nearby headland. It came close by, and we could see the Malaysian family on the deck, equally curious at our presence.

A verbal request for anyone with quinine was passed from mouth to mouth. An Army private was suffering a bout of malaria. Our little group were lucky. Despite the hot days, and cool nights, we were all well.

"Here we are again – big eats," announced a nearby voice, and a sailor appeared, carrying a mound of corned beef on a large plate in one hand, and an enormous container of boiled potatoes in the other.

'I like this dining out on deck. Pass the mustard please."

"What. No mustard," said Pots, as we tucked into our limited rations.

That evening, the anchor came up cleanly, and we had no problem in moving off, churning out of the muddied waters.

We tried to calculate our approximate position.

"Must be something like 200, even 250 miles from Singapore now," speculated Yeoman Jones. "We must have made good progress all through Saturday night, and also on Monday night, after we got ourselves unstuck. With a bit of luck, we'll be close to Java the day after tomorrow."

I must have dozed off with that cheerful thought in mind.

The next I knew was that I was rudely awakened by a flashing light, and sat upright to see a distant lighthouse beaming its warning across the still sea from our port side. By now, Jones and Ainsworth were also awake, rubbing their eyes in the gloom.

"What the hell's going on? Where are we? What's that light doing on the port? Surely the coast is on our starboard side?"

We couldn't answer any of these queries. They were unfamiliar waters. The shafts of light spun through the darkness, and the pointing finger suddenly flooded us in a pale light. Almost immediately, there was a further stabbing beam from way astern. A cold, silvery pencil, added to the former, and held steady, as the lighthouse radiance curved away.

Then, an intermittent, and stuttering signal, flickered through the darkness. Difficult to comprehend in my early wakefulness. Then more deliberate.

"... –   – – – .– –."

"... (S) – (T) – – – (O) .– –. (P)"

"S T O P   S T O P."

There were shouts aboard Tapah. In the pitch black, it was quite impossible to determine the source of the searchlight, or the Aldis lamp, spelling out its hesitant morse message.

Were we lucky enough to have been picked up by an Allied ship? There was a surge of optimism. We knew there had recently been Dutch warships in the area, and this might explain the slow deliberation of the message. Or was this a Jap far south in the Java Sea?

The engines still drove us on, as now, all alert, we strained our eyes astern.

The scream, and splash, of a shell ahead, quickly followed by another, rather nearer, gave no identity. There was another, another, very close, too close for comfort.

Then again, S T O P, very deliberately, but with no clue as to the sender.

A large white ensign was hoisted, and Lieut. Hancock gave the order to obey.

Clearly, with our almost absent armament, and our complement of refugees, including women, we had no alternative. Accordingly, the throb of the engine was stilled, and the only sound was the gentle lap of the water, as we waited developments.

Out of the night appeared a light cruiser – I believe it had four funnels, very high out of the water, but my memory isn't clear on that.

There were some more signals flashed. Yeoman Jones had, by this time, made his way up on to the small bridge, and I found it impossible to interpret the quicker morse.

"They're sending a boat across. Do nothing until we are sure who they are," came a message.

Soon a motor launch appeared off our port side.

The tension grew, as we awaited identification.

Then the shout from Tapah's bridge.

"They're Japs."

We knew then what was required – each had his own urgent duties. Mine once more, was to dispose of the confidential books. I dragged out the canvas bag from under the wireless set, and took it to the ship's side.

Others made sure that the radio was made quite irreparable, such parts as could be stripped off the gun were removed, and I believe that the ship's engine was sabotaged in some way.

The zip fastener on the top of my bag was reluctant to close despite my anxious tugging, so the few heavier books, each with its caption inside 'Weighted with lead, and if thrown overboard will sink' were dispatched, one by one, into the ocean.

I was left with just a few light books, rather like school exercise books, and these I rolled in the bag, with the burdening weight of a dud shell, bound it quickly with a piece of string, and hurled it into the night.

Even as it splashed down, there were hurrying feet at the back of me. Nippon sailors, ran, bayonets glinting, to secure their capture.

"That's it then," said Pots, "We're prisoners of war."

"What now?" added Jones.

Lieutenant Hancock passed round the ship, urging calm.

What would the future hold?

Indeed, what now?

We couldn't begin to contemplate what lay before us.

I think that despite the calamities of the last two months, we were still, even then, optimistic enough to feel that Allied retaliation would be swift and effective.

We didn't know of the fate of that Armada of small ships which had fled from Singapore during that dismal fortnight in the middle of February.

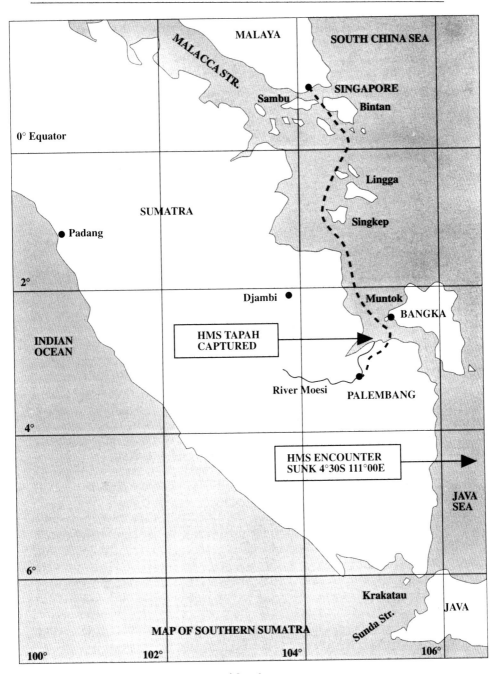

Map 1

It was only later, during capture, and even later still, on release, that the full extent of the disaster became known.

Personal stories told of the Li Wo, and her heroic Captain. They related details of the sinking of the Grasshopper, the Dragonfly, and the Scorpion. Survivors passed on details of the massacre of the Australian nurses off the Vyner Brooke. Information was sought as to what became of M/L 310, the Giang Bee, the Shu Kwang, and many others.

But most of these disclosures were yet to come.

The realisation that, despite everything, we were among the lucky ones, would have been difficult to imagine as we awaited developments. Impotent to help ourselves, and now subject to the whims of these little yellow men.

Muntok, and Bancka Island*

The events of the night prevented further sleep, and we sat on the deck, huddled in groups, contemplating what might lie ahead. We cursed that we had not turned north from Singapore, and retraced our path from Ceylon, not 3 months previous. Why had we not been made aware of the situation in the Java Sea, and instead of negotiating a course close inshore to Sumatra, perhaps of heading outside of Bancka Island? We may even have gone to the nearest point opposite Malaya, and taken our chance of getting across Sumatra (This was proved by history to be the only viable escape route). We ruminated on what might have happened had we not spent two abortive nights on our journey southwards – we were soon to learn.

As dawn broke on Wednesday, 18th February, we were escorted slowly along the coast to what we learned was Bancka Island, which lay just off the coast of Sumatra, near to the mouth of the River Moesi.

Anchored, were numerous warships, and merchant vessels, and we realised then that we had run straight into a gauntlet of Jap ships stretched across our escape route. Perhaps, had it not been for that lighthouse beam, we might possibly have crept through in the darkness. However, we were but one of some eighty small vessels that had shared the same, or worse, fate.‡

We eventually came alongside a long planked jetty, at a place called Muntok. We disembarked to curt commands, and were prodded forward, carrying those possessions we had brought with us from Singapore. I had

*Sometimes spelt "Bangka" or "Banka".
‡See Appendices I, II and III.

my leather suitcase, and a small knapsack.

"Try and stick together," said Pots.

The comfort of familiar faces was a lucky liferaft in these uncertain seas.

The jetty was a bustling hive of activity, and struggling along, we were jostled by other bodies moving seawards. Along the sealine, we could now see some buildings, one of which was some form of warehouse, and into which we were unceremoniously herded.

A rough count was taken, and we were then told to leave what bags, and trappings we had, and fall in outside. Our captors were already pressing into service all available labour, and the rest of the day proved an almost endless procession up and down that jetty, unloading the cargo boats, with their invasion material, and then carrying various spoils on the reverse journey.

Our first eyeball-to-eyeball encounters with the enemy brought the verdict that we were in for a hard time, and by that evening, all of us bore blisters on our hands, shoulders and feet, that were to be the forerunners of many more.

For a seemingly endless week we toiled along that jetty, the physical pain of our exertions, competing with the growing pangs of hunger, our emotions clouded in numbed submission. I had one consoling thought. Could this body of yellow, myopic dwarfs, in their motley uniforms, possibly be a match for our forces, once our terrible unpreparedness had been remedied?

It is really only now that I can recognise that in those early days of captivity, my mind refused to register the grim fate which had overtaken us, while my body worked passively, as we were driven to unaccustomed degrees of labour in the tropical heat. For us there was no siesta. Indeed mad dogs and prisoners of war went out in the noonday sun. We were on a treadmill of gigantic dimensions, and days and nights merged into unaccountable weeks.

The only punctuation marks in this nightmarish charade were the occasional brief raids by Dutch Blenheim planes, which vainly interrupted the post-invasion activities of the Jap troops. These lifted our spirits somewhat from the depths into which they had plunged.

Even in those early days, we were hazarding guesses as to when the friendly forces would hit back. Had we known the truth then, I think many would have given up the unequal struggle.

One day, we watched quietly, as two Australians seized the opportunity to paddle away in a small craft, in a courageous attempt to reach freedom. They disappeared from view, leaving us envious of their heroic venture. Our hopes and prayers for them were later shattered by a guard giving a graphic demonstration of a plane diving, and machine gunning them.

"Bastards," said Yeoman Jones, drawing back the veil of his Welsh reticence.

"Apa," (what?) enquired the guard, in his newly acquired Indonesian, sensing the curt disapproval, and kicking out viciously at the defenceless Petty Officer.

Despite our present physical discomforts, our over-riding thoughts were for those at home, worried at the lack of personal news, amid the overall tragedy of the fall of Singapore, and the thousands of households and families who would be directly affected.

"I expect the Red Cross will arrange something," said Pots, "even if it takes a month or two."

The subject was never far from our minds, but became submerged beneath our immediate difficulties, only to surface again in the quiet of night.

The Allied officers were endeavouring to compile a list of personnel, service numbers, next-of-kin, etc., and to persuade the local Jap authorities that we should be treated as Prisoners of War in accordance with the Geneva Convention, that contact be made with the Red Cross, and names passed on.

I recollect that among our naval officers, my rank as 'Coder' caused some concern, as it might be thought that I had some valuable insight and knowledge – I was promptly 'converted' into a Writer! This foresight possibly spared me from the none- too-gentle means of persuasion that were a characteristic of the Japanese Kempei Tai.

Even the night time rest from labour, while so welcome, had become a restless battle to sink into unconsciousness. The hard unyielding floor was causing sores to hips and shoulders, and skin irritations caused by bites, and unceasing perspiration, were a constant discomfort. Only too often when sleep had won, despite the grunts and snuffles, snores and sighs of all manner of men, the necessities of nature would impose an early reveille. There were also many occasions when our captors rampaged through the recumbent figures, unceremoniously kicking, pushing, or prodding awake anyone who might lie in their path.

At times there would be a shout of "Tenko", and we would be mustered outside, while an interminable count was mounted, accompanied by kicks and punches for anyone not alert in seconds, or who happened to be paying a visit to the vile trench which served as latrines for many scores of men.

Frogs and toads would set up a cacophony of grunts, and monkeys in the nearby trees took up the chorus. Mosquitoes plagued us in their thousands, and our restless assembly became an untidy parade of bare arms swatting bare legs and faces, until the relief of "All men, resto," returned us to our hard floor.

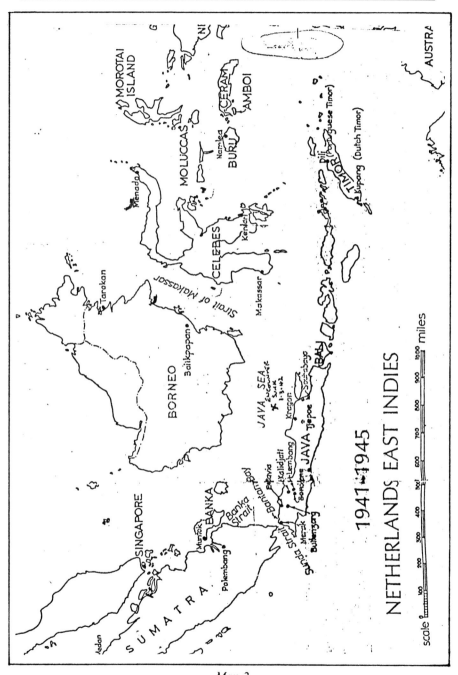

Map 2

The first signs of dawn, and preparations for the day's grind, had us rubbing limbs into life, donning the shirt and shorts which had been folded together and converted into a pillow – those same articles, which, pristine white, had seen our departure from Singapore, were now grubby, soiled, and much in need of replacement.

Queues formed at the trenches, while others, according to rapidly organised rotas, wended into crocodiles, to use the few buckets of water provided, for a quick sluice and refresher. Another party went to collect the kerosene tins, now used as containers for the thin rice slop which was the inevitable breakfast, on which to work a day of hard non-stop labour.

Even before the last few mouthfuls had been eaten, we would hear "Mashi finishu," (Food over). "Oru me' mari sini" (All men, come here). How we interpreted this mixture of Malay, Japanese, and bastard English, I don't know. It was more the peremptory signs, flailing rifle butts, and rough pushing and shoving, that in those days had us out in the open. A motley crew we were in dirty uniforms, unshaven, and topped off with whatever head covering we could lay our hands on – straw hats, uniform caps, even pieces of cloth, arranged burnoose fashion. But we were then mostly fit, mostly in our twenties or early thirties, and able to a great extent to cope with the excessive demands of our physical tasks.

Our victors themselves gave us some cause for humour as we watched their sloppy attempts at disciplined drill. Some in peaked caps, some a kind of legionnaires hat, with neckshield, some in their army round hard helmets. They had a mixture of hard boots, soft, canvas, black ankle boots, with a cleft compartment for the big toes, and occasionally NCOs and above, with smart calf length high boots. Some wore puttees, some wore socks. Their shirts, of various hues of fawn through to brown, bore a small red and yellow badge, with pips, or stars, to indicate their rank, and we gleaned that even the privates were one, two or three pip – the former being the lowest of the low – even then much superior to their prisoners. The humour however was mainly caused by their shorts. The Nipponese, are of course, mainly small in stature, but to see them with shorts well past their knees, sometimes loose, sometimes tucked in socks, outshone even the strip of that famous Arsenal footballer, Alex James. The most ludicrous of all, however, was the sight, generally of an officer, officiously strutting with sword very nearly touching the ground, wearing shorts, and socks – held up by suspenders. It was as well we could see the funny side of it, there was little else to find amusing.

It was during our early labours on the jetty that we heard that in the previous 48 hours, when the Japanese had first landed along the coast, they had been allowed to run amok, beating, raping, pillaging and looting. It was then that the dreadful massacre of the Australian Army nursing sisters, survivors off the Vyner Brooke, had taken place. They had been lined up along the shore, at the water's edge, and killed in cold blood, together with some of the other escapees from Singapore, who had reached that point only two days previous to ourselves. The frustrations of our 48-hour delay were fortunate blessings in disguise.

It seems that the Japanese Navy had exercised a little more restraint than their army. Or perhaps, our value as slave labour swung the pendulum in saving our lives.

By this time, I had met up again with Johnnie MacMillan, and Able Seaman Shaw, who had both been with me at Singapore, and in Fort-canning. Johnnie, heeding the developments on Singapore Island, had fortunately discharged himself from the Alexandra Hospital before, only hours later, the Japs, on the pretext that shots had been fired from the windows, stormed the building, stabbing and bayoneting the unfortunate and helpless patients.

Finding our quarters deserted on the late afternoon of 13th February, and knowing our plans, he had made his way to the harbour, where he was allocated to a naval torpedo boat, only to have this order cancelled, and to be transferred to another craft, the hand of Lady Luck thereby saving him from early death, as the MTB, with Rear Admiral, Malaya (Rear Admiral E. J. Spooner) aboard, and also the Senior RAF Officer (Air Vice Marshal Pulford) was attacked by aircraft, and beached on an island, where the occupants all died.

As day succeeded day, we became inured to the same dull, repetitive routine. Reveille as dawn broke. Quick, soapless wash, small bowl of porridge rice, march to the jetty, then the laden tramp up and down its ever increasing length. The midday break was the only punctuation of the dragging hours, and we found whatever shade there was to receive another bowl of rice – dried out in grains this time, with perhaps a lime, or a banana, and a mug of milkless, sugarless, tea. Then more burdensome hours, until the gathering piles of stores and ammunition were depleted, and we were allowed to drag our bodies back onto the foreshore, and our 'home' in the warehouse. The day ended with another bowl of rice, and a mug of coloured water, patronisingly called 'soup', with perhaps a few bits of tropical vegetable, or a microscopic piece of meat floating in it.

Against this sparse routine, we faced also the comparative opulence of the Dutch troops, and their ability as resident colonials to converse freely with the natives. By the roll of the dice, they had fallen captive on their 'home ground', and consequently had ample clothing, pocketsful of guilders, and the acquaintanceship of the locals, dubious though that might be. They rarely shared their good fortune, as they blamed the British for the disastrous collapse of Malaya, and we regrettably felt the same about their swift capitulation in the East Indies.

This then was the inauspicious start to our years of captivity.

To Pastures New

The depressing scene at Bancka changed but little. However, we were aware that one by one the anchored ships were moving off, and so it came as no surprise to be told one evening that we ourselves were to be taken inland. There we were promised we should find a proper camp, we should be better organised, and we should have regular rations.

Hardly had the evening rice been served out, and quickly eaten, than we were warned to be ready with our kit, and march down to the pier.

Preparations for such a move needed careful deliberation on our part, on two scores. Firstly to select those absolute necessities to the limit of our carrying capacities. We had already got into the habit of collecting any oddment which fortunately might come our way – a rice sack to lie on, bits of cloth to be made into bags, pillows, clothes, or protection against the sun or mosquitoes, chunks of wood to burn for cooking, or to carve into a rough eating utensil. The debris of human existence was soon recycled, and became prized possessions.

Secondly, there was a need to disguise, or conceal those objects which, we were already learning, might be confiscated, by the guards. Watches, rings, and fountain pens were eagerly sought by the Japs, and more often than not, taken without recompense, though occasionally, a very one-sided barter was conducted. Such items as penknives, razors, and scissors, were considered as potential weapons, and were removed on sight, while diaries, and books of any description were viewed with suspicion, and needed to be censored, and stamped.

Amid the usual gruff shouting, haphazard counting, and counter checking, we shuffled off – for the last time – along that wooden pier.

Alongside the jetty lay a small freighter – I don't suppose she displaced more than 1000 tons – until she was laden down with 3 or 400 men.

We had felt some discomfort crowded as we were on HMS Tapah. But this was a new experience – it wasn't exactly 'standing room only', but it was 'crouching, squatting, sitting'. On the deck, on the hatches, in the bows, wherever there were a few horizontal feet of space, everywhere was covered with bodies, and gear.

We now too had our first walking wounded, and extra space had to be found for the several men who were either suffering from malaria, or high temperature, or had sustained some injury while working.

As evening fell, there was a slight breeze, and without any additional clothing, we shivered after the intense heat of the day. We sought what bit of comfort there was under tarpaulins, and wore every scrap of clothing we could muster. The Bancka mosquitoes came down in their hordes to bid us farewell.

It was early the next day, before the ramshackle engine was tempted into life, and we set off westwards. Before long, the grey blue of the sea turned into a muddy brown, and we realised that we were entering a river estuary.

"What's the latest buzz, Stubbie?" asked Pots "Have you heard where they are taking us?"

Cut off as we were from news, papers, and radios, all kinds of speculation and rumour were rife.

"No, you're as wise as I am," I answered, "but I hope it doesn't take long. Looks like some pretty heavy weather on the port there". The sky was occasionally lit by a flash of tropical lightning, and a distant rumble heralded a possible storm.

Before long, a heavy downpour squalled across the sea, which in a few minutes left us drenched to the skin, while the water ebbed, and scurried, across the vibrating deck.

On the day previous we had been fortunate enough to acquire some small, dried, fish. They were unhygienic, black and grey, shrivelled things, with vicious looking spines. A trader had them spread out on the ground near the jetty, and unusually, was willing to trade them for some of the last of our Singapore money, while also to our surprise, the guard turned a blind eye.

Normally we would not have considered these fit to eat, but we were crossing boundaries unknown before, and the fish offered a savoury contrast to our eternal rice.

Someone on board had a deep bowl, and as soon as we could, we filled this with sea water to soak and swell the fish, so that we could pull the meat off the bones with our fingers.

Alas, the only toilet facility was one bucket, regularly tipped over the side, and dragged in the sea to scour it. In the darkness of the night, our bowl was mistakenly used as a lavatory, and our luxury of fish was again consigned back into the ocean!

Cramped and uncomfortable though we were, somehow we contrived to sleep.

Dawn found us in the wide mouth of a river, trees crowding the banks on either side, with just an occasional row of spars marking a native fishing trap, where the ebbing tide would snare the catch.

The boat chugged slowly on, churning the thick, brown water, and now as the banks became closer, sending a ripple of waves against the mangrove wilderness.

The wide course of the river turned round hidden bends, and we looked hopefully ahead, optimistic enough to think our destination was just around the corner, and we would soon be reaching new quarters, and then looking forward to having some kind of a meal. Perhaps things would be better.

There was little to be seen. Sometimes a canoe, or native fishing boat would glide by. Curious black faces turned towards us, but no sound, no wave, no recognition. Crocodiles, recumbent, lay half-submerged on the muddy beaches which sometimes breached the tangled undergrowth.

The morning sun strengthened, and we were glad to feel its warmth, our clothes steaming as the damp retreated.

"We've been on this ruddy boat over 18 hours," mused Pots, glancing at his wristwatch, surreptitiously withdrawn from the pocket of his shorts. "It's lunch time – what would you like? I think I'll have the chicken, with roast potatoes, peas, and sprouts,"

"I don't think we're getting anywhere on this wretched schooner," said Jones, ignoring Pots' attempt at light-hearted conversation. "Not even a damned drink."

And so it proved. Towards late afternoon, some buildings appeared round a broad sweep of the stream, and soon after we pulled across to a rather elementary dockside. We weren't very interested in the scenery, but obviously on the far side there were some industrial installations, and where we now moored, some wooden and corrugated iron warehouses. Two or three small freighters completed the picture that this was quite an important centre, though virtually a day's sail up river.

We clambered ashore, stretching aching joints, mustering at the river's edge and securing our kit, while we waited for further instructions.

"So this is Palembang?" said one of the officers. "It's a Dutch oil centre – that's the oil installation over there, I believe, place called Pladjoe."

Nobody seemed to know whether this was the end of the journey, or whether we would be going on elsewhere by foot, or by lorry. There seemed to be a masterly lack of co-ordination about everything. The Jap guards who had been with us on the boat were impatient to be off down river again, having delivered their charges.

Eventually, a small detachment of troops, in the charge of one NCO appeared. There was an obviously angry exchange between the two parties, and then the first lot were mounting the gangplank of the small ship.

"Keirei – Engrishu offica mari sini." (Hey, English Officer, come here).

The NCO was peremptorily flapping his hand downwards in that strange

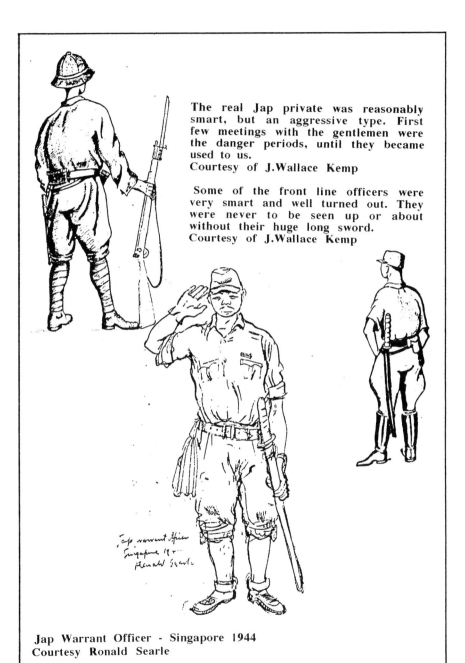

The real Jap private was reasonably smart, but an aggressive type. First few meetings with the gentlemen were the danger periods, until they became used to us.
Courtesy of J.Wallace Kemp

Some of the front line officers were very smart and well turned out. They were never to be seen up or about without their huge long sword.
Courtesy of J.Wallace Kemp

Jap Warrant Officer - Singapore 1944
Courtesy Ronald Searle

way they had of beckoning. The words obviously failed to register quickly enough.

"Speedo, offica, Nippon gunzo speak."

Someone stepped forward. The army officer's cap and tunic indicated the rank of a Lieutenant Colonel. We had not at that stage progressed to knowing identities, apart from the few officers we had known at Singapore, and on the journey into captivity.

The Jap sergeant swung a stick at him, to show his annoyance at being kept waiting. By signs, he demonstrated that he wanted the men paraded in fives – they could count reasonably in fives, but they never mastered fours.

Once fell in, and the count satisfactorily concluded, we were marched off. Our long column had two guards in front setting a smart pace, two on the flanks, and two behind pressing the stragglers, and sick, at the rear.

So this *was* Palembang. We passed through a large open market, the wooden stalls, single and two storey buildings, shuttered and closed. Beyond, we could catch a glimpse of fingers of muddy creeks, fronted by stilted wooden houses, and occasionally, a sampan, or even a larger kind of houseboat.

We soon joined a tarmaced road, which displayed the desolate atmosphere of an out of season jaded shanty town. The only signs of movement came from the small flags draped from the shut doors, and shuttered windows. The natives proclaimed their new allegiance by the 'poached egg' Jap flag. The days of the Dutch empire had come to an end.

As we came into the centre of the town, and some rather more substantial buildings, we passed occasional natives, curious at our appearance, but unwilling to meet our sidelong glances. I noticed that some of them wore armbands, on which had been daubed Jap writing.

The only physical contact we had on that eerie kind of march was with the small children, perhaps 5 or 6 years old, who ran from the side of the road, pulled our clothes, taunted us, or spat. The short period since hostilities had exploded in Palembang, with the coming of Japanese paratroops, had erased their respect for the white man, and replaced it with uncertainty for the Indonesians, coupled with a Quisling-like acceptance of the new régime.

We must have marched – if that is the right term for our straggle – something like two miles. That part is plain. Strange that for the next short period, my memory is clouded. I have a very vague recollection of finding myself in some kind of stone-floored room, with a raised boarded platform down each side. These were to be our quarters for a week or two. Outside was a field – probably the play area of the school, for that is what it was, into which we had come. The field was already carved across with foul ditches.

38

The main street, Palembang.

Native huts, Palembang, Sumatra.

I have wondered why this patch should have submersed in my mind, but can find no reason. A name had been put to these quarters. It was the Hua Chiao school, but even that sheds no light on an apparent amnesia of that brief spell. I believe during that time, the strange diet, and distressing sanitary conditions caused violent outbreaks of stomach and bowel disorders, and the word dysentery became part of our vocabulary.

Personalities

"So this is Chung Hwa, and this is our mess room. Suppose it could have been worse. At least, we have got electric light, water, and toilets, and a good roof over our heads. Anyway, we've got to make the best of it, so I don't want a lot of moans. Any real problems, come and see me, and I'll do what I can."

The commentator was Leading Seaman Frank Downing, who had been put as 'killick' in charge of the other 15 or 16 of us, who were contemplating the confines of our new quarters, a square room measuring, I would think, some 16' each way, giving us about 2' by 6' or 7' each, allowing a narrow passageway to the door.

It was a bare stone-flagged room, with a single window, barred, but not glazed, giving light from a paved courtyard, where we could see the green of two large trees.

Frank was not of dramatic stature, and being well into his thirties, was distinctly 'old' compared with the rest of us, but he left us in no doubt of his intention to have an orderly and well behaved mess, and imposed a fair and rigid discipline, which he had acquired over his years as a regular serving rating.

We were a mixed bunch. Apart from 3 'youngsters' who had not reached 20, and were regular 'boy' entrants, we comprised 'hostility only' men, from very mixed backgrounds, and drawn from all over the country, plus two sailors from Australia and New Zealand.

There was my 'oppo' from HMS Sultan, Johnnie MacMillan, the only Scot in our room. Tom Wannop, from Manchester, and Johnnie Flood, an unusually quiet Liverpudlian, represented Lancashire, while Tout and Aston were Bristolians. There were two inseparable Londoners, Ernie James, and George Byworth, while Stan Orton, a near neighbour of mine from Palmers Green, in North London, and myself, made a quartet from the capital. Signalman Harry Gosden hailed from Surrey. Then there were the three 'boys', 'Bungy' Edwards, Biddulph and Shewring. The Royal

Australian Navy was represented by Kim Mendelsohn, and we had Maurice 'Kiwi' Verry from Wellington.

It seemed a long shot that we would all settle down together, but fortuitously, apart from the occasional rumble, or instant flare-up, we learned to accept our lot, and soon appreciated that we had been fortunate in our grouping.

Charlie Tout had been a showman with a travelling circus, and happily kept us amused with his stories of those earlier days. Foolish minutes were spent bobbing up and down, aching limbs forgotten, as we took on the role of various fairground rides, and mimicked the whistles and hisses of the mobile organs.

"Roll up, roll up. Here you are, sir, try your strength. Fifty woodbine, if you ring the bell. Good lord, no lady, you didn't give me half a dollar, you gave me a bob." In the meantime pretending to show the bare lining of his pocket to prove the absence of the higher value coin.

"Made a pile that way," he grinned.

Johnnie Mac had us all licking our lips at the thought of a juicy pair of Loch Fyne kippers, so real they could be tasted, while Tom re-lived the roar of the news presses from his night duty experience on the Guardian.

Friendships were forged, compatibilities established, and the whole strange jigsaw of our too-close existence sorted itself out, for a time at least into a united pool, a mutual and necessary foundation on which to build and maintain sanity.

We were expanding from individuals into groups, from blank existence into an acceptable level of subsistence.

We had been dumped in the asphalted playground of this former Indonesian junior school, and as soon as we were able, we explored what was to be my home for best part of two years.

Chung Hwa school was solidly built of brick, with a tiled roof. It was approached off an alleyway leading to the main street, and the passing Indonesians, in their colourful saris and sarongs, who had now found their tongues again, chattered animatedly as they passed by.

A courtyard, overshadowed by several large trees led across to a warehouse or store, recently occupied by the local Chamber of Commerce, made evident by the literature, and correspondence, which now cluttered its floors.

There was a large assembly hall, with a stage, and a two storey block, which was taken over as the officers' quarters. At the rear was a large roughly gravelled yard, flanked by another public passageway, and off the playground, was a series of doorless, continental type water carriage toilets, and a series of antiquated, perforated pipes, which ostensibly were to serve as showers. We had little idea then of how futile it would prove to be for

41

Commander Philip H. S. Reid, RN – Soon after capture in March, 1942.

several hundred men to use these doubtful facilities, which had previously been installed to meet the needs of a comparatively few native children.

Through the Embassy of the Republic of Indonesia, and via the Mayor of Palembang, I have endeavoured to obtain an interpretation of Chung Hwa, but have been unsuccessful. My local Chinese restaurateurs have also been unable to assist. One theory is that the characters mean 'Middle Flower' appertaining to 'People's Country', signifying China, but this train of thought seems to be as inscrutable as the Chinese themselves.

Apparently, the new authorities had no intention of continuing with any educational facilities for the local population, and for our part, we were pleased to find accommodation which was watertight, and at least offered even minimal toilet facilities.

Chung Hwa was to be known as 'B' Camp.

Other prisoners, mainly redundant officers – a highly suitable term – had been taken into bungalows formerly owned by Dutch colonials, in a small locality, known as 'O' Camp, while the Dutch troops, and some sick, went into another school – Mulo – which was designated 'A' Camp.

A visible pattern was emerging of our own service organisation. The army, navy, and air force personnel were being separately assembled, and a few names were becoming recognised as the higher ranks in each force.

At 'A' camp, for a short time, we heard there was an Air Commodore – Modin – but I never saw him, and we gathered he was taken away from Sumatra, at the time when all high ranking officers were moved north to Singapore, or Japan. Three Squadron Leaders remained, however. Of these, Clouston and Howell had served as pilots in the Battle of Britain, and the third, Moore found his niche in the spiritual side, acting as a Chaplain – all three being very respected leaders of the RAF contingent.

The army had four Lieut-Colonels – Hill, Fox, Long, and Percy. The former was of ex-Indian Army experience, of somewhat unflinching and aggressive manner, eager to maintain the rigorous discipline previously imposed on his Imperial troops. The latter was a reserve officer, and father-in-law of my own superior naval officer at Fortcanning, Lieut. David Christie. The army other ranks were largely from the Argyll and Sutherland Highlanders regiments, and also included troops from the Royal Artillery, Service Corps, and the Ordnance Corps.

The Royal Navy was well supplied with Officer ranks, many of whom had survived from HMS Prince of Wales, and HMS Repulse, and again from the slaughter of the ill fated journeys south from Malaya. There was Commander Philip Reid, later to become Camp Commandant, and Commander Scott, a round and humorous character, who hailed from Penang. We had two Lieut-Commanders, Victor Clark, very much a man's man, and Spaull, whose background I never got to know. There were numerable Lieutenants, and Sub-Lieutenants, the majority of whom were of high calibre.

From Australia, we had a contingent of the Australian Imperial Force, under the command of a young Lieutenant, Bull. In these early days, the question of their escape from the besieged island of Singapore was under scrutiny, and for that reason, they were somewhat distanced from the rest of us. The Aussie General Officer Commanding, Lieut-General Gordon Bennett, had allegedly left his troops to their own devises, and made good his own escape, and in fact, the whole matter smouldered on into post-war history.

In other rooms, the Liverpudlians and the Scousers, clanned together, in a tough, uncompromising band, matched perhaps by the Geordies, with their almost impenetrable language barrier, understood in the main only by the border Scots. The Welshmen retreated into their characteristic earnestness, serious in their attitudes, as if still hedged in to their valley strongholds.

The Royal Marines (mainly off Prince of Wales and Repulse) occupied yet another room, and despite the change in circumstances, under popular

Sergeant King, retained for a long time, and most outstandingly, an element of smartness.

Of course, we sought out our 'townies', be they from any of the other services, and when the day's labours were done, sat for many an hour exchanging reminiscences of familiar landmarks.

We relived our teenage experiences, and recounted our local knowledge. Sometimes, it seemed that that brought the comfort of home and loved ones nearer. Sometimes it accentuated the divide.

However, life at last had some kind of pattern, and some kind of order.

Acclimatisation

By now, a familiar daily pattern was beginning to formulate. We had become somewhat acclimatised – we thought – to the Jap guards, though individually, they had shown themselves to be of very diverse characteristics. The officers, dressed in their tall, polished, brown boots, breeches, and uniform jackets, with badge of rank, very generally immaculate, white, open-necked shirts, certainly looked the part, whereas, the other ranks really were a motley band, usually in black, canvas shoes, with individual compartmented large toe (known as TABIs), trousers tucked into puttees, and ill-fitting shirt cum jacket, laden with water bottle, cross shoulder ammunition packs, and capped with soft, shapeless, peaked cap, carrying a rifle, seemingly as tall as themselves. The officers had red badges, with yellow stripes and stars, and the other ranks had gold stars on red, three stars for a 'superior private', two stars for a 'first class private', and one star for the 'second star private', the lowest of the low.

I don't think that we ever came to terms with the not infrequent sight of longish shorts, being worn with socks, held up by garish suspenders or their bespectacled, virtually hairless, sepia, smooth faces, and high cheekbones, generally devoid of all expression, except bad temper. These troops, used to guard prisoners of war, were certainly not the cream of the Japanese Imperial Guards.

"Just look at Gladys," said a voice outside.

"My God, what a great big nit."

"Look at me girls. Anyone for afters?"

Gladys was one of the guard sergeants. He was mincing across the playground, seemingly unaware of the attention he was receiving. As Japs go, he was thin, with slightly bow legs, emphasised by his foppish gait. His uniform, as always, was spotless, but several sizes too big, and he was sporting a pair of bright red elastic suspenders. He was a post-graduate of Tokyo University. We soon learned to our cost, that despite his educational background, and his rank, Gladys was one of the most vicious, and bestial, of the guards. His lack of stature was supplemented by an extreme and uncontrollable temper.

As part of our rapid indoctrination, we learned to submit to bowing to our captors, as soon as they hove on to the horizon, and God forbid anyone who overlooked this enforced act of submission. It was not unknown for a guard to lurk out of sight round a corner, and when a prisoner passed, without seeing him and without bowing, the man would be called back and given a beating for not doing so.

One night, we were warned that by the end of the week, just 3 or 4 days off, all men must have their heads shaven, as indeed, did the Japs. The difficulty was that among many hundred men, there were very few pairs of scissors, and a few, by now blunt, razors. The Japs took no steps to provide any utensils, but repeated their orders. We did not really object to this, as it would clearly be more hygienic, though quite incongruous, seeing that most of us had bushy beards, with no means to shave or trim them. Those few days saw us all reduced, quite painfully, to patchy scalps, as hair was cut, trimmed, wrenched, singed, and otherwise removed. I must say that this was all accompanied by a good deal of mirth, as we took on the look of a crowd of moonmen. It had the great disadvantage that with little or no headcovering, a sunburnt pate could be extremely painful.

About the same time, we had a pleasant surprise. We were issued with soap.

"Now don't all go raving mad," said our Leading Hand, as he distributed the ration. "If you rub hard enough with this stuff, you might just get back to your skin again, but go easy because we don't know how long this has got to last."

'This' was a yellow block, like a bar of sunlight, but was as soft as butter, and needed to be baked hard in the sun before use, otherwise it went in a flash. After drying, it became like a strip of wizened toffee, though very precious. With reasonable use, to wash ourselves, and our few bits of clothing, it would probably have lasted best part of a week. An allocation was made erratically, about every 6 or 7 weeks, and then disappeared completely.

The 'galley' as the kitchen was termed, probably because it was under the command of the rations officer, Navy Lieutenant McMullin, was the centre of most interest.

Our rice ration was nominally to be 500 grammes per man per day, or between 17 and 18 ounces. However, that ration was only supplied for each man who went out on working parties. Those who were on light duties, or sick, had a much lower allocation. Then, since it was evident that many of the 100 kilogram sacks had been pilfered, were leaking, or worst of all, were the warehouse sweepings, and included cement dust, and rats' dirts, in effect, our daily ration in 1942, probably hardly amounted to 400 grammes.

At first we had white, polished rice – preferred by the Japs – but as shortages became felt, we had what they considered inferior grade brown rice – to the delight of Dr Reed, who recognised the better vitamin contents.

The bulk supply delivered to the galley was cooked and distributed evenly to all personnel, divided into three meals – the breakfast portion was the smallest, and served like a wet porridge rapidly named as Glop – this was the basis for a day's hard labour of 10 hours at least. The midday meal was plain dry rice, usually eaten wherever we were working, on the docks, aerodrome, jungle, or wherever we happened to be. The evening rice, was usually accompanied by 'soup'. Almost invariably the bulk of the soup was made of 'kankong', which was a river weed, after the style of spinach, to colour the water pale green. Occasionally, this green liquid would be bolstered by a whole, or part, of a tropical pig – a scraggy animal – shared between the whole camp strength.

In the rare event, there would be perhaps a supply of say 50 duck eggs, or 20 unidentified fish, like herring, and these intermittent arrivals were cooked and issued on a rota basis, according to mess number, or alphabetically. Generally, anything special in this way would be largely fed to the sick, and we were left wondering whether our own number or letter would ever be reached. I found myself wishing that my name began with 'A' or 'B' and not with an 'S'.

To my knowledge, never were any eating utensils provided, and my only implements over 3½ years, were my army mess tin, which I had acquired on HMS Tapah, an empty vegetable tin (which was also useful for ablutions), and a carved wooden spoon, which in fullness of time, was replaced by an aluminium scoop, hammered from a piece of aircraft body.

From somewhere, there came an irregular provision of tobacco, or cigarettes. The tobacco was sparse and coarse, sometimes in leaf form, and the cigarettes, few in number, in crushed packets, and worm eaten, but they were manna from above. For non-smokers, they were so much in demand, as a good swap value for sugar, or salt, or some other food.

The clothes we had when captured were now rapidly falling apart, and he was a lucky man indeed who boasted of footwear. In due course, the Japs issued us with 'fandushis' – these were long oblong strips of thin, white, material, tied round the waist with two tapes, the unattached end being pulled between the legs from behind, to contain the essentials, and then looped up behind the tape at the front.

46

To save our feet from cuts, bites, hookworms, and other dangers, we made clogs for ourselves – shaped like a Dr Scholl, and held on by a narrow band of rubber, leather, or cloth – whatever was available, usually salvaged from something else, which had reached the end of its useful days.

Being the height of fashion, with bald heads, fandushis, and clogs, we made light of what the well dressed gentleman was wearing.

At night time, we dragged whatever we could over ourselves, be it rice sack, old shirt, anything to keep the mosquitoes at bay, and form some protection from the chill damp. So far as the Other Ranks were concerned, and generally speaking, the Officers were rather more fortunate, mosquito nets and bedding were unheard of, and I made myself a cover for my face and head from old curtain and cardboard, something like a large lampshade.

As the tropical night swept rapidly over Chung Hwa, so the pariah dogs began their nocturnal wanderings in the optimistic search for food, and, as if by one accord, the rats scuttled from their day time hides. We partially resolved both problems, by making large wood and barbed wire traps, baited with burned crusts of rice, with a stone weighted shutter. The early morning saw the chief rat catcher, old Bagsy Baker (a Royal Fleet Reservist, who probably was only about 40, but seemed to me then to be like Methuselah) releasing the rats, one by one, for the dogs to chase, and satisfy their pangs. Barbarious, no doubt, but there was little choice.

To complete the picture, I must not forget the cockroaches, which crunched underfoot in the night, or the lizards which slithered silently over walls and ceilings.

Home Thoughts from Abroad

"Oh to be in England now that April's there."

So ran Robert Browning's immortal poem, and never more true was the wish from the prisoners in Palembang. After the first impact of our capture had sunk in, our thoughts naturally turned more and more to home.

Would the lists of prisoners assiduously made out at Muntok be transmitted, and our next-of-kin be informed of our fate? What would be the effect on them of this news, coming as it must on top of the trials which they were enduring themselves?

My own birthday towards the end of March, my twenty-second, had passed as just an ordinary day. I cannot recall that even I had thought any more about it than that. But at home, what of them, not knowing whether

Envelope in my Father's handwriting, overstuck with label
'Return to Sender'.

I was alive or dead. What harrowing thoughts must have been in my parents' minds, as that day dawned, and passed?

Shortly after the outbreak of war, my family had moved to Southgate, on the extreme northerly boundary of London. Our modest, three bedroomed semi, adjoined the Green Belt, where soon the trees would be bursting with their new green, and the chestnut candles, of pink and white, would herald our English summer.

The preceding year and a half had seen heavy air attacks, as even the suburbs contained some vital military targets. I knew from personal experience of the nightly air raids, on even the outskirts of the capital.

My two brothers were awaiting call-up, and my younger sister had already been evacuated with the War Office staff to Cheltenham, so my mother and father would be on their own.

I had written home of my transfer from HMS Encounter to HMS Sultan (the Singapore shore base) early in December of 1941, but I had no idea, except from intermittent mail received, of the time lag between dispatch and receipt. From subsequent confusion, it appears that this move had not then been communicated to the Admiralty, or my home depot of Chatham.

What a shock it must have been at home, when my father's letter, posted on 17th February, 1942, was returned, with a cryptic sticker over the address.

Then, on 12th March, a handwritten telegram was addressed to my mother, as next-of-kin, setting out in misspelled detail, some explanation. A confirming letter arrived from Chatham, dated 13th March.

Home Thoughts From Abroad.

POST OFFICE

No. T 118 30.

OFFICE STAMP

Charges to pay
___ s. ___ d.

RECEIVED

TELEGRAM

Prefix. Time handed in. Office of Origin and Service Instructions. Words.

69   5.30   Cheltenham 36

From T S V   B OHMS   To

Mrs RA Stubbs 68 Hampden Way Southgate N.14

Deeply regrette to inform you that the ship in which your son Raymond S Stubbs Coder believed to have been

For free repetition of doubtful words telephone "TELEGRAMS ENQUIRY" or call, with this form at office of delivery. Other enquiries should be accompanied by this form, and, if possible, the envelope.

Charges to pay
___ s. ___ d.

RECEIVED

POST OFFICE

No. T 118
OFFICE STAMP

N 14
13 MAR 1942

TELEGRAM

Prefix. Time handed in. Office of Origin and Service Instructions. Words.

70

From T S V   To

serving has been sunk in the battle of the Java Sea he must therefore be regarded as missing on Act of Service letter follows Commodore RN Barracks Chatham

For free repetition of doubtful words telephone "TELEGRAMS ENQUIRY" or call, with this form at office of delivery. Other enquiries should be accompanied by this form, and, if possible, the envelope.

```
Mrs. R.A. Stubbs,                R.M. Barracks,
88 Hampden Way,                  Chatham.
Southgate, N.14.
                                 13th March, 1942.

Dear Madam,

          In confirmation of the telegram already sent to
you, I deeply regret to have to inform you that
H.M.S. "Encounter" , in which your son,
               Raymond Stanley Stubbs,
          ( Coder ),

is believed to have been serving, has been sunk in
the battle of the Java Seas.  He must therefore be
regarded as missing on active service.

          There is insufficient evidence at present
to show whether your    son    may be alive or not,
but I will write to you again as soon as possible.
In the meantime, please accept my deep sympathy
in your time of anxiety.

                              I am, Madam,

                                 Yours sincerely,
          [signature]
          Commodore.
```

My sister caused further enquiries to be made because of my change of
ship, and on 30th March, the Commodore, Chatham, wrote in the following
terms:—

```
Mrs. R.A. Stubbs,
88 Hampden Way,                R.M. Barracks,
Southgate, N.14.                 Chatham.
                                 30th March 1942.

Dear Madam,

          With reference to my telegram and confirmatory
letter of 13th March concerning your son, reporting
him missing in H.M.S. "Encounter", as the result
of a special wireless message sent abroad
to ascertain if he was still in "Encounter"
when that ship was lost, a reply has now been
received from the responsible authority on the station.
It is regretted that, although this reply confirms
that he had left the ship and was drafted to a shore
signal station at Singapore, he is now reported
as missing, in consequence of having been in Singapore
at the time of the Japanese capture of that place.
          Every endeavour is being made by the British
Government to obtain from the Japanese authorities,
definite information about all personnel who may be
in enemy hands, and as soon as any news is received
it will be forwarded to you.
          Please allow me to express my sympathy
with you in this time of anxiety.

                              I am, Madam,

                                 Yours sincerely,
          [signature]
               Commodore.
```

50

So that was the news at home, or lack of it, during the month of March, 1942 – when I became 22 years old.

But no, from the end of March, 1942, until 3rd June, 1944, a period of 26 months, there was no news. What distress and sorrow that silence must have caused – it can have no measure. For my shipmates, who were taken to Macassar, in the Celebes, there was no communication at all for over 3½ years. The pain and distress inflicted by our yellow enemy was not limited to the prisoners of war.

I learned when I got home that kind persons wrote home to Southgate. Letters still preserved, from my office, my athletic club, my friends and relations, provided comfort and hope for those waiting for news.

In Southgate, a Prisoners of War Relatives' Association (under the able Secretaryship of Councillor H. S. Beardow) provided a valued centre for disseminating advice, help, general news, and much needed social contact and recreation.

Meanwhile, in Palembang, we dreamed of homes, and mothers and fathers, of wives, sweethearts, and those we had left behind. Each town of any size had its knot of men, who formed a common identity, linked by the place of birth, of education, or of livelihood.

From our segment of North London, and nearby, there was RN Signalman Stan Orton, who had been a swimming pool attendant and life guard. Private Tickner was a male nurse, now helping with the sick in the camp. He came from that now famous, or infamous (!), road in Tottenham, the home of Tottenham Hotspurs, White Hart Lane. A near neighbour of George Bernard Shaw, in Ayot St Lawrence, just into Hertfordshire, was Marine Donald Brown, a survivor off HMS Prince of Wales. Quite close in Enfield, were the homes of Private Donald Richardson, RASC, and Lance-Bombardier Groves, RA. A particular friend was Alan Anstead from Golders(berg) Green, whom we ribbed over his semitic connections. After the war, he was to prove himself an able sales manager.

How many hours we reminisced over our families, the familiar haunts, the picture palaces where we had taken girlfriends, the Wood Green and Finsbury Park Empires, where we had enjoyed first class variety shows. Pubs, restaurants, fish and chip shops, all came under review, but these centres of gastronomic delight soon became a mutually taboo subject, as it did nothing for the unassuaged pangs of hunger.

We recollected, and argued over, our favourite sports. Old rivalries never died, and while some would prefer standing under the clock at Highbury, watching the Arsenal, others could recall the schoolboy enclosure at Tottenham. The defensive merits of Male and Hapgood, for Arsenal and England, were contrasted with the attacking abilities of Willie Hall and Willie Evans, of Spurs, England and Wales.

Quite out of the blue, in June, 1943, we were issued with a blank postcard each, to be written in block letters, for forwarding home. Precise instructions for their completion were listed. Of course, there had to be no mention of military matters, and anything vaguely critical of our captors would clearly lead to rejection. Also, there was the need to convey messages which would allay any fears back in the UK. I cannot recollect any restriction on the number of words to be used, on that first card, though this was conditioned by the size of the card.

This card was delivered on 3rd June, having taken twelve months in transit. It arrived home at the same time as another, written in January, 1944, by which time the Japs had imposed a limit of 20 words, with some mandatory phrases, and a few permissive.

The Palmers Green and Southgate Gazette of 16th June, 1944, reported their arrival, and my sister's comment: "When we saw the cards with the Japanese markings, we nearly fell upon the postman."

It was a contact, and it was wonderful. It gave the prisoners a boost to be able to send something, and it must have been a tremendous fillip at home. It was only after the war, that I learned that the Japanese had taken many of the cards, and burned them. Also, of course, by the time they were delivered, many of the senders had died.

The real red letter day for me was 29th October, 1944 (strangely enough it was to be precisely one year later that I arrived home), when part of a letter, dated 7th March, 1943, from my mother, was brought in for me.

Petty Officer Writer Bill Bolitho, relying on his prodigious memory, had earlier been sent to Jap HQ to sort through some bulk mail, and extract, for censoring, those destined for our camp at Sungei Geron. Each day, as he came back, so he would be besieged by enquirers.

"Any for me?"

"What about me?"

"No, sorry. Yes, Brown, there are three for you. Ah, Stubbs, Raymond Stanley, C/JX 205607, Coder, RN – one for you."

Some lucky lads later received up to 9 or 10, some, none at all (the unfortunate Bolitho included).

Since my mother wrote every week, and family and friends several times a month, I have often wondered what happened to the other 300 to 400 letters. Once again, the attitude of the Japanese authorities was inexplicable. Was this intended as part of the mental torture, or had they no organisation?

The news in the one curtailed letter which I received – I imagine that my mother had not veiled her views, and the censor did not take kindly to part – informed me that life was going on as usual at Southgate. My little dog, a Manchester Terrier, had (as I learned later) surprisingly paired with

"THE FIRST CARD
HOME"

WRITTEN 10/6/43
RECEIVED 3/6/44

RAYMOND STANLEY STUBBS,
C/JX 205607,
WRITER, R.N.

MY DEAR MOTHER,
    I AM A JAPANESE PRISONER-OF-WAR, AND AM BEING
TREATED QUITE WELL. THE FOOD IS ALRIGHT, AND WE
HAVE PLENTY OF BOOKS, GAMES AND CONCERTS. GIVE MY
LOVE TO EVERYONE IN THE FAMILY AND KEEP ON SMILING
I AM QUITE FIT AND WELL — I HOPE YOU ARE ALL THE
SAME. BEST OF LUCK TO ALL MY FRIENDS. LOVE
UNTIL I AM HOME AGAIN.
                    YOUR AFFECTIONATE SON,
                            RAYMOND.

Commander P. H. S. Reid, RN, was Senior British Officer at Palembang from
April 1942 until May, 1945.

MALAYAN PRISONER-OF-WAR C/JX 205607. WRITER. RAYMOND
CAMPS.   STANLEY
                                                                              STUBBS.

MY DEAR MOTHER,

STILL WELL AND CHEERFUL. LOVE TO ALL AT
HOME. SEVERAL FRIENDS HERE FROM NEAR
SOUTHGATE. KEEP SMILING AND HEALTHY. LOVE,

RAYMOND.

MALAYAN P.O.W. CAMPS C/JX 205607.
WRITER RAYMOND STANLEY STUBBS.

DEAREST MOTHER,
KEEPING QUITE WELL. RECEIVED
MAIL. ORTON, PALMERSTON CRESCENT
HERE. LOVE TO ALL FAMILY. REMEMBER
TO FRIENDS AND OFFICE. CONGRATULATIONS
BESS. LOVE.
RAYMOND

WRITTEN   9/11/44   RECEIVED AUGUST 1945

R.N. Barracks,
Chatham.

26th September 1944.

Dear Madam,

With reference to my letter of 30th March 1942,
information has now been received that you have heard
from your son as a prisoner of war in Japanese hands,
and he has been noted as such in records.

I am to state that correspondence with your son
may prove difficult, and it is suggested that you should
communicate with the British Red Cross Society,
Prisoners of War Department, Lord Chamberlain's Office,
St. James Palace, London, S.W.1, for information and
guidance in this matter.

A copy of a handbook is enclosed for your information.

I am, Madam,

Yours sincerely,

Commodore.

Mrs. R.A. Stubbs,
88 Hampden Way,
Southgate,
London, N.14.

March 7. 43

88 Hampden Way
Southgate
N 14

My Dear Boy.

Just a few words to let you know we all are
quite well. including black Bess one of
her pups we often see the lady calls it
Rajah good name, double the size of Bess
Dad takes her out for a walk half doz times
every day, well things are going on as
usual at Southgate, Mrs Cooks got a son
two weeks old, Carol is now three years old
I dont hear from Dick much now
I expect Gerald will soon now be called

The only letter received for three and a half years. Received 29th November, 1944. Note the Japanese censor's stamp.

EXAMINER 3315

Service des prisonniers de guerre.

Coder, STUBBS CI 205607
EXTENDED. DEFENCE. OFFICE
C/o FLEET. MAIL. OFFICE
SINGAPORE.

BRITISH. PRISONER OF WAR.
Co. JAPANESE, RED .CROSS.
TOKYO.

Envelope to letter dated 7th March 1943 and received 29th October, 1944.

a large, black Labrador, and produced several large, first class pups, which had been recruited as police dogs. I was able to acknowledge this happy event in my third card.

Palembang

"What a godforsaken dump this is," said Johnnie MacMillan, as we balanced precariously in the back of a lorry, as it rumbled and swayed on its journey.

But as time went on, we learnt a little more of our surroundings.

Palembang, we discovered, was the centre of one of the world's richest oil deposits, and held over half of the Netherlands East Indies oil reserves. Well over 4 million tons of oil were produced here, per annum. Undoubtedly, this was the main reason for the Japanese air borne attack on the town on 14th February, the day before Singapore fell.

The enemy had dropped shock paratroopers in an attempt to capture the oil refineries, and the aerodrome (known as P1), and in support, thousands of men had swarmed up the River Moesi, from the invasion fleet in the Bancka Strait.

In what has been described as the greatest voluntary destruction ever seen, the Dutch blew up the installations, refineries and equipment, and denied the Japs those precious stocks at Pladjoe, across the wide, swift flowing river from the town of Palembang itself.

Millions of barrels of petrol, crude oil petroleum products and aviation fuel were consumed in inextinguishable flames, and the oil pipe line itself, running up the Djambi road, was severed every few hundred feet, by dynamite charges.

Oil surely must have been the only reason for the existence of this township, situated some 75 kilometres from the Moesi estuary in the Bancka Straits, and about 500 kilometres due south of Singapore. It had rail communication with the southern tip of Sumatra, and road connection with Djambi and Padang to the north and west. Apart from these tenuous links, it was isolated in the equatorial jungle, on a latitude of 2 degrees 59 minutes south of the equator.

It was an untidy conglomeration of east and west. There was a main street of two storey, somewhat Victorian looking, stucco faced shops, or bazaars, with domestic quarters over, some with balconies, and bedecked with Chinese flags, streamers, and advertising signs. The bazaars gave way to the trappings of the Dutch influence, comprising a cinema, a sprinkling of offices, and further on, a modern estate of attractive

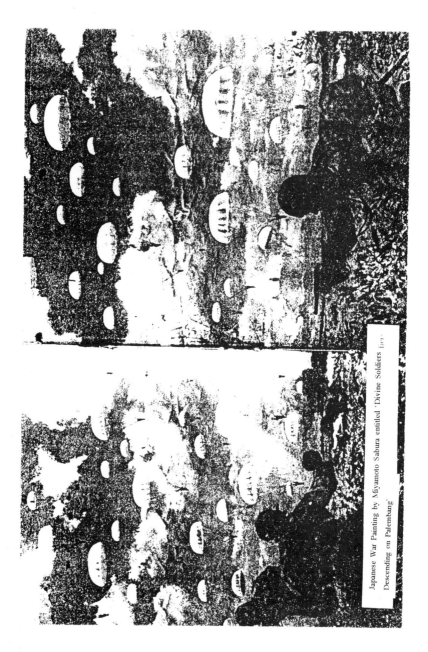

Japanese War Painting by Miyamoto Sabura entitled 'Divine Soldiers
Descending on Palembang'

From "Hurricane over the Jungle" by Terence Kelly.

bungalows. It was here that 'O' and 'A' camps were situated.

The Governor's House, and a water tower, serving the mains water system, were evidence of opulence between the wars, and the 'Charitas' Catholic Hospital on the outskirts of the town, treated some of our sick, until medical supplies were exhausted, and prisoners of war were excluded.

In the main, however, native bamboo huts very largely predominated, approached by slatted walkways over the mud and slime of the river flood, its tributaries and inlets.

The centre of the town was paved, and etched red with expectorant betel nut, seemingly chewed endlessly by the locals. A concreted roadway connected the railway station and the docks, on the one hand, with the aerodrome, a few miles outside the town, on the other.

Ox carts and pedal rickshaws jumbled with rather antiquated motor cars and pedal cycles, which rapidly gave way to the lorries and vehicles of the Japanese invasion forces.

The open market bustled with life, while the saronged natives harangued volubly over the available fish and vegetables, laid out for inspection on the ground. Commerce was clearly dominated by the Chinese and Indians, who principally conducted their businesses in clothes, and manufactured items. The native Indonesians dealt in the foodstuffs, and basically, provided the labour.

Even many weeks after the peace of this isolated town had been disrupted by the airborne invasion, there were still the signs of the short lived hostilities. Here and there was a burnt out, or wrecked vehicle. Out along the road towards the air field, was the ghastly remains of a human being, stark in a ditch, shrivelled and stinking in the sun. Occasionally, a rough wooden cross, by the roadside, marked the grave of a victim of the violence. The Dutch 'scorched earth' policy was emblazoned by the sight of a dynamited oil line, and the Jap ruthlessness was depicted by a decapitated head surmounted on a pole.

Above all, the scorching sun daily pursued its path across the thundery sky, sometimes clearest blue, and at others, heavy and oppressive. The heat produced a dank humidity from the foetid earth, and a variety of smells from the foods, the storm trenches and the decaying foliage.

We gazed around us, generally from the grandstand of our swaying lorries, at the colourful sarongs, and bajus (small native coats), which added a kaleidoscope of brightness to the green fruits, golden bananas, baskets of red and green chillies, and delicious pineapples for sale, by the roadside. We envied the natives their freedom, and wistfully gazed at the apparent plentifulness of the food, denied to our aching stomachs.

Heigh Ho, Heigh Ho, It's Off To Work We Go

There was the sound of heavy boots in the corridor.

"Wakey, wakey, rise and shine, the sun's burning holes in your blankets." The loud voice echoed through the presently silent room.

"Oh gawd, why doesn't someone shoot that twit."

This remark ignored, the voice, now at the door.

"C'mon lads, let's see you. Cooks to the galley."

It was a voice of mixed authority and concern. Authority, because of a lifetime as a naval policeman, it was bred in the speaker, Master-at-Arms Hitchens, and concern, because he knew that that command meant the end of a comparatively peaceful night, and the start of another day of labour and trial.

There was barely light in the sky, as we roused. The end of the sleeping hours was generally the most restful, when sheer exhaustion claimed its captives, after hours of restless tossing and turning on the hard floor. The constant buzz of the mosquitoes, and the occasional scamper of a rat competed with the sighs, groans, snores, bowel sounds, and the occasional sob, or subconscious cry, as our bodies endeavoured to cope with our discomforts. But just before dawn, all seemed to become silent.

"Right, duty party collect the rice." This time it was Frank Downing trying to organise the still drowsy bodies. The room was emptying rapidly, as we left, one by one, to join the endless queues, either for the lavatories, or to the sparse water supplies, to immerse our faces and hands, and wash away the sweat in a soapless ablution.

"Blasted Hollanders" came the words from an open lavatory pen a few yards away. "I can't get used to this damned water idea."

The speaker was squatted over the channel, which served as a communal toilet and bidet combined, endeavouring to wash himself from an upturned bottle, while balancing, feet astride on the marked plinth.

"Why couldn't they have put in proper loos. What would I give for a roll of Izal."

"Come on, come on, look sharp, we haven't got all day," came an angry shout from the queue. Little sympathy was available for those who griped about this lack of elementary facilities. Our personal desires and feelings were taking priority over the needs of others.

Eventually, back in the mess room, we eagerly watched the distribution of a bucket of wet rice, as it was slopped into our individual containers, one ladle apiece. In a cup, or mug, it nearly reached the top, but on a plate, it barely reached the edge.

"Hey, watch it" claimed someone. "Even stevens."

"You've got your wack," said the killick.

The inquest into the fairness of the distribution hummed on while we consumed our rationed spoonsful of this tasteless, glutinous grey mess.

"Any lagi?" (any more)" called Charlie Tout, optimistically.

"Any more?" said Frank. "Who are you, bloody Oliver Twist? You can scrape the bucket."

"He had it yesterday," claimed Aston, despite being townie with Charlie.

"Alright then, whose turn is it?"

A metal spoon scratched the pail, as the fortunate recipient retrieved the two or three scourings, and left the receptacle bare. The argument was brought to the end by a guard clattering down the corridor, banging his rifle butt on each door jamb, as he passed.

"Tenko, tenko, orru me," (Count, count, all men)

Bungy Edwards had barely stirred from the floor. Being in the darkened corner, by the window recess, little thought had been given to the shape still recumbent, shoulders and face mostly hidden under a rice sack.

"Hey, Bungy, tenko," called Shewring. "Eat your rice – quick."

He pulled back the sack, and saw the red face of his friend, wet with perspiration, yet shivering and convulsed now and then with the rigors of malaria.

The killick came over.

"Sick, lad?" he asked, though he already knew the answer.

There was no answer. Only a slow nod of the head, as Bungy drew the rice sack closer round him.

Again. "Tenko, tenko, lekas" (quickly) More shouts.

Out on the parade ground, we stood in vague ranks – equipped for the day. Some were barefoot; some, luckier, had boots, or shoes, but most of which should have long since been discarded. Some had shirts and shorts, while some were bare-backed, and forced to tolerate the tropical sun. Others had garments roughly cut from sacking, and some had fashioned tunics from curtaining. There were forage caps in khaki, or Air Force blue, navy caps, straw hats, coolie hats, cloth hats, peaked caps, any kind of cover for our shaven heads, from the intense rays of the equatorial sun. The Japs being fearful of disease and infection had insisted that within a 48 hour period all men must have their hair cut off. Of course, they provided no means to do this, and having confiscated cut throat razors, and scissors of reasonable size, several hundred men were subjected to the attentions of a few Sweeney Todds, who operated with old blunt safety razors, and a few and scarce pairs of nail scissors, leaving us shorn of our locks, and left

Dawn Parade
*[Ronald Seale's sketch relates to the Thai-Burma Railway – but life at
Palembang was just the same . . .]*

with untidy and unequal trims, looking more like tramps from Mars than the smart troops of only a few months previous.

Each man had his eating utensils hung from a cord, or belt, around his waist. They ranged from dixies, metal plates, tin mugs, to hub caps off lorries. Each individual had a spoon of sorts. Some were metal, turned from a wrecked car, or a cigarette tin. Some were wooden, carved from a piece of packing crate, or even the bough of a tree. In 3½ years, the Japs supplied nothing.

"Ichi, ni, san, shi, go . . ." The Jap sergeant traversed the ranks counting, childlike, making use of his fingers, as he went along the rows. At the end he turned angrily to the Master-at-Arms.

"More, twelve men," he shouted, emphasising the figure with his fingers.

"Twelve men, bioki". (sick) was the reply.

"Bioki, nei." Incredulous that any could be sick in these conditions.

He strode into the building for proof of the absentees. At each door, he stopped, looked, counted, to reconcile his figures. Angrily, he pulled back the inadequate covering of the half conscious figures, prodding or pushing with his rifle, as if to ascertain the degree of life.

A heavily bandaged foot, or leg encased in rag, was ample satisfaction. A fever, or stomach disaster needed greater proof, and generally a long harangue took place, usually necessitating the presence of one of our doctors, the interpreter, and at least an officer, to plead for the exclusion from work of the suffering party.

By the time the tenko was completed, various Jap NCOs from other units had arrived in the courtyard to demand the number of slaves they needed for that day.

In the early stages, the greatest demand was from the regiment in charge of building anti-aircraft gun, and searchlight, emplacements, but there was also a requirement for timber cutting in the jungle, and for the movement of rice and stores.

The former was soon found to be the most onerous, and despite protests from our senior officers that this work was incompatible with the dictates of the Geneva Convention, as it was war work, the objections were contemptuously dismissed, and we were carted by lorry to the sites on the outskirts of Palembang to dig enclosed redoubts, with sandbagged walls, to house the anti-aircraft guns, and lights, for the defence of the town.

The timber party offered the benefit of being able to 'win' some off-cut wood for fires, for cooking purposes, or even through cuts of trees, which were readily converted in to very acceptable dartboards.

The men fortunate enough to be chosen to work on supplies, or at the docks, had the best jobs of all, because though it was hard labour, it always offered the chance of a little extra food, given by a better disposed Jap, or more often, pilfered.

As a result, there was always a lot of shuffling of ranks, as the Jap contingents became familiar to us, and it was a battle of the fittest and most subtle to jockey for position, and be included in the party which offered the best perks.

For my part, I seemed to land the Sakasa, or gun site party day after day. Many of these were constructed along the banks of the River Moesi, and it meant clearing the dense undergrowth, and then working knee, or thigh high, in clogging mud. Our footwear was worse than useless, and to preserve them for other occasions, we worked barefoot, only to incur grazes and scratches on our feet, and up our legs, and to be plagued by constant leeches, worms, and sometimes small water snakes.

It seemed also that the guards on these units, having little else to occupy their minds, delighted in a constant 'Speedo' or 'Lekas' as they drove us on. I think perhaps we hoped that this desire for rapid defence gave us then some hope of Allied retribution. None came.

Yasumé

'Yasumé' was the most welcome word in the Japanese language. It was variously interpreted as 'rest', 'break', 'stand at ease', or as the guards themselves sometimes put it, 'resto'.

It had been a harrassing day on the gun emplacement, and tired, hungry, and caked in mud, we arrived back in camp. The journey back had been hectic, crowded in the back of an open lorry, standing, because there was no room to sit, we had been hurled from side to side, perilously close to being flung out, gripping the side, or tail boards, for dear life, legs and thighs tensed, hoping that our neighbours would not collapse against us.

Now, following the tedious count, within the camp perimeter, we were dismissed. 'Yasumé'. Casting our headgear, pots and pans, and everything except one article of clothing about our middles, into the mess room, we ran to get to the shower pipes.

"Blast, there's not a drip of water."

We were late back after the other parties, and the sparse water had been consumed. Only an occasional drip came from the rusty pipes, and we tried to collect these, and wipe our filthy bodies with a piece of old cloth.

But it is always darkest before dawn, and there was a buzz around.

"Heard the gen?"

PRIVATE COOKING

Drawing by Peter Bivand – later Art Master at Chipping Sodbury Grammar School 13 October, 1944.

It travelled like lightning, through the milling, naked bodies.

"There's meat come in this afternoon. Pork soup tonight."

I suppose that food was more important than cleanliness, and wiped down, we made our way back to the room.

"That true, there's meat tonight?" All other aches and discomforts were set aside. Meat – magic word, after but two months without.

There was a new atmosphere. We had been given thin rush mats to lie on, and these automatically became our individual and demarked 2' or so, by 6', on the floor. Rough shelves, supported in a cantilever style, by coarse string or rope, were fixed at our bed heads, and made a home for our crude, but valued possessions. A home-made dart board swung from the door jamb, and washing lines ran between the bars at the window.

"Rice up," came the call, and there was no hesitation to fetch it. The carriers soon returned – they had two tins – both steaming. One contained dry, grained, white rice – the other a greenish liquid.

"There is meat in it," announced Frank, as he ladled it out. "There you are – pork soup." We crowded round to see this gastronomic delight.

65

I think I was one of the lucky ones, because I had a small cube about the size of an Oxo. Boiled so much, it was tasteless, but something to chew.

Over the past week or two, other developments had taken place. The officers, few of whom were called upon to go with working parties, were to receive a pay allowance, the men were to be paid 10 cents a day for each day they worked, and the corporals, sergeants, and their equivalents, received 15 cents a day. Because of this, the Japs brought in a number of items we could buy, such as small green beans (kachan ijau), discus like moulds of sweet brown sugar (gula java), and pieces of coconut toffee, about the size of a domino (gula klapa). Sometimes, there were bananas, limes, or oranges. Occasionally, there were a few duck eggs, dry tea, and peanuts. In this way, a week's hard grind on working parties would yield some tasty little titbits to jazz up the stark reality of the inevitable rice, and make our meals a little bit more palatable. The Japs, of course, got their money back for food they should rightfully have been providing anyway.

This system had two very great advantages, however, from our point of view. Since the beans needed to be cooked, and the tea boiled, a system of domestic cooking developed, and the rough yard at the rear was the Mecca for numerous little groups gathered around, tending improvised ovens, and fires on which were balanced all kinds of pots and pans. The Nipponese quartermaster needed to allow this in order to feather his own nest.

The second advantage was that if we came across any spoils while outside the camp, we now had the means of cooking them, though this was a hazardous operation should a guard stroll over to see what was being prepared.

"What's the menu tonight then, Jock?"

"Green beans, and duck egg soup. How about that?"

Not quite the Ritz, but it went down well.

Anything remotely edible was baked, boiled, fried, burned, incinerated, cremated. Even the charcoal served to assist some of our digestive problems.

Social life picked up too.

The playground became the centre for various physical activities. A ball, mysteriously obtained, made football, and handball, realities. A ring was set up for inter service boxing, and wrestling matches.

On one Jap festive holiday, we even had a match against the guards, who were ever anxious to demonstrate their superiority in the martial arts. It was our boxers versus their ju-jitsu experts. The evening closed with each of their representatives retreating with a bloody nose, split lip, or black eye. Nippon was proven not to be omnipotent – the occasion was not repeated.

Here and there a precious set of draughts, or chessmen, or a pack of playing cards made their appearance.

Dart boards proliferated, and darts made out of thin bamboo, and a nail, came thick and fast, progressing to inter mess, inter-service, and individual championships.

Sundays were generally rest days, and when the rooms had been cleaned, the communal parts swept, and our personal chores of clothes washing, mending and making were done, we had a few hours to read, to chat, or just have a little kip.

Very often, in the evening, we were allowed to organise concerts, and we were privileged to use the school piano!

I well remember Petty Officer 'Bish' Hardman, who in his tatty shorts, but sporting a white cardboard 'dog' collar, with exaggerated expressions of piety and prayer, would play the part of a Bishop. He would read the Sunday announcements from the platform 'pulpit'.

"The Christian Men's Society," he said, "will meet on Monday at 8.00 pm. I regret that due to a previous engagement I shall not be there."

"The new Brownies will be admitted on Wednesday at 5.30 – I am sorry that I can't attend until later, but I will meet Brown Owl at the back of the hut – privately."

"The young wives have a toast and crumpet, and lucky dip night on Friday – the vicar and I will both be there."

Likewise, I shall never forget how 'Bish', having exchanged his dog collar for two nearly white cuffs, led the Chung Hwa Sympathy Orchestra of piano, triangle, and various home made wind instruments in an hilarious presentation of Suppe's Poet and Peasant Overture.

Then there was LAC Roy, who brought that ailing piano to life, with 'Begin the Beguine', and several of his own compositions.

There was 'Heaven just over the Wall', which harkened back to life outside of barbed wire. I should mention, in passing, that just over the wall (or fence, as it was) was a row of bamboo built, palm leaf huts, set on stilts, and approached up several wide wooden steps, wherein the oldest profession was practised by a number of dusky maidens (!) but I don't think that was the heaven referred to. From the first floor window of the school, we could often see them, sitting on the steps, combing their long black tresses, and mending their sarongs, making good the ravages of the previous night, and preparations for the business of the day.

These women, who had probably reached the depths of degradation themselves, felt some sympathy for our plight, or maybe we were just men, for quite often, they would risk their own skins to push below the fence, or drop over the top, a banana, a hard boiled egg, or some morsel of Indonesian cooking, which came like a birthday treat, and more importantly showed to us all that there was an awakening friendship for us among the native people.

Another song was 'What about you?'
"What about you in times such as this?
What about you when things go amiss?
Are you wearing a smile,
Making life seem worthwhile?
I'm smiling, but what about you?"

One of the British Naval Officers was Surgeon Lt. Reed, and 'What about you?' was his familiar opening question to each of the straggling crocodile of men waiting to see him with skin ulcers, cuts, malaria, ringworm, prickly heat, and the many other early health problems which beset us.

Then we had Petty Officer Bill Bolitho, who as I have mentioned previously was our Memory Man. When challenged by any member of the audience he could straightway recite their Christian and Surname, Regiment or Ship, and Service number. In a mobile encampment of some 800 men, this was indeed a feat.

A story went round the camp that he had won a wager with a guard over eyesight. From the early weeks of our capture, we had to wear a number. Originally these were punched out of raw edged tin, and fastened to our shorts where the serations caused painful tears and scratches to our skin. Later, they produced a stamped cloth number, with Japanese symbols. The Japs considered themselves very superior in eyesight to the Westerners, and despite their slit eyes, and often heavy glasses, boasted of their visionary capabilities. Bill bet one that he could read any prisoner's number before the guard. Of course, recognising the man at a distance, and remembering his number, he beat the guard hands down.

We also boasted a home-made magic lantern, and some hilarious cartoons and slides were produced. The guards were always fascinated by this, and seemed perplexed as to its operation.

Invariably, the entertainment was brought to an end by a powerful rendering of the National Anthem, and Albert Hall itself has never resounded to such enthusiastic patriotism. There came the day when our temporary overlords, perhaps fearing the uplift of those spirited performances, first banned 'God Save Our Gracious King' – swiftly replaced by 'Land of Hope and Glory' – and when the Kempei Tai seized the magic lantern as a suspect secret weapon, totally withdrew permission for gathering of more than four or five men.

An additional facility which we managed to build up at this time was a library. Some of us, more fortunate, who had not had to ditch out of a plane, or swim for the shore from a sunken ship, had books of various descriptions – some paper backs, favourite novels, Readers' Digests, school books, bibles, instruction pamphlets, guide books, and the like. These had previously been passed hand by hand among friends, but now by common

MALAY HOUSE

Peter Bivand.

Official 'cloth' POW Number, which replaced original 'raw tin' number.

consent, were pooled, registered and indexed, and issued on strict principles, and time limits, to those interested. Working parties near the vacated Dutch houses managed to snaffle more, and even some of the guards, anxious to improve their knowledge of English, produced some welcome additions, with the result that we had some 600 items circulating. All of these were carefully scrutinised by the Jap interpreter, and duly stamped as 'Censored'.

In retrospect, these were the comparatively halcyon days. It was not to be long before the enemy attitudes hardened, rampant inflation made our few cents worthless, the Greater South East Asia Co-Prosperity Sphere was recognised as a non-starter, a black market economy flourished, and even duck eggs disappeared, though I am sure the ducks didn't cease laying.

Search

With nice precision, and no warning whatever, there had been a rush of booted feet, and a strident call to 'Tenko'.

In the pitch black, we had been thrust out into the night air, to assemble in the school playground, again to be subjected to the farcical Japanese attempts at a roll call.

"Orro me, speedo, lekas." (All men, quickly, quickly.)

No chance to pull a rice sack over our nearly naked bodies. No time even to collect our muddled thoughts, as we were awoken from our fitful slumbers. Certainly no opportunity to collect anything suspect, or incriminatory, in the eyes of our captors.

The sight which struck us when we returned to the mess was one of utter devastation. Our few pathetic belongings were strewn all over the floor in untidy piles. The wooden shelves, so carefully constructed, had either been ripped down, or left at crazy angles on the walls. A small photograph frame lay smashed, its shattered glass obscuring the middle-aged couple who were someone's parents. Underfoot was scattered uncooked rice, and a small patch of pale brown showed where a tin or jar of sugar had been emptied over the floor. One amateurish pillow had been slashed, and the rag contents emptied out. Cases and knapsacks had been opened, their contents tipped out. Books lay ripped and jumbled, and odd sheets of paper untidily joined with mess tins. The faint solitary unshaded electric light bulb cast its ray on a scene of havoc.

It was now early morning, and after reclaiming what we could, we spread our thin bed mats in the chill dawn, and tried to settle for what remained of the night.

There was the choked sob of someone whose precious sugar now laid crunched into the stone flagging – a valuable ration, almost worth its weight in gold – the pitiable level of our chattels – and our morale.

A voice at the door.

"Quiet now everybody." It was the Master-at-Arms.

"Commander Reid, and the interpreter, Captain Ringer, are at the guardhouse now. We'll have to wait till the morning, to see what happens. In the meantime, for your own sakes, try and get some sleep."

The morning was a long time coming. The clarion call of 'Wakey, wakey' found bleary eyes, restless shapes on the floor, but tenko took place as usual, the rice pap was served up, as usual, and working parties selected, and set off, as usual.

However, following the evening tenko, we were told not to move off, but that the Commander needed to address us. He told us that the Japanese search of the camp had been fairly unproductive, though a couple of knives, and several pads of writing material had been confiscated. It was believed that the main objective was to see if there were a secret radio hidden away. Next priority was to look for arms, of any description, and then any stolen goods, food, clothing and the like, and also any diaries.

Although the Jap guards were well aware that we were all a little light fingered around the docks, they professed anger at the amount of illicit rice uncovered – I suppose it was something to do with 'loss of face'.

Anyway, there came a warning to go easy for a time, until matters simmered down.

That same evening, as if to underline the warning, we had a visit in the mess, by one of the guards – not one of our favourites – nicknamed by us 'Pig Eyes'. He came to tell us how badly the war was going for the Allies. Here we go again.

With much arm waving, gesticulation, and positive crude suggestion, he sought to convince us that none of our womenfolk back home were safe from the lecherous depredations of the visiting American Forces. We must know, he stressed, that the war in the Far East was already lost, and both in Africa, and in the Middle East, the Germans were pushing our forces back unremittingly.

Had it not been for the night before, we might well have believed a lot of what he was saying, but even against the evidence – our personal experiences of the last twelve months – we determined not to be subdued, as his claims became more and more unbelievable.

When he flapped his arms, in imitation of a bomber taking off, and mouthed the words "Tokyo – London – boom boom", it was time to draw a halt.

I think it was Charlie Tout, with some of his fairground nonchalance and cheek, said with mock gravity.

"Nippon pilots bagus." (Japanese pilots very good).

"Nippon pilots very clever to bomb London from Tokyo."

'Pig Eyes' warmed to his audience, his geography became even more exaggerated, until there wasn't a major English city that hadn't been razed to the ground by the omnipotent pilots of the Emperor.

In tones of great condescension, Charlie raised his hands in surrender.

"Nippon pilots, bagus. Nippon navy bagus. But you, you little slant eye twit, are a lying bastard."

"Arigato" (Thank you) said 'Pig Eyes', not understanding the definitive noun, or suspecting Charlie's carefully intoned words.

It was dangerous ground. Some guards were beginning to learn a few words of English. But for all that, I think we slept a little better that night.

Benjo Tuan Besar

The toilet facilities for several hundred men at Chung Hwa soon proved grossly inadequate. Spare paper from the Chamber of Commerce building was easily available and suited our Western habits. The drains meant to carry only fluid were constantly becoming blocked, causing flooding, and its accompanying stench.

To alleviate this, the guards brought in 6 or 7 large oil drums. These were installed in the rear yard, and staging, approached up a few wooden steps, was constructed around them.

Each day, the contents had to be emptied, and these duties were carried out by the 'benjo' working party.

In charge was a short, bow-legged Chief Petty Officer, Shorty Eccles, a cheerful little Lancastrian. I wonder what His Majesty's Admiralty would have thought, having expended finance and training, to produce a CPO who was then employed emptying lavatories.

My 'oppo' Johnnie MacMillan, having suffered a hernia, became a more or less permanent member of this party, and though this might be considered anomalous, since it involved lifting these heavy, slopping drums onto a trek cart, and pulling and pushing it a mile or so through the streets of Palembang, it soon proved to have benefits. But it meant only about 2 or 3 hours work in the morning, and again in the afternoon, foul though this work was. Also, there was sometimes the chance to pick up some food from the natives.

I, too, was co-opted onto this job for a short time, together with Johnnie Flood, and Harry Gosden, until I was elevated to cleaning the officers' quarters, where I was in sole charge of their toilet and urinal. I was to remember this with some amusement after the war, when I was studying the principles of drainage and sanitation for my examinations.

However, once the outside working parties had departed, the camp party, i.e. those with some injury, or recovering from illness, and termed light duty, would rally for their various chores, be they cooks, medical orderlies, camp cleaners, or the benjo party.

The guard appointed to supervise would stay his distance, while Shorty gave his orders.

Having inspected the drums.

"Right, I think it will all go into three drums this morning. All together round the end one."

We would heave the end drum out from under the platform, rolling it carefully on its rim, as not to spill its putrid contents. Then up a plank, and on to the trek cart, which operation was hazardous in the extreme, and took every ounce of our combined effort. This was repeated three times, and then any remaining soil was bucketed out from those still on the ground, until the loaded drums were a foot or so off the brim.

Once the cart was satisfactorily balanced, rice sacks were thrown over the cargo, and we set off. All of this performance was necessarily the subject of some ribald wit, and Shorty the butt of anyone who might have observed the whole struggle.

"Where are you going to my pretty maid?"

"Put that lot on my rhubarb."

"Blimey, Shorty, is that you that smells?"

The procession consisted of a guard – well in front, Shorty ambling along behind him, then the cart with a man on each side of the shafts at the front, and a man steadying the cart, on each side at the back. Lastly – well behind, the second guard.

Fortunately, the route was fairly level, and once the large wooden wheels started turning, unless we struck a rut, it was not too difficult to keep going, meandering through the native quarter, via the market, and down to the river bank.

The guards, particularly on the way out, were barely to be seen, and generally apart from the effort of pulling or pushing, we were not under pressure, or observance.

There was one occasion, though, when we were all taken by surprise. A Jap staff car passed by, and we could see from its fluttering pennant, that it clearly carried an occupant of rank.

"Kurrah!" came the agitated shout from inside.

We stopped in our tracks, and gently let the cart rest.

"Engerisso gunzo?" (English Sergeant?)

Shorty bowed at the appearance of the red badges, and yellow stripes and stars, as the officer clattered out of the car, narrowly avoiding tripping over his dangling sword.

He let rip in a torrent of snorts and unending vowels.

Though we couldn't understand a word, the gist was clear.

What were prisoners doing out without a guard?

The front soldier had disappeared out of sight, and the rear one was hanging back, keeping well out of smelling distance.

"Where are you going?"

Shorty, if anything, a little more diminutive than his Jap questioner, stood silently, but not fully comprehending, pointed vaguely towards the river.

His arm was knocked aside, and a fourpenny one landed across his face.

By this time, the officer was working himself up into a frenzy, as he felt his rank affronted.

"Apa" – said the officer, now trying Malay to break the impasse, and moving nearer to the cart.

"Apa sini?" (What is that?)

Unfortunately, Shorty didn't know the Malayan answer, so he replied using an old English four letter word, which absolutely and correctly, described the cargo. As well the Jap didn't know that word either, but Shorty stopped another wallop. By this time, a crowd of inquisitive natives were peering from behind the various shacks and structures, which served as stalls and shops. Impatience now at its height, the Jap tore the rice sack off the nearest drum, and peered inside. To say that he recoiled would be a gross under-statement.

By this time, the rear guard had caught up with us, and vainly tried to explain.

"Benjo, benjo," he said. Of course, the officer had no need for further explanation. The private unwittingly became the target for the officer's spleen. He was sent reeling to the ground, rifle clattering on the cobbles. As he tried to regain his footing, a long, shiny boot swung at him, and sent him over again.

Red faced, and ill trying to conceal his anger, the officer jumped back in his car, and shouted at his driver, who accelerated away.

One guard, now brushing himself down, mouthed oaths as he watched the officer's car disappear, and when we demonstrated how he had peeped into the drum, with one accord, both Jap and English were all convulsed at the crude humour of the situation.

Eventually, we came to the edge of the river. Now it was a case of holding back the cart, as we reached the sloping bank. It was a scene of colourful hubbub, but as we made our appearance, the natives, from early experience, discreetly withdrew.

74

Down river, as the muddied waters eddied by, a group of chattering women hastily withdrew their dhobying, out of the way of the discharge that would shortly foam past.

A little nearer, we recognised two of the prostitutes from the houses close to Chung Hwa, as they ceremoniously washed, inspected, and dried for further use, the tools of the previous night. I remember thinking how strange that they should be in possession of contraceptives, but the more likely reason was as a protection against venereal disease. Dunking them in the river was hardly a sterilising process!

With a heave and a splash, the drums were tipped into the current, and rolled back and forth to cleanse them. When all three had been emptied, they were left for a few minutes in the eddying flow, while we had a short break. The two guards lit cigarettes, and Shorty also produced a few strands of tobacco, and proceeded to make himself a smoke.

Once loaded up again, we resumed our trek back to the camp. Passing through the market again, we were regaled with calls of "Benjo tuan, benjo tuan besar," (Lavatory man, chief lavatory man). The natives thought it great fun to see the big white man acting as sewage disposal workers. However, having witnessed the earlier incident, they were more on our side, than against us, because one or two broke off a few bananas and offered them to us. The guard didn't seem to mind, but we quickly threw them into the drums, so as not to be seen by the sentry on the gate. Actually, this became a regular thing, and grew into a barter business, when we could afford a few extras.

"Ananas tuan?" (Pineapple offered)

"Tidak ananas, ada ubi kayu?" (No pineapple, have you sweet potatoes)

"Ada tuan – lima cent dua." (Yes, 5 cents for 2)

"Besar ubi?" (Big potatoes)

"Banyak besar." (Many big ones)

"Lima cent tiga ubi." (5 cents for 3 potatoes)

"Okay, okay". This universal word concluded the deal, and probably in the end, we got four each for our 5 cents apiece. We strolled in through the camp gates, our spoils hidden where the sentries would never look. Some we cooked and ate, some were given to friends, and some were sold at a profit, or exchanged with others, for sugar, or tobacco, or whatever was available.

"There's no sentiment in business," quoted my Scottish financier friend.

Shorty halted at the gate, between the cart and the guards. He stood as upright as his bow legs would allow.

"Couldn't stop a pig in a passage," my mother would have said. With his wide straw hat crumpled on his head, and his droopy shorts revealing his navel, and covering his knees, he came to attention, saluted, and bowed to the guard house.

We were safely inside, with extra food for the evening. Mission accomplished.

The Djambi Road

Our killick came in through the messroom door. He had a puzzled look on his face.

"Working parties tomorrow are to go out equipped to be away for several days," he said. "Don't ask me why, because I don't know. That's all that we have been told. So if you have got any spare clothing, take it, and don't go without your eating utensils."

It didn't take much preparation for these unusual circumstances. All of us had virtually what we stood up in, and that wasn't much. In addition, we would need to take our bedding, which generally meant one or two rice sacks, soap, for those still lucky enough to have a sliver, and for the very few, who still had a razor (cut throat types had been confiscated) and any toilet items, these would go as well.

Next morning, we were roused early, and after the usual routine, drawn up outside the school buildings. In the playground was a pile of equipment, large toothed tree saws, chungkals (an Indonesian tool, like a large hoe), pick-axes, several large ridge tents, with poles and guys, kwalis (rice cooking pots, like big woks), and sacks of rice.

Over the weeks, we had begun to be able to deduce our working destination, by the identity of the accompanying guards, and by the direction in which we set off. But today was clearly to be something different. We humped all the equipment into the half dozen or so lorries, which were standing outside, and then, were ourselves counted onto the vehicles. Perched on top of all this gear, our journey was to be even more uncomfortable than usual.

Past the Charitas Hospital we lurched, northwards, skirting the fringe of the aerodrome, and on and on until the jungle seemed to press closer, and closer, and the road itself became merely a cleared track, marked only by the elementary earth embankments, and ditches, on either side. It rose and fell with the terrain, and in the hollows, where the torrential rains had swept down, it was a sea of mud.

Over recent weeks, various of our men, capable of driving lorries, had been recruited for this purpose by the Japanese. This had caused a lot of bad feeling at first, as many thought there should have been no assistance given whatever, unless it was forced under duress. But the Japs knew that there were drivers from the Ordnance and other Corps, so it could not be denied that there were some available. Passions cooled after a time, when it was learned that surreptitious acts of sabotage were gradually removing vehicles off the roads, and relegating them to the scrap heap.

On the treacherous, slimy surfaces, however, it did not take any deliberate act, for a vehicle, laden down with its human load, together with all the extra equipment, to skid in the morass, and finish, wheels slipping madly, in the storm trench. Then everyone had to jump off, to manhandle the lorry to the next piece of serviceable track, harangued, and driven on by the guards, and deluged by the mud flung up from the skidding wheels.

After some hours, we came to a small Indonesian village, or kampong, built round a clearing near the roadside, and here we disembarked.

Several small children, playing by the track, looked up in amazement, until summoned to their huts, by their nervous mothers. "Anak, mari sini, lekas." (Child, come here, quickly)

An old man emerged from one of the stilted huts. He walked with a stick, and his sarong drooped from his thin, rounded shoulders. He bowed low to the Jap sergeant.

"Salamat pagi, tuan." (Good morning, sir). "Apa mau?" (What do you want?). His toothless mouth slurred the cryptic phrases.

In the background, we could see brown faces, peeping from door-ways, and peering round the sides of the buildings.

The sergeant made it clear that he wanted accommodation for his men for the night, and room for us to erect our tents.

A young Indonesian girl emerged from one of the huts, carrying a basket in which were some oranges, a pineapple, and some tiny yellow bananas. She shyly offered them to the Japanese, averting her eyes, and bowing deeply, while she held her sarong modestly around her.

"Bagus, arigato." (Good, thank you) said the sergeant, in that strange mixture of tongues, which we all were cobbling together to make ourselves understood.

The old man led the sergeant away, calling as he did so in the direction of the huts. Several women emerged, and he gave them sharp instructions. After a while, he came back, and pointed to a piece of fairly level, rough ground, indicating that we could put up our tents there.

We fell to, and struggled with our strange native tools, to level the ground, and fix our poles and guy lines.

Sergeant King (Royal Marines) called for some expertise from ex-boy scouts.

"C'mon then. Who learnt to be prepared?"

"Spread yourselves out a bit. Leave plenty of space for the guys."

"Hammer those pegs in well."

Of course, we had to have that corny joke about the pegs.

"Now you hold the peg upright, and when you nod your head, I'll hit it."

We had been left to fend for ourselves, while the guards went to explore what room was available for them. The atmosphere seemed strangely relaxed.

Nearby was an occasional banana tree, bearing hands of these same tiny, orange coloured fruits, hardly longer than a man's finger. 'Pisang mas' we learnt they were called – golden banana.

Scraggy chickens strutted and squawked through the rough undergrowth, and pecked at the newly disturbed earth, as we dug it with our long handled hoes. I think every man had visions that night of something rather special on the menu.

We had arranged ourselves in groups; a wood party to find and cut wood for cooking, a galley party to fetch water, boil the rice, and make tea, and the rest of us working on the tents.

"Don't be a B.F." shouted King, "there'll be a right shindy if you collar that."

'That' was one of the plumper chickens, which had wandered too near one of our Scouse mates, who had contrived a noose with a piece of rope, and was clearly well ahead with his supper plans.

He grumbled that surely one wouldn't be missed, but was eventually persuaded that softly, softly, we might persuade the natives to give us a few gifts. Indeed, our contacts with the inhabitants of the kampong, who showed us where to find water, resulted in some rapid barter. Johnnie came back with a very satisfied look on his face. "What have you got there?" I enquired.

"Banya ikan, pisang, garam, sambil. Just leave it to us Scots – Empire builders."

"Four courses tonight then?" said Harry Gosden. "Fish, rice, fruit, tea!"

"Don't forget the sambil dressing, and the salt," added George Byworth.

We were like a crowd of schoolboys looking forward to a midnight feast. There was much laughter and joking, and we worked with a will to make ourselves comfortable in this oasis in the middle of nowhere.

That evening – a fine night – we sat in our new surroundings at comparative peace with our world – our stomachs more satisfied than they had ever been during the previous months of captivity. We chatted round the embers of the fires, topping up our vegetable soup, fish and rice, with the delectable small golden bananas and mugs of smoky, sugarless and milkless tea. We listened to the noises of the jungle, the cackle of the monkeys, the croaking of bull frogs, the shrill chirping of the cicadas. We didn't seem to care about the insects which winged across the clearing, perhaps kept at bay by the smoke, and watched as fireflies fleetingly illuminated the clearing.

The count was taken, and we retired for the night into the obscurity of our tented accommodation. The soft earth was infinitely preferable to the hard floors of Chung Hwa, and with our boots and shorts serving as pillows we were soon all away in the oblivion of sleep.

As dawn broke the next day, raucous bird noises heralded the daylight and the big black pots were soon bubbling away. Before long, we were sitting round with our rice porridge, this time with pineapple and our tea.

In due course, the guards appeared on the scene and motioned for us to line up for the count. This done, we mounted the lorries and were off further northward.

"Do you see that they are all fully armed, and have machine guns as well?" posed Marine Sergeant King. "Don't like the look of this. Surely they haven't bought us all this way up into the jungle just to bump us off."

It was a chilling thought, but then the Nips seemed to retain the good humour of the day before. There were very mixed feelings, as we rumbled on. Only a few weeks earlier the Australian nurses had been unmercifully slaughtered on the beaches of Bancka, and a number of service men had been gunned or hacked to death. In fact, one of our number, a big chap, Hodgson, had lost parts of two fingers fending off a sword, in the same incident.

The first lorry reached a high point of the road. We saw it stop. The convoy slowly drew to a halt behind it. The sergeant waved his arms for us to alight. We weren't too eager.

Eventually, we were all standing in a bunch by the side of the road. The Japs were busy by the first vehicle. They had pulled back a tarpaulin, and were passing what looked like machinery over the tailboard.

"They're mortars," said Blue Axton, one of the AIF chaps.

"What the hell have they got those for?" asked Cyril Pye.

"We'll soon find out," replied Captain Ringer, who by now was watching with intense interest.

The guards carried one of the mortars onto the roadside bank, and with the assistance of another, was busy assembling it, and laying its projectiles alongside.

"Keirei," shouted the sergeant, seeing our watchful eyes.

He made us form into fives, and marched us a few hundred yards up the road.

"What's the range of those things?" asked Stan Orton, one of our naval ratings, off HMS Dauntless.

"I hope we don't have to find out, as target practice," was the reply.

We marched on, down into a valley, and out of sight of the lorries. The road at this point was virtually impassable, the mud oozing off the hardened surface, and filling the storm ditches.

A lorry rattled to a halt, and two more Japs unloaded a second mortar. They carried it on up the road, until we could just see them on the crest of a hill.

The thick undergrowth encompassed us to left and right. In front was a mortar team. Behind was a mortar team.

It was some very considerable relief, when via the interpreter, we were told that we had got to repair the road, and in some way render it passable.

One gang had to drag the mud off the top of the road, pulling it into sagging heaps, which were then loaded into wicker baskets, and tipped a few feet into the jungle margin. Others sieved stones across what was left of the slurry, while a party armed with axes and saws went off into the trees, and struggled back dragging branches and saplings. These had to be interlaced, and pegged down onto the mud surface to make a rough foundation for more stones and gravel.

We worked without haste, but the steamy atmosphere and intense heat sapped our energies, and the undergrowth tore and scratched at our unprotected legs and bodies. Dragging the saplings out through the binding creepers, and avoiding more substantial trees and bushes strained at our arms and shoulders.

Both captors and captives were glad of the temporary breaks which were frequently necessary. During one of these rests, we could glimpse the mortar party, on ahead, now dug in on the next piece of high ground, one of them scanning the road further on through binoculars.

What could this mean. Who were they searching for. Could there still be Allied troops in Sumatra?

At several points along the road, we had seen huge holes, and scorched debris, where the roadside oil pipe line had been breached. Like many others, I had often wondered what had happened to our other companions from Singapore. Some, rumour had it, had headed north up the Malacca Straits towards Colombo, and others had chanced a trek across Sumatra to Padang, or one of the other west coast ports. Sumatra was a very large, inaccessible island. Were the Dutch and others still possibly holding out somewhere to the north?

The sight of what now proved to be defensive outposts for our working party resurrected these thoughts, and seemed to indicate the concern which the Japs had for pockets of resistance in the vicinity. It could be, of course, that the local natives were proving more of a handful to force into submission than their counterparts in the town.

However, there was cause for some speculation.

That evening, the conversation scarcely moved away from this overwhelming possibility.

On our return to the pitched camp, the first job, as usual was to get the fires going, fetch water to wash ourselves, and make a brew of tea. It was during this that I came across the Scouser of the previous day. He was smuggling a dead chicken back to his tent.

"Big eats, tonight, again," I said.

"Yeah, they won't miss another one," he smirked.

"What, you've just picked it up, and wrung its neck?" I queried.

"So what's it to you?" he challenged.

"Nothing, except that these folk in the kampong have been very good to us, and if we go just pinching their goods, we've had it."

"If we don't pinch, we don't live. They won't miss it. Anyway, it's dead now."

"You can't see further than your nose," I argued.

Next minute I was flat on my back. His head had come down, and butted me, as his knee had come up. Stoker Farron knew all the tricks of dockside strife. I writhed in agony. Fortunately, the incident was seen by several chums, who manhandled him off, and were equally annoyed at his stupid theft. But I never forgot Stoker Farron.

I sat by the tent flap, dabbing at my bleeding nose, and rubbing my aching stomach. We had enemies within.

Meanwhile, Johnnie, Frank, and Harry were searching for more timber. Just on the edge of the clearing were a number of felled trees. They were some two feet across, and had obviously been cut for some time, as they were completely dead and dry. I helped roll them over, as others wielded axes to reduce them to burnable size. Once we had dealt with the top ones, we came to those resting on the ground. We heaved at one and eventually got it to move off its damp bed. As we did so, we were startled to find small, dark, crab-like creatures scuttling for cover in the dead creepers and undergrowth on which the tree had rested. Scorpions. We beat at them with our tools, but in the moment, they were gone.

Long after the evening meal, and the evening count taken, we sat, resting our aching limbs, speculating on the next day's work, and the presence of the mortar parties.

I was very tired, and my head ached.

"I've had enough, I'm going to lie down."

I was stopped in my tracks by Johnnie, and Tom Wannop, who were standing by the door of the Niger.

"Don't go in there," they grinned.

"One of the scorpions is in there – right by your kit."

I was in no mood for skylarking.

"Oh come off it, I'm clapped out. Pull someone else's leg."

"No kidding," they said.

Anyway, I wasn't convinced – it was all too pat. I crawled in in the dim light, and reached out my hand for my bundle. As I put my hand forward, there was a slight movement, and I could distinguish this creature, half raised on its pincers, almost imperceptibly rocking, as its tail curved menacingly forward over its body. My exit was rather more sudden than my entrance – my fatigue forgotten, and in my case, overcome by the hilarious laughter of my two 'friends' who had watched the whole pantomime. After that, the offending animal was duly dispatched, but none of us laid down until the tent had been completely cleared to ensure that there were no more intruders.

Eventually, we settled in again. There were a few quietly whispered conversations, then quiet. An occasional snore, or grunt, and then peace.

"What was that?" Harry Gosden sat up alongside me.

There was a very subdued murmur at the tent door.

"You chaps awake?" It was one of our naval Petty Officers.

"Listen quickly, and no noise. You all know about the mortar parties – We think there is a good chance of friendly forces not far away – and two of the lads want to make a break for it. It has been discussed with Captain Ringer, and he approves. The only thing is that they will need a few more bits and pieces, and we are rustling up any spare guilders, change of clothes, and anything which might be useful."

We soon found a bit of cash, some matches, and a vest, or shorts, from our tent, and the furtive visitors departed, leaving us all excited at the prospect.

In the tropical jungle, there were no man made barriers, or penetrating searchlights to prevent escape, and I think that, in spirit, we all went with these two, brave, and as yet unnamed, men.

Next morning, word soon got around that the two who had gone were two Royal Navy friends, Petty Officer Britt, and Barber. They were two tough, regular service men – they would need all their reserves of energy and resourcefulness to make it in the hostile jungle.

The next difficulty was 'Tenko'.

If we could keep them covered for a day or two, they could possibly put fifteen or twenty miles between us, but if their escape were found immediately, their prospects were virtually nil.

Fortune was on their side. A single guard took the count, working on his fingers the lines of five.

"Roku me ada?" (Have you six more men)

"San bioki, ichi benjo, ni machi." (Three sick, one lavatory, two preparing food).

He trailed off behind our NCO to the far tent. No-one there. He made his way to the middle tent. By this time, someone had broken ranks, and came hurrying back from the direction of the toilet pit, clearly adjusting his shorts, as he did so.

"Satu orang," announced the NCO.

By this time they had got back to the nearest tent. There were three figures on the ground. One sat up rubbing a bruised and swollen ankle – the other two mostly hidden under their sacks.

"Tiga orang bioki." (Three men sick).

They turned towards the cooking area. It had been ridiculously simple.

We managed to cover for I think three days, but then the day before our return to Palembang, all hell let loose. Evening tenko by the sergeant, while another guard stood idly watching, prevented any rigging of the numbers. Diversions were tried. One man 'collapsed', but though he was sat at the side, it was not possible to half shuffle into his space and 'add' another one. Another, clutching his seat.

"Benjo," he pleaded.

"Benjo, nei," said the guard, giving him a cuff round the face.

The game was up.

"Ringer. Ringer. Mari sini, speedo."

By now the sergeant was showing his fury.

Capt Ringer stepped forward, saluted, and waited for the onslaught. He had lived in Japan before the war, and was fluent in Japanese. But no interpreter was required. There are two men missng. Where are they? How long have they been gone? What are their names? If no answer, then all men will be punished. Interminable question after another.

Every prisoner had been brought out into the opening in front of the tents. Four 'real' sick were on the ground. The cooks had been brought from cooking the evening meal. The handful of British officers, and NCOs were stood in front.

"Two men, more two men," shrieked the sergeant. When it was discovered that these were naval ratings, all of those in the same service were punched and kicked. Men in the same tent were kept standing out in the open, as daylight faded, and were badly beaten.

Our return to Palembang was subdued. We hoped for our comrades, but we dreaded what might happen now. We had heard of the Kempei Tai.

Strangely, nothing. We did hear that the Jap sergeant himself received a beating. There was no understanding the oriental mind.

It must have been a month – possibly two, when two dishevelled bodies were brought into Chung Hwa. They had long, straggly hair and beards, their skins burnt deep brown, their eyes sunken, their emaciated bodies displaying every bone, as they shuffled barefoot, manacled into the playground.

"Engrishu Commanda," the strange guard shouted. "Two prisona."

They were released into our keeping. Two new names were added to the roll – Blake and Jackson.

Despite their privations, both men had retained sufficient common sense to relinquish their previous identities – Barber had become Blake, and Britt was now Jackson. These men of courage were henceforth to have no communication to, or from, home whatsoever.

'Jacko' Britt wrote to me in 1983: "We escaped from the working party in a sampan left in the rushes by a Chinese. An officer by the name of Ringer was in charge, and he gave us help by giving us extra biscuits. We spent two days on the river, and then started on land. After about four days, we came to a hut, on the river bank. We spent two days there, and Blake had a touch of malaria. On the second day, we were confronted by a native with a big parang, all ready to use. I got him to understand we meant no harm. He then shouted something, and a woman came out of the bush, with a baby, and went into the hut. I made him understand that we wanted to go north, and he took us through the jungle to a path, and left us. We had a day on this path. We came to a Chinese kampong. They took us in, and gave us some rice and fish. We stayed with them for a week, and then on we went. We met three Malays, and they took us to their village, on the banks of a river, took us to a house, and gave us some food. The next thing we knew, two Japs were at the door, with fixed bayonets. We were put in a lorry, and taken to Djambi. There we were put in jail, with a lot of locals, and fed on corned beef. We went before the commanding officer, and he wanted to know who we were and where we came from. We said our ship had been bombed. We had swum ashore, and made our way through the jungle.We were put back in jail, and the next day brought back to Palembang. We gave false names, in case they knew we were on the working party, up on the Djambi Road."

Change for the Worse

We, who were prisoners could, I suppose to some extent, expect and understand the ill treatment meted out to us, because we were enemies, but the Indonesians themselves were also abysmally treated, despite the

Ronald Searle 1942 – Japs beating up a Chinese.

Nipponese ideal of 'Asia for the Asiatics'.

Three separate instances come to mind to demonstrate the bestiality of our captors upon these hapless natives. Life at its best was a very basic existence for them, but the inhuman usage they suffered, apart from starvation and slavery, was incredible.

Since these three happenings all took place in Palembang, they can only be interpreted as being warnings to other transgressors.

The first was the sight of a young man, completely naked, tied to a tree by the edge of the road, his arms stretched and bound to a crosspiece of wood, the tips of his toes barely able to touch the ground. The weals and bruises on his face and body clearly told of the beating he had endured, and the terrified suffering shown in his face was an almost audible pleading. We didn't know his crime, but it was probably something paltry.

Being physically exposed was very repugnant to an Indonesian and would have hurt him even more than the physical injuries. When we had been near the river we had seen local men and women covertly bathing in their sarongs, careful to avoid the slightest indecency, and it would have been unthinkable for them to be put on such very public exhibition.

Small groups hurried by, aghast at the scene, chattering in fright, on the other side of the road.

In the evening, returning from our day's work on the lorry, the motionless body hung there, flies clustering around the mouth, eyes, genitals and now congealing cuts and wounds.

On another occasion, a party of us were moving timber in the town, long, rough baulks, which cut our bare shoulders and tore our fingers. The guards, bored with the monotony, turned their attention to two native women passing by. One was heavily pregnant, and the guards' comments needed no interpretation. The expectant mother showed her disgust by spitting on the ground. The tone of their banter switched with dramatic suddenness.

"Kerei, mari sini." (Hey, come here!) one soldier shouted.

Apprehensively the two women walked slowly towards the guards, who grabbed them roughly, shook them, and scolded them for their reactions. Their struggles to free themselves only resulted in more ridicule, and loud smacks. The pregnant girl, at whom most of this was directed, was thrown to the ground. Eventually they used the poor demented girl as a pivot for a plank, on which two of Sumatra's 'saviours' rode see-saw on her distended womb. Her petrified cries will never be erased from my memory.

Most of the guards were given nicknames, usually as a result of their behaviour at some incident or other. The guard accompanying a lorry party one particular day was named Watari Jiro. The lorry had slowly rumbled and jerked its way through the congested main street of Palembang, with

Watari standing in the back, leaning on the cab, berating all who hindered its path.

Suddenly, from a side alley, a rickshaw ran out, causing the driver to swerve and brake hard. We, and the guard, standing in the back, reeled violently. Watari did not hesitate. He leapt over the side-board and laid into the defenceless rickshaw boy with paranoiac fury. The next we knew he had taken the crank handle from the driver's cab, and had beaten the boy senseless. Blows rained down on him, head, shoulders and body, anywhere. With scarcely a glance at the crumpled, bloody body, Watari climbed back into the lorry and ordered the driver to carry on. Watari from thence on was called 'Starting Handle'.

These were only three of many examples of the bestial tempers of our guards. They underlined the feelings of impotence, helplessness and inadequacy to which we had been reduced.

I found myself quite unable to understand the ruthless military rule, which the Japanese were imposing on these conquered territories, and their people. The eastern and western sociological cultures were so diverse that there was no common ground for the appreciation of the other, but I felt that there might have been a closer concord between the coloured peoples.

Having subsequently learned a little more of Shintoism, and Bushido, my lack of understanding has increased, rather than diminished.

'Shinto' is said to be the way of 'kami', a mystical, divine nature which transcends the cognitive faculty of man. Daily life is made possible by 'kami', and the personality and life of man are worthy of respect. Man must therefore revere the basic human rights of everyone, regardless of race, or nationality.

'Bushido' is the code of warriors, revering athletic and military skills, and fearlessness, but having regard for frugal living, kindness and honesty, while the Samurai class equated with the Confucian 'perfect gentleman'.

How could these precepts be reconciled with incidents like these, and the many other violent and cruel acts towards natives, prisoners, and even animals?

The few months of relative stability were first disturbed by the sudden arrival of Sikh soldiers, who had joined the pro-Japanese Free Army, as guards on the gates. Virtually no communication took place with them, and they did not patrol inside the camp perimeter – possibly they were well aware of our reactions, since only weeks earlier they had been alongside British Empire troops.

When very shortly afterwards, the Sikhs were replaced by the Koreans we did not appreciate then the coming violent change for the worse. These men were rather bigger in stature than the Japs, mostly of peasant stock, and treated with contempt by even the lowest grade, one pip, Nippon soldier, with the result that their captives presented to them the opportunity to vent their spleens on beings even lower in status than themselves.

Such conversations as took place with the Japs or Koreans ran a fairly predictable course. At the outset, they despised us for allowing ourselves to be taken prisoner, something which they indicated was quite incompatible with their own beliefs (A view which did not materialise in August, 1945, when the roles were reversed).

There would be enquiries about our families and wives.

"You, wifo ga?"

"No."

"You, perampuan, ga?" (Girlfriend?)

"Yes."

Lewd signs inevitable.

"Anak ada ga?" (Have you children?)

Why did they persist in adding vowels to everything they said!

"Tidak." (No)

"Engreeshu tidak bagus. Nippon ada banyak kechil." (English no good. Japs have many small ones)

Once this elementary dialogue had run its customary course, and the vulgar virtues of Jap virility had been established to their satisfaction, perhaps the topic would change to the invincibility of the Imperial forces of the Emperor. By much arm waving, and nasal and gutteral sounds, a frequent tack was repeated over and over again, following their own indoctrination. "Japan/Tokie/London/Boom Boom," from which we were meant to deduce that Jap planes flew the many many thousands of miles to wreak havoc over England. They seemed surprised at our lack of concern at these miraculous feats, and their claims got progressively more preposterous.

They would always be on the lookout for rings, watches, fountain pens, any valuables or mementoes, such as photographs, insignia of any kind, most of which were unashamedly stolen, but on the odd occasion a one-sided barter took place. I was careless enough to be sitting one day, indexing the precious camp library books. I was using a Waterman fountain pen, which had been presented to me when I left my first job, after leaving school.

My colleagues at Hornsey Borough Council had kindly allowed me to choose it as a parting gift. It was black with tiny little random insets of red, green and silver crystal. It was precious to me.

The first I knew of the presence of the guard was the scrape of his rifle as he rested it against the table. I expected trouble as I had not heard him come in and therefore had not bowed, but fortunately he had his mind more on my pen. His hand stretched out and took the pen, and he walked over to the window to examine his find.

"Watermanga?" he said, having read the clip on its side. "Engrishu?"

I nodded. He paused in thought. He then pointed to 9 on his watch, laid his rifle on the table, put three fingers on his badge of rank and made as if to remove his cap and rest his head.

"Ah," I said. "Sembilan, kashkan resto." (9 o'clock officer off duty.')

He nodded. More charade demonstrated that after that he also came off duty, and would then return. I could have kicked myself for my stupidity at not being more alert. I thought to myself that I'd be damned if he was going to have my pen. The more I thought about it the more doggedly determined I was that he should not have it. Then in a flash I had the answer. I unscrewed the case, removed the rubber ink sac and replaced the pen back together. The sac I hid behind some books on the shelf.

A few minutes after nine, he returned, grinning, hand extended.

I stood, bowed, picked the pen up off the table, and gave it to him.

Delighted with his acquisition, he made to write on a scrap of paper, which was on the table. Nothing. Querulous, he handed it back to me, and by unscrewing the nib, I showed him with my limited Malay vocabulary, that it was "Tidak bagus" (No good), "Mati" (dead), and it needed to be constantly dipped in the ink bottle, to write at all.

Realisation was slow, and then holding his arm out, with hand flapping downwards, in that odd Japanese way, he motioned me to come from behind the table. As soon as I was within reach, he smacked me hard, several times, round the face, his features distorted in rage.

"Bakayaro," (Idiot) he screamed.

"Kono yaro," (Damned fool) he shouted, as more slaps and punches rained on my bare chest and arms.

The pen was flung across the room. I stood motionless, hoping that my outward calm might somehow show his attack to be not worthwhile. No such luck. He drew back his foot, and kicked hard at my shins. Fortunately, he was still wearing his soft boots, and the kicks, while painful, did not inflict wounds. We had already learned that to stand upright was the best remedy to avoid the ferocity of such attacks, and with the table behind me, I managed to stay passive and erect.

We also knew that any retaliation was useless, and could be fatal.

The monologue continued unabated, his eyes peering upward, searching my face, which I could feel reddening and dripping with sweat.

Then he grabbed his rifle, swung it round my hips and buttocks with shattering blows, finally stabbing the steel-shod butt repeatedly down on my unprotected legs and feet. I felt the skin tear, the sharp pain, as the blood trickled down.

I don't know whether it was the sight of blood or his fury being spent, as he hurled one more "Bakayaro" over his shoulder, and stamped off, penless.

Perhaps I could have saved myself a lot of pain and anguish by letting him have the pen – perhaps I had been foolish for my pride. I don't know.

It was a relief to regain the haven of the stone floored mess room where at once, Johnnie MacMillan found an old shirt to bind my legs and feet, and someone else contrived a cup of hot milkless tea, sweetened like nectar, with more than one spoonful of their precious sugar.

Strangely, the Korean's name has long since disappeared from my memory – only the scars remain.

That was my first individual beating – but it was not the last. I was fortunate that at that time I was fit enough not only to withstand the physical barrage but also the shock, which came later to under-nourished bodies and could prove the breaking point. At that time too, flesh healed, whereas later, because of vitamin deficiencies any cut or abrasion festered or ulcerated, turned septic and refused to heal.

Six years later, in a green meadow by a lush stream near Calbourne, on the Isle of Wight, as I cantered with my young bride on honeymoon, that pen must have jumped out of my pocket, and was lost to me for ever.

Aerodrome Working Party

The aerodrome at Palembang (referred to as P1), situated several miles outside the town, close to the road north to Djambi, had only been used for commercial purposes. As I remember it, there was one main runway, virtually, north/south, parallel to the road, and bisecting it another runway, reaching towards an incline and a valley to the west. The perimeter disappeared into close jungle. Here and there were earth banks, which acted as dispersal bays.

It gave us consolation to see the wreckage of many Zero fighters, which had been destroyed in the hard-fought battle for mastery at the time of the invasion.

The Japanese soon took steps to extend and improve the field, and the British and Dutch prisoners of war, together with many hundreds of natives, provided a much needed working force.

The main project was to move the long incline, into the far valley, so that the shorter runway might be extended. This necessitated shifting hundreds of tons of earth, and for us weeks of unremitting labour through the heat of long tropical days.

This was done by constructing several radials of a small railway from the hill top, down to a concentric point in the valley. On each converging line were a dozen or so small V shaped tip up trucks. These were loaded with soil at the top, and then run down the gradient, to the lowest point, where the soil was deposited.

"OK lads, let's get fell in, otherwise there'll be the usual ructions." It was a young naval sub-lieutenant speaking, Sub-Lt. Lyle. We had jumped from the back of the lorry, and piled the pick-axes, chungkals, long shovels, and baskets on the ground. The Jap guard was pacing about, anxious to impress his sergeant that he was well in charge. Apart from an occasional purge, the Allied officers were not required to work, but a few, generally the younger, and more subordinate ranks, accompanied working parties, in a supervisory capacity, and as go between. Lyle, who had spent a major portion of his young life in the East, and spoke one of the Chinese dialects, was a welcome officer among the other ranks.

The Jap, seeing some patent signs of order, called us to attention.

"Kiotsuke. Orru me ojigi." (Attention. All men bow)

"Bow. Bow to that stupid little twit." One of the Aussies didn't like the idea. Nor did any of us come to that.

"Better bow than be bashed," came wiser counsel.

"Tenko."

"How many more bloody times?" said the Aussie.

"Alright. From the left," said Subbie Lyle.

"One, two, three, four . . . eight, nine, ten, Jack, Queen, King, fourteen, fifteen, sixteen . . ." There was concealed laughter at this little diversion.

"Told you he was a little twit," repeated the Aussie.

The count eventually completed, we were marched off to the head of each individual line, where stood a row of empty trucks. Three, or sometimes, four, men took up position by each truck, and started shovelling loose earth into them, while others dug up the hard-baked soil. Once the line of trucks were full, the wooden chocks were knocked away, and gradually they gained speed, clattering noisily down towards the valley. Since it was necessary to tip and empty the truck at the bottom, and then physically heave it up to the top again, the crew had to ride down with it. One man at the front was the brake man, having a long spar of wood, which when needed acted as a lever against the angle of the truck side, and on to the front axle. The other two men hung on precariously to the sides. The whole operation was fraught with extreme risk of physical injury, and many a sprained ankle, or twisted leg, or bad bruising occurred, when the wood spar sprang back, or as sometimes happened, the whole truck, and its contents, jumped the rails, and ran out of control, until arrested by some softer earth.

The guards, of course, were insistent on the whole line moving as quickly as possible, and woe betide the last truck to be loaded, for it held up the descent.

Always present, a strutting Jap, with soft cap, and cloth protection to his neck and back – Legionnaire style – shouting "Lekas, lekas," (hurry, hurry) while we strained and sweated with our primitive instruments, mostly barefoot, with only shorts, or fandushis, as cover against the sun, dirt, and curious gaze of the natives.

As the many tracks converged on their downward journeys, and some hundred or so trucks discharged their loads, so the valley level rose daily, and the hill top flattened out. Armies of natives laboured with us, the men with chungkals, and the women struggling with palm baskets, bulging with earth and debris, which they dragged to fill holes and crevices.

Occasionally, when it was the all too brief yasume period, we would seek what shade there was behind the trucks, or under a bush, and we began to discover a common identity with the Indonesians, who seemed to be able to squat endlessly on their haunches in seeming comfort. Our few words of 'pidgin' Malay expanded into increasing dialogue, and after a while, a small market grew, we bartering with our few precious cents, and the natives finding a ready sale for their gula Java (lumps of hard brown treacly sugar), gula klappa (a form of peanut brittle), chillie sambals (highly seasoned sauce pastes, wrapped in banana leaves), a few wisps of tobacco, or baked ubi kayu (wooden potato).

Now and again, when the guards became impatient with our progress, one would demonstrate for a few minutes how quickly he could fill a truck, and then retire under a tree with his water bottle, fully expectant that we would follow his example, hour after hour. Sometimes, when this ploy failed, and tempers and swearing subsided, they set a target to be reached before we could return to our camp – 16 trucks per team – then if that was achieved, it was 18 the next day – then 20. Even the tough dockies from Liverpool and the North East, more used to physical labour, soon rumbled that one, and the pace dropped back, despite the anger and hostility of our overseers.

We worked with Zombie-like precision, the monotonous boredom and the desire to conserve our draining energies overcoming any wish to talk, our only interest the next fleeting chance to sit, and perhaps have a few sips of the strictly limited water ration. Even this encouraged the sadism of some guards, who would force a prisoner to hold a kerosene tin of

A prisoner performs a rock-holding endurance test for the amusement of the Japanese guards.

From 'To the Kwai and Back' by Ronald Searle.

precious water at arm's length, until strength flagged, and it spilled in the dust and rubble.

Sometimes, if the work rate did not come up to their standard, an unfortunate culprit would be made to stand, holding a pickaxe above his head, for an indescribable length of time.

There were some sharp moments of drama.

I recall the hurried withdrawal, and excited chatter of the natives, as we struck a tarantula nest, and these huge, rather beautiful spiders, their irridescent bodies shining in the bright light, scattered among us, then temporarily froze in the scorching afternoon sun, before scuttling off to a hiding place. The anxious warnings of the Indonesians had alerted us.

On another day, after much vicious punching and bad tempered treatment of a small group of natives by two guards for some passing misdemeanour, the natives were led away, out of sight. Shortly afterwards, the guards returned, unaccompanied. As we were marched back to the lorries at the close of day, our particular guard was keen to demonstrate how he would have carried out the beheading, much more cleanly, his sword ripping off small branches of bushes as we passed, until he tried his luck at a young sapling, and the mild steel wrapped itself neatly round the resilient green wood, leaving him annoyed at his personal embarrassment.

While away on these outside parties, the rice rations were generally prepared in the camp, and distributed as lorries or other transports were available. It was in these early days that the vagaries of the eastern diet were thrust at us. While they were later to become occasional luxuries, at this stage, they were odd tasting, but necessary, food.

We had fish soup, complete with heads, bones, fins, the lot. There were plums, apparently of several years vintage, salted and packed in small wooden barrels, Seaweed, Mangka, or Jackfruit, mangoes, soya beans – so hard, and completely indigestible – (they emerged exactly as they were taken in) – all these things provided a strange variety.

After some weeks, the plateau became a reality, the runway was far longer and wider, and our work there was ended.

Minor Ailments

'Grannie' Grandidge tottered precariously into the mess room. His 6 foot frame bent, and his arms outstretched as he threw his weight one way, and then the other, while he placed his feet very cautiously down on the stone-slabbed floor. That was it – his feet.

"Who's the Fairy Queen then," asked Charlie Tout. "Wouldn't the silver slippers fit?" We had become accustomed to many forms of footwear. The carefully boned black army boots, the blancoed gym shoes, pristine white, the carefully preserved leather sandals – a souvenir for back home – all these had long since become holed and worn in mud, rain, and baking sun, and would no longer even find a place in a tramp's possessions. In their place was a selection of wooden clogs, hewn from scrapwood, and held on by a solitary cloth or leather strap across the toes, discarded Jap canvas jungle boots, and a motley salvage of useable parts of former uniforms.

But Grannie's footwear was something special. His feet were swathed in layers of buff coloured rice sacking, ill fitting like brown cloth bags tied round his ankles. He sank down on the floor, and as if unconscious of the jibes, peeled off the covering to his left foot, wincing as he did so. As he revealed the ball of his foot, we could see the raw flesh spreading towards his toes, which themselves appeared like strips of evil coloured meat.

"Good God," said Charlie, "Can't they do anything about that?" 'That' was Athlete's Foot, which starting from crevices between the toes, had now spread from the soles of his feet, as the skin disintegrated, leaving only the raw and bleeding flesh. 'Chinese Rot' as it had become known throughout the camp, was insidious as it crept from joint to joint, and person to person.

"What can they do?" replied Grannie. "The sick bay tiffy hasn't got any ointment, just swabbed it with a boiled rag."

It was no surprise to us that this tall, elegant fellow, clearly from a good class background, should be reduced to a shambling wreck by this creeping scourge, for which he had no cure.

"The doc says he has asked for some of that purple stuff that they paint on in the Navy, but a fine hope of getting any."

So it was with most things.

The Jap doctor who visited the camp occasionally, paid scarce attention to even more accentuated problems. It was only the need for working parties that prompted them to provide the most essential commodities.

"Well, I suppose that when I'm sitting down, it's not as painful as your tooth-ache," Grannie said to Harry Gosden, who for some days had had a swollen face.

"Hope it doesn't spread to your backside then," came in Frank Downing.

By this time, there weren't many of the men that couldn't show the distressing weals of ringworm, or the irritant specks of prickly heat, but now the absence of medicines, and the pathetic attempts at hygiene, were reaping a rich harvest.

We had discovered lice in our rice sacking bedclothes, the evidence of nightly visits by the rodent population was an accepted part of our conditions, and the latest scourge was to find that several of the chaps had pubic lice. 'Crabs' they called them. I was reminded of that rhyme scribbled on the door of the lavatory in Gibraltar.

"It's no good standing on the seat,
Gibraltar crabs can jump ten feet."
Then, I didn't know the meaning. Now I did.

Each night there was the necessary routine of self examination to find these minute creatures, which burrowed into the skin, and caused painful irritation. Of course, you knew you had caught them, even before the debasing proof was seen, but this proof of being unclean was, even in these circumstances, a degradation difficult to accept. Of course, no medicaments were available to deal with this condition either, but we did discover that rather than try to pull the pests out, leaving the head under the surface, only to grow again, a flame applied to the small body, would cause it to retract and fall out. You can imagine the ribald comments that accompanied this nightly procedure. Sex had long since ceased to be a priority in Service conversation, but it had a wry humour as a lighted taper, or red wire was carefully applied to the visible end of the lice.

"Careful now, Andy, don't burn it off."

"What's the matter, can't you find it?" And, of course, rather more colourful remarks.

The Japs did sit up and take notice if something which was likely to affect *their* troops, ran through the camp. When dysentery was at first diagnosed, and began to spread among the prisoners, we even had a water cart brought in to supplement the variable water supply. This was to provide water to scrub the insanitary loos. In order to guage the extent of the outbreak, the Jap doctor arranged for a physical examination of each man. He sat at a small table in the open, with a medical orderly at his side. As each man was presented, so a glass tube was thrust between his buttocks, wiped onto a slide, and then swabbed with a piece of lint. No apparent record of name, or identity. Just how many had, and how many hadn't. Of course, the glass tube was a convenient way of transferring infection from one man to another, but one of the strange quirks of the oriental nature was that they were demonstrating their reaction to the spread of the disease, and by this quite useless action, they were not losing face.

Though we did not realise it at the time, the gradual process of devitaminisation was taking place, and this manifested itself in a multitude of ways. Hip and thigh sores, caused by our nights on hard unyielding floors, spread and worsened. The beginnings of pellagra raised blotches on the skin. In many, eyesight was affected, and even temporary dementia, little understood, was easily triggered by some unforeseen and critical event.

One phase which brought untold misery was precipitated by the arrival of the cement boats.

The dock party – generally a favourite because of the chance to find a bit of extra food – was suddenly plunged into what was probably the most depressing task. On these small cargo vessels were thousands and thousands of 50 kilo bags of powdered cement. These had to be loaded onto our backs and carried into the warehouses. The labour in the open was bad enough, but down in the stifling holds, choked with the acrid dust, it was a penance. To carry 110 lbs weight, hour after hour, was now an accepted task, particularly as rice was in 100 kilo bags, twice the weight, but the cement dust penetrated every crevice, in our eyes, up our noses, in our mouths, everywhere, and mixed with perspiration chafed, and rubbed. It was misery to clear one's eyebrows, or to blow your nose, and even a sip of welcome water, was accompanied by the grit.

On return to Chung Hwa, we were walking grey bodies, caked from head to toe, and often there was no water. We had no change of clothing to relieve the coarseness, or ease the bite of the acid on sores, ringworm or other skin eruptions.

After a few days of this, we were all walking like cowboys. The pain and misery was intense. Scrotal dermatitis became the order of the day. It is perhaps wry humour now to look back to the sick parade, which then wound itself round Chung Hwa playground, leading towards where Lieut. Reed, our naval doctor sat, awaiting each individual.

"What about you," he would say, with hardly a glance. He knew there was nothing he could do, but each man hoped to be spared the next day at the docks.

"What about you." Another torn pair of shorts, or a Nip fandushi would be lowered, to expose the rawness hidden underneath. A weeping, horrible mess.

"Next." That was it then. No remittance from the next day.

Back to the mess.

"What did he say?"

"Nothing."

"You can't be that bad then."

It was all comparative.

One day, the Japanese, perhaps concerned that the cement boats were not being unloaded quickly enough, sent across a bowl of water, with some evil smelling disinfectant in it. It was something. One by one, over three hundred men stooped over this one bowl, gingerly bathed themselves, and passed on – at the end it was more like cement slurry.

From then on, the term 'rice balls' had a new meaning.

However, it still continues to amaze me, the phase passed, perhaps our bodies were able to react, or we found a cure.

We had seen the natives running their fingers around the black oil on axles and then smearing it on cuts. This crude treatment kept off the flies, and excluded the air, and the cuts and sores healed. We watched the 'ladies of the night' in their quarters adjoining the school, as they ran tapers over their bed mats, and we followed suit, and so kept down the lice which inhabited the seams. We found that coconut fibre cleaned our teeth, and that charcoal helped our bowels. Doc Reed boiled leaves, and plants, and found by accident or design some palliatives to our ills.

In 'B' camp, at Chung Hwa school, too, we were lucky. We really didn't notice, unless it was a close friend, that occasionally someone was taken away to 'A' camp, where there was some provision for a sick bay, or even to the Roman Catholic hospital in the town, Charitas, which for a time was able to continue its works. Sometimes, they didn't come back.

Chung Hwa School POW Camp – Front Entrance – Guards' washing on the line.

A Chink of Light

The dreary months of mid 1942 dragged on.

The intense heat and humidity, and the unaccustomed labour, drew heavily on our physical resources. The incessant diet of rice, and weeds dredged from the river, which were the basic ingredient of the evening watery soup, provided little sustenance.

As he scraped his metal plate clean, Tom Wannop looked up, and quietly announced: "Do you realise that that must be about our six hundredth meal of rice?"

"Just fancy all those little coolies planting out their paddie fields just to keep us all in luxury," commented Charlie Tout, with mock sarcasm.

"What wouldn't I give for a nice plate of fish and chips," broke in Boy Edwards.

"That's enough of that." Up spoke killick, Frank Downing. "As if things are not bad enough. There's no point in torturing yourself. I thought we had agreed not to talk about grub."

He was right, of course. But on the other hand, if we couldn't talk about food, there was no point in talking about home, about girls, about families, about sport, about any of the things which were now so remote.

Perhaps this was the insidious effect that the incessant bombardment of Jap propaganda was having on us. With our bodies strained to the limit, our brains and thoughts were more easily persuaded.

We were daily assailed with depressing news of defeat.

From our first hand knowledge, we were only too well aware of the miserable situation in the Far East. When the Encounter had left the Mediterranean, towards the end of 1941, the naval and military position in the Middle East was posing all kinds of problems. We were being forced into retreat everywhere.

At home, many who had experienced the bombing of London, and other big cities, were fearful for their loved ones, and apprehensive of the possibility of invasion from the Continent.

The Japanese were flushed with their rapid advance down the Malayan Peninsular, and through the Dutch East Indies, while the other prong of the pincer had closed tightly round Pacific island after island, until the chain reached temptingly towards Australia.

Their excitement was spelled out large in the headlines of the Syonan (Singapore) Times, still printed in English. Whole issues, page after page, recited details of their victories in Java, the capture of Rangoon, the bombing of New Guinea and Darwin, and their all powerful race towards India and the Australian continent.

There seemed to be little variation from week to week, apart from the change of scene.

The Axis bombing of England, and Malta, was intensified, Tobruk had fallen, and the Germans were advancing into Egypt. The Americans had suffered grievous losses in the Battle of the Coral Sea.

These newspapers were gratuitously exhibited on a large notice board, and even then, the more vociferous of the guards took great delight to remind us that "Ingris soldjar no good, tena"; "Nippon, number one"; "America tida bagus." (No good).

Near at hand, we could see the consolidation they were achieving in Palembang, quite unhindered by any counter attack by Allied forces.

We wearied of reading these chapters of woe, and being taunted by these little yellow devils, so it was not surprising that after some months, only the front page of the newspaper was displayed, for our benefit.

One day, we came across some Jap troops at the railway station, south of Palembang. The line ran south to Oosthaven, a port at the most southerly tip of Sumatra, where the Sunda Straits divides that huge island from Java. A line, which we learned too late for our advantage, carried many refugees away to safety.

These troops were on transit north, and we had the task of unloading their equipment into lorries. There were casualties among them, and perhaps fleetingly, we had feelings of exuberance, not at their sufferings, but perhaps because now there was some tangible evidence in our favour.

We trudged along by the rail track, eying enviously the itinerant salesmen, with fruit, and peanuts, and coffee. At the end of the road was an embankment. There stark against the sky, was a funeral pyre. On top was a uniformed body. The war for that soldier of Nippon was over. As the flames leapt round the still form, I felt that despite our privations, we still clung to life. It was a strange moment.

Perhaps also, this incident had an effect on our guards, because we were invited to share a small mug of black, sweet coffee. The Chinese woman who had the coffee stall was fat and blousy, but somehow had the compassionate air of understanding about her, as she ladled out the hot liquid.

She took the proffered cents from the guard, and held out the mug towards us.

"You like?" she queried. She really had no need to ask. We did like.

"Gula mau?" she added, as she kindly dug a spoon deep into the brown sugar on the stall.

It was real nectar, and the mug was lovingly caressed as it was passed from mouth to mouth, and consumed, sip by sip.

She turned her head away from the Japs, and there seemed to be a smile which lingered briefly on her bland face.

Alongside her was an Indonesian trader, parang in one hand, and pineapple in the other. He spun the fruit nimbly, while the razor sharp knife rose and fell, cutting shallow 'V' shaped troughs in a descending pattern around the orange and yellow skin, removing all the tough inedible portions, and leaving only the juicy flesh to be cut into luscious slices. I marvelled at his dexterity, and cared not for the obvious lack of hygiene, as various winged creatures alighted on the finished objects.

He too gave a slight sign of recognition, nodding his head slightly, as eyes met, but sadly, wanted money for his wares.

By now, there was a crowd of prisoners around the coffee stall, all anxious to take advantage of the unexpected show of generosity. Inevitably there was a shout of "Kerei", and it was back to work again.

The day ended, and thankfully we climbed back into the lorry to return to Chung Hwa.

It may have been a couple of evenings later that Frank Downing was summoned to a meeting of NCOs of messes, quite a usual routine whenever camp matters were to be discussed, and instructions from the Senior Officers were issued.

On his return, serious faced, he indicated that there was something of importance to tell us. First, we must make sure there were no guards about. We posted one man in the doorway, and another by the grilled window onto the yard.

"Does anybody know where Midway is?" he asked.

"What's this, a joke?" said Aston. "Never heard of it."

None of us had, in fact, heard of Midway.

"Well," continued Frank, "it is an island between Hawaii and Japan, and according to the Chinese woman at the station, there has been a big naval action close by, ending in an American victory. Good news at last. A chink in the darkness, you might say. Anyway, the Commander has asked that everyone be told – it seems reliable – but not to breathe a word within Japs' hearing."

"You know, it's strange," said Johnnie MacMillan, "there hasn't been anything about it in the Syonan Times, and in fact, they only let us see the front page now."

It didn't seem to matter that we could not pinpoint the location of this island – it was an item of good news – to be carefully preserved among us.

After that, each evening, as the working parties returned from their labours, particularly if they had been near the station, the overwhelming query was whether there had been any more contacts with outside sources, especially the Chinese woman. Our hopes had been awakened, and I believe that from that time on, we were all confidently expecting a rapid turn of events.

Because of the necessity for secrecy and security in these things, a system was evolved by which any gen, however obtained, was passed direct, by the senior hand in each mess, to the British Commander. It did not then lose its accuracy in being passed from mouth to mouth, and the Commander, with his Aides, had to filter what was thought credible, back to the various messes.

There were at times strong rumours that a radio set had been put together, but this was strongly discounted, though everyone was agog for the latest 'buzz'.

We did see that, in time, the uncensored front page of the newspaper became more and more a propaganda statement than actual news items, or two or three extracts would be cut out, and exhibited for our attention. Gradually the printed news coverage dried up altogether.

Hopes rose, and were dashed. Hearsay, and tittle-tattle were fed by optimism, and regretfully, sometimes by pessimism, and swept the camp. Sick men were bolstered by their expectations, but sadly, died later by their disillusionments.

We began to speculate not only on when release would come, but how? I think that only Jock MacMillan had any firm ideas. He always anticipated as a Scot with his deep roots would, that there would be a skirl of pipes, and a Highland Regiment would march in. We had to wait a long time, and it was nothing like that.

It was not until after the war had ended, that most of us discovered the truth that the news did not come at all from the friendly Chinese, but actually from a secret radio hidden in the camp, operated by Graham Chisholm of the Australian Imperial Force. Also from time to time, our interpreter officer, Captain Ringer, and others, were able to smuggle Japanese newspapers in from Jap quarters across the road, and glean some precious information.

The penalty for discovery would undoubtedly have been death, and with the surprise searches that took place at any hour of the day or night, these clandestine operations demanded the highest level of courage.

Also, as time went by, the effects of malnutrition, and some diseases, affected mens' brains, and an unguarded word in delirium, or nightmare, could have had dire consequences.

I believe that it was news of the naval successes at Leyte, in the Philippines, towards the end of 1944, that inadvertently escaped from a very sick man, that caused great consternation to us. It was a stroke of good fortune for us that the demented rambling of this naval rating was overheard by a guard who was not intellectually very bright, and probably could only understand a few basic words of English, for a rapidly concocted explanation satisfied him, and luckily prevented the matter escalating.

After the war, Graham received the British Empire Medal (Military Division) for his fearlessness and ability in building and operating the set. His citation read

"He knew the penalty for discovery was death. This soldier exhibited courage and skill of the very highest order over a very long period."

'No Escape' Document

Towards the end of August, 1942, the Japanese produced parole forms for each man to sign, indicating that since we had been treated as military captives, and accorded proper recognition as such, we should not make any attempt to escape. They clearly were under the impression that the conditions so far had been benevolent in the extreme. Of course, nothing was further from the truth. The Geneva Convention, to which the Japanese unfortunately were not signatories, had been breached in every respect possible. The edict – to require our signatures to these documents – appeared to come from high authority, and the issue was pursued quite relentlessly.

After a brief preamble, the wording was something like:

"I solemnly swear on my honour that I will not, in any circumstances, attempt to escape" and referred vaguely to the grave consequences of breaking that undertaking.

The possibility of escape was something that we had all considered in varying degrees, from time to time. There would have been no difficulty at all in getting out of Chung Hwa, or fleeing from one of the working parties, but what then? We were many miles inland, with no maps, surrounded by virtually impenetrable jungle and swamp. By reason of our colour, and clothing (or lack of it) we were easily identifiable. Then, of course, there was the language barrier. Also, there was unlikely to be any assistance from the native population, many of whom then remained hostile, and all of whom had been indoctrinated as to the dire consequences of helping any of the Allied forces. Others were generally not averse to currying favour, or reward, from the yellow invaders. Even if we could reach the coast, Australia to the South, or Colombo to the west, were many hundreds of miles off. In the very early days, a Captain Jennings, and a Bombardier Hall, had set sail in a little native boat 'Gilca' from the west coast of Sumatra. After weeks of privations, and terrible hunger, the tides and winds had brought them back to within a few miles of their departure point. (See

'Ocean without shores' by Cyril O. Jennings). They now shared our fate in Chung Hwa, so we had first hand experience of the difficulties. We knew what had happened to Britt and Barber, and the sheer hopelessness of making a successful break.

After due deliberation, we were advised by our own senior officers, for each of the services, that such a document was contrary to our military code, and ran counter to the agreement accepted by the signatories at Geneva. En masse, therefore, on August 30th, the forms were returned unsigned by the British.

"What happens now then," said Pots Ainsworth, as we broke ranks, and returned to our quarters.

"One thing's certain – they'll be bloody annoyed," said Jones.

"Well, in any case, there's no chance of getting very far from this one-eyed dump. Can't understand why they want these signed anyway."

Retribution was swift. A massive search of the camp was launched – presumably for arms or contraband – in the course of which many of our few remaining personal articles were deliberately smashed, or confiscated. The already inadequate rice ration was halved, such facilities as we had for recreation were taken away – no darts, no handball. Private cooking was halted, and all work outside stopped – this of course, was a mixed blessing. Worst of all, the men (mainly Dutch, and Officers, and sick) from Mulo School camp were brought in and concentrated in the insufficient space of Chung Hwa. The overcrowding became intolerable, the water and toilet facilities, already grossly overstretched, became impossible. Very quickly, our emotions and pent-up feelings reached bursting point, and petty niggles flared into heated arguments, and occasionally, into fighting.

Within a few days, the Dutch had given in, and this fact concentrated the growing dislike and mistrust which had simmered under the surface since our original capture. In broad terms, they had blamed the British for the dismal defeat in Malaya and the capitulation of Singapore, while we had been similarly critical of their attitudes and weakness in the Dutch East Indies.

Many of the Hollanders, being captured in situ, had bags of kit, were not short of guilders, and had some local contacts, which eased their difficulties on their initial detention, after a few days of fighting. On the other hand, most of us had virtually nothing, after being chased from pillar to post, in other theatres of war. Then having been thrust into this area, insufficiently armed, and ill prepared, we felt that they could have been more co-operative. This situation was not helped by the attitude of the Dutch colonials of mixed blood, who seemed to take every opportunity of adopting a superior stance to the white British. Hostility grew against our former Allies, and from then on, apart from rare individual friendships, the 'Gott verdommers' were considered generally with some reserve.

The British senior officers, Commander Philip Reid, RN, and Lt. Col Hill, Indian Army, were taken away to solitary confinement. This must have been quite terrifying, and the privation was intended to exert the utmost pressure. The scant medical supplies, infinitesimal as they were, were stopped entirely, and the usual ill-tempered treatment escalated into wholesale oppression.

Eventually, on September 8th, the decision was taken that the 'Non escape' forms should be signed, but that the Japs should be informed that since this was done under duress, we considered them to be of no significance.

This done, the two Senior Officers were released, and conditions slowly reverted to 'normal'.

From post-war accounts, it seems that this procedure occurred throughout the areas occupied by the Japanese, and although communication between British Officers in remote prisoner-of-war camps was quite impossible, identical action had been taken elsewhere.

The "Library"

I have mentioned earlier (Yasumé) that in the Camps, we were fortunate enough to have a number of books, including novels, and short stories, some fiction and some non-fiction.

Following a bout of malaria, I was in such a low state of health as to be excused from outside working parties for a time, and it was then that Lieut. David Hamilton Christie, RNVR, formerly of the Colonial Education Service in Malaya, and one of my Officers at Fortcanning, asked me to try and maintain and repair the books, and to organise a library system.

Since this was about the only mental diversion we had, it was a highly prized facility, and I was very fortunate to have this job, which allowed me spells of comparative peace inside the camp, and at the same time, provided a satisfying and rewarding occupation.

It was not long before the paperbacks started to fall apart, and the bindings of the more substantial publications split, and pages, or whole sections, were loosened.

We had some paper and card from the Chung Hwa School records, supplemented by cement bags, and coarse thread from rice sacks. Among my own necessities, which I had brought with me, I had a naval 'housewife' (hussif) containing a few needles, and some cotton, and some mending materials of various sorts. Nothing of possible recycling use was ever thrown away.

With the aid of a few daily spoonfuls of rice pap, I took books completely apart, page by page, then stuck and sewed them into sections, and made new covers and spines, which were then printed with titles, and reference numbers. I must admit that sometimes temptation got the better of me, and part of the rice pap (amounting to just enough to taste, went into my tum). Books of short stories, or larger volumes, where possible, were split into sections, to enable wider circulation.

For the benefit of the working parties, the 'library' which consisted of a table on the first floor landing, was opened for an hour each evening. Queues formed like a sale event, in the effort to secure the more popular novels. A reservation system was introduced, together with a necessary check method, to keep track of each book.

I also organised a visiting system for the sick, both in their messes, and later, in the so called 'hospital huts', in order that the many, unable to fend for themselves, were not omitted.

Entry into the hospital huts was strictly controlled, to try and contain the spread of disease, and the method of decontaminating the books was simply to spread them in the hot sun, whenever possible, turning the pages periodically. We hoped that this would kill off any germs. It certainly caused the bugs to crawl out from the crevices, and vacate the pages.

As time and malnutrition took toll of health and senses, group reading sessions were arranged. Those whose eyes had succumbed to the effects of devitaminisation could enjoy, not only hearing a story, but company for an hour or so.

The temporary joy that short, fictitious period brought to those pitiful wrecks was a tremendous reward to those of us rather more fortunate.

I don't think that ever a radio serial was more earnestly anticipated than some of those times, which became a real source of pleasure to both reader, and listeners.

The mute nod of a head, the squeeze of a hand, and even a tear of gratitude, were cogent recognitions of this very minor service.

Many times, I found, that at the next session there was an empty space, or a new face.

(See Appendix V for Library 'contents')

Docks Incidents

"Oh, well, could have been worse," said Charlie Tout, as we swayed from side to side in the lorry, heading for the docks. "There might be a chance for a little bit of 'lagi' (extra) today".

"You must be joking," said Harry Gosden. "I expect there's another cement boat in".

"Did you see who the guard was, on the other lorry," commented Aston.

"It's that bastard 'Pineapple' (Kimura)."

"He's got eyes in the back of his arse," said someone else.

Well, it turned out right. We did arrive at the docks, but it wasn't cement this time. It was rice. There was a small coaster alongside, and already, there were Chinese coolies carrying the large brown sacks into an adjacent godown. These bags weighed 100 kilos (220 lbs), but the Chinese seemed to manage them easily enough. Once they were on a man's back, they seemed to dance away, with a smooth rise and fall, something like the movement of a horserider. Only their smooth, yellow skins, glistening with moisture in the humid atmosphere betrayed the effort that was needed on this treadmill from gangplank to warehouse.

With the arrival of our working party, a large square steel dray was brought into use, to lift the rice from the hold, and then swing it across the deck and down onto the dock side.

In the hold, conditions were stifling, with the fine dust filling the enclosed space, but it had its advantage, in that four men, one to each corner, took the bags, only a few paces, and dropped them on to the steel plate.

On the dockside, four more men then raised the bags individually onto the backs of the queue of men, who had to trot them into the nearby store.

From time to time, duties were reversed, so that each man had a share of carrying and lifting. As the bags were lowered onto each back, and the unwilling 'donkey' underneath took the weight, we all had our unspoken words and thoughts as to how long we could possibly withstand the strain of this incessant labour, on such an inadequate diet.

Two things kept us going. Firstly, a Jap bayonet had amazing powers when pushed just hard enough into our buttocks, when flagging limbs could scarce go another pace, or backs were breaking under the weight. The other was that we all hoped that at the end of the day, we could manage to smuggle back a few ounces of the precious grain, which would satisfy our hunger pangs for just a little longer.

Inside the warehouse, we would inevitably find one bag which had a tear in it, depositing here and there, on the concrete floor, a small pile of gleaming white gold dust. Of course, if there wasn't one with a hole, it didn't take long to make one, as opportunity presented. So, with the Jap guard out of sight, sitting musing with his rifle between his knees, out would come our little swag bags, and as quick as lightning, scoop a handful of pearls into the receptacle. Even 'Pineapple' couldn't be everywhere at the same time. Hung from our fandushi strings, pushed into the crevices of a straw hat, or even brazenly carried in our crude food bowls, it was amazing how much went undetected.

So hour after hour passed. Inside, the mound grew, as the ceaseless crocodile, ever slower, wound its way in from the riverside. As the day wore on, so the mobile contents of the bags became even more difficult to manage.

"Surely, it must soon be yasumé. Certainly there can't be many more bags left in the hold." Our worn out thoughts found vent in tired expletives, as now that the stack was several feet high, the final move was to strain, and heave the leaden weight upward.

Suddenly, outside there was a shouted warning, followed by silence, as even the monotonous pad of human feet stilled.

"What is it – what's the matter?"

The shrilled call of alarm. Had 'Pineapple' wreaked his cowardly revenge on some transgressor over a few grams of rice? We knew the penalty was likely to be swift and heavy.

With almost one accord, work was abandoned, and we ran out into the sun. There lying on the ground was one of our number, lying motionless, a circle growing round him, including two guards, now alert, and gesticulating loudly with their arms.

The heavy metal tray swung drunkenly over the ship's side. One of the four chains hung limply down, while the other three still secure, wrestled slowly to a halt. By the victim was a pile of about a dozen sacks of rice, even now just coming to rest.

The British officer in charge was kneeling by the body, assessing the situation. As he did so, there were words of explanation from those that had been on hand.

"As the load jerked down, so one corner gave way, the rice slid off one side, and the cradle was sent spinning and hit Usher in the middle of the back."

Usher was a naval rating – seaman, I believe. A wiry little chap, not of commanding stature.

The officer slowly climbed to his feet, and indicated to the guards that it was a stretcher case. The lads made him as comfortable as they could on the ground, awaiting further action.

The only immediate action was a piqued snort from the guard that we

Market and docks, Palembang.

Strange things in strange places – Dutch Island, once British Portuguese warehouse – Japs capture English Coolies and a book on the life of Albert Dührer (1471/1528) a painter and printmaker generally acknowledged as the greatest German Renaissance artist; famous for great altar pieces and religious works. The POWs are carrying 100-kilo sacks of rice while the guard sits at the door.
Drawing by Peter Bivand

had all temporarily stopped work, and swinging his rifle butt menacingly urged the early clearance of the heap of rice bags.

The injured sailor was left, as we picked our way past him, to complete our task.

The lorry that evening took back to camp our semi conscious comrade. I believe he was taken to Mulo School, the other camp in Palembang where the sick, and most of the Officers, were interned.

We variously heard that the impact had broken his back, and that one of his kidneys was badly damaged. I believe that our wonderful doctor, Dr J. G. Reed, with the aid of a piece of rubber tubing, was able to fit up a catheter. The Japanese contribution, and by comparison, this was generous, was a roll of sticking plaster. Miraculously, Usher survived the tedious months which were to follow, but would never walk again.

Some way short of the actual docks, a little way down the river, we had become used to the sight of the superstructure of a small vessel – probably a casualty when Palembang was stormed by the Japanese in February, 1942. Whether our captors now considered this a hazard to shipping, or whatever their motive, one day, a team were sent to salvage whatever cargo it had on board.

The swirling, turgid water of the River Moesi had flooded over the wreck for many months, and now the secrets of its contents were to be disclosed.

The difficulties of this operation were great, but at least the cooling water had its blessing.

We were rewarded with crate after crate of tinned vegetables, and even soups, like MacConochies meat and vegetable. We gazed incredulous, as the sodden tins were heaved onto the riverside, their labels detaching with the unaccustomed handling, after laying in their grave of clogging mud.

A windfall. The Japs carted away the whole crates, and as a bounty we were rewarded with those that had burst open, releasing the rusted, and bent tins. I need hardly add, that we made sure that several more crates burst in the cartage.

What luxury there was for a few nights. Real thick, meaty gravy with our rice. Tinned tropical fruits as dessert.

I don't think one of us thought for a moment of the very considerable health risk there was. We had to discard much that had been 'blown', but a mere buckle in a tin, or one very nearly rusted through, had not a moments consideration.

Another incident worthy of mention is the day we caught the iguana.

Work was in progress as usual, by the river, when this creature made its unfortunate appearance. It must have been at least four feet long, as I remember it, humped, a cross between an alligator and a lizard.

"Food," went up the yell.

The guard, very interested, allowed us to trap the poor animal. We weren't sure of its fighting capability, or indeed, whether its flesh was suitable for the pot, but we decided to take a chance. The guard wanted its skin, and we wanted the meat. This convenient arrangement led to success in our chase, and of course, allowed us to carry it back to Chung Hwa without secrecy. Needless to say, once the scaly outer covering had been removed and the internal organs disposed of, there was precious little left. However, nearly a thousand men that night swore that they could taste the meat among the habitual kancong.

I think that was the first wretched animal that finished in our stewpots – it certainly wasn't the last.

Thank God for the Red Cross

No birthday parcel, no Christmas parcel, no gift ever could have been more gratefully received than the Prisoner of War packages received from the American Red Cross.

It was early November, 1942, when the glad tidings came. We had been prisoners for 9 months. It was a 'rest day' at Chung Hwa, when one representative from each mess was summoned to collect rations.

Those men who were in the room, stopped their conversations. The many who were out in the field at the back of the school, coaxing their private cooking fires, brewing tea, or concocting something tasty out of virtually nothing, halted what they were doing, and hurried back to their messes.

"Did you hear that pipe?" enquired Harry Gosden. "Something about collecting rations, or something like that, anyway."

By now, there was a steady stream of bods, out into the front playground. There wasn't one person from each mess. I think that there was pretty well a hundred per cent turnout.

Lieut. MacMullin, who was the British Officer in charge of rations, was standing by a large pile of open boxes, surrounded by a crowd of jostling, half naked bodies.

"Right then, one man from each mess only, with your mess numbers."

At his side were Petty Officer Bill Bolitho, and Corporal Warburton.

"Don't all rush. You'll all get the same. Just give us time."

The rough queue moved slowly forward, into and through the now complete dense packed circle of men, near the playground entrance.

As each recipient received his allocation, his mess-mates clamoured round, to see what wonders there were, and to assist in hurrying the valuable goods back inside the buildings.

Frank Downing was well back down the expectant crocodile, but as we waited, there were excited cries from those further forward.

"I think it's bully in those square tins," was an optimistic forecast.

"Cor, what would my guts say to a nice bit of old bully."

"There's packets of something there too. Some kind of powder."

The playground began to empty rapidly, as little knots of men filtered away. Now it was Frank's turn.

Bill Bolitho passed a small cardboard box to the Lieutenant, who already had two of the square tins in his hand. Then there were four round tins – some kind of stamp marked on them, but no labels. Half a dozen mixed packets followed – varying shapes, with small printed white labels, unreadable at any distance.

"Royal Navy mess. Sixteen men, Sir," as he saluted.

"OK that's it. Next."

Frank, with box, and superfluous escort, almost ran into the small mess room.

Every man jack crowded round. Dhobying, cooking, mending, all other chores forgotten.

"Right let's see what we've got. Two tins of bully beef." He scrutinised the round tins.

"Gosh, look at this. Four tins of meat and vegetable. Two tins of mixed fruit." He drew in his breath in pleasurable anticipation. Then as he picked up the packets, one by one.

"Dried fruit – soup powder – cornflower – biscuits – salt – and what's this last one – ah, Camels," as he pulled open the torn brown covering.

"Four packets of twenty fags."

"What about the non smokers?" came the question.

"What do you want to do?" Frank asked.

"We can't very well divide the tins up. The bully beef would be one tin to eight men. I suggest that when our rice comes up tonight, we each have a couple of slices. Then tomorrow, someone can warm up the meat and veg – that's one tin to four of us. We can have the fruit tonight as well, if you like. The packets are best left until we are cooking something else."

In answer to another prompt about the cigarettes, he split open the small, soft, coloured wrappers, and gave each man five smokes apiece.

That evening, we had a three course meal. The usual kancong soup, followed by boiled rice, crowned with two chunky slices of real corned beef, and finished off with tinned fruit and a small helping of rice porridge. Oh, I forgot – the mug of milkless, sugarless tea – bit smoky, but lovely to wash down the solids. The Chef de Cuisine at London's Ritz never got a greater accolade than our cooks that night.

And what is more, at Tenko, it was announced that there was more to come. It turned out that there was tinned Spam, butter, salmon, marmite, dried milk, and glucose.

In addition there were some clothes. I think that most men received a hat like a trilby, a thick tweed like jerkin, and some had boots, or shorts.

Much of the food, such as the powdered milk, the marmite, and the butter went exclusively to the sick, and some of the tins were kept safely by for the Christmas menu. There was also a small amount of lint, and bandages.

I suppose in all that we each got about a packet of cigarettes, half a tin of spam, half a tin of corned beef, a taste of salmon, a few biscuits, a few spoonsful of cocoa, and various small quantities of the other goodies.

At the bottom of each box, there was a small postcard, which was to be returned as a receipt to the American National Red Cross, through the international committee. The Japanese were not interested in their completion, or return. It was later obvious why.

The real joy of those few days was that we had been remembered, and contacted, by the outside world. Naturally enough, we anticipated that this manna from heaven would be now a regular thing. This was the end of 1942 – there was only one more very tiny distribution, well into 1944. We know that the Japanese and Korean guards stole a great deal of the parcels, and I heard tell that after the war, many undistributed parcels were found in the warehouses of the Far East.

Nevertheless, what we did receive lifted morale enormously, had a marked effect on the sick, and made me, for one, eternally grateful to those who had worked to provide these aids and comforts.

High Days and Holidays

"Tojo presento," said Kanemoto, the Jap guard.

He held out an opened packet of American cigarettes.

"What's the catch?" muttered Harry Gosden.

We were sitting on the floor of our mess room, some reading, some trying to mend their tattered garments, others just doing nothing in particular.

Kanemoto – 'Cats eyes' as we knew him, because his eyes were even more slit like than the usual Japanese – gestured again.

"Presento, smoko."

It was too good to be true, but the offer was there clearly enough.

"Api ada?" asked Charlie Tout, as he took one of the proffered cigarettes, and queried whether the guard had a light.

The packet was passed round the room, until it was empty, and the smiling recipients were happily puffing away with their unexpected gifts.

"Arigato," said Frank Downing, in thanks.

'Cats eyes' inclined forward, in a slight bow, as he acknowledged the grateful response.

"Bagus tena. Ini hari resto. Hirohito er, er . . ."

The guard hesitated as he sought for his words, So that was it. That was why there were no working parties today. April 29th was the Emperor's birthday. It was good, and we were enjoying a break from our oppressive tasks.

In expansive mood, Kanemoto turned on his heel and went. Six or seven cigarettes among about 12 men. 'Presento' had a different meaning among us. It usually referred to a wallop around the face, but today, a few puffs on a cigarette, was a highlight. Of course, we weren't to know until later that these cigarettes had been pilfered from the very rare American Red Cross parcels that found their way to Palembang, and those that did were stripped of all those things which the guards enjoyed.

"Well, here's to the Emperor," said Aston, as he raised a mug of cold tea to his mouth. "May he have lots of little ones, and lots of birthdays, then we can have lots of days off."

Birthdays. Mostly they were just dates on a non existent calendar. Sometimes, if friends knew, or remembered, there might be a spoonful of sugar, a banana, a few green beans, a couple of chillies, anything that had been hoarded, or tucked away, for a special occasion.

Usually, we had one day a week, or part of a day, when we remained in camp. Often it was a Sunday, but whether this was an acknowledgement of our Christian habits, I never knew. Then there were camp chores to be attended to. The place had to be tidied, the mess rooms swept out, stores brought in, the toilet drums to be emptied, and the storm drains unblocked.

When these communal duties were finished, there were always the personal matters to be looked after. The broken clog had to be mended, hair more than a centimetre long had to be shorn, cuts and sores had to be cleaned, and bound as best possible, our bits of dhobying had to be squeezed in when there was water, and some kind of utensil available.

Then usually the canteen was open for an hour or two, and we could spend the few cents we had earned on foodstuffs to supplement our rice. 'Canteen' might sound pretentious. In fact, it was a small storage place, next to the squatting latrines, where a few sacks of goods, purchased in bulk through the Jap quartermaster, could be dispensed. At odd times, there were lumps of solid brown sugar with a candy like texture, brown or green beans (kachang ijau), occasionally there were duck eggs, until after a few months these disappeared from Palembang altogether, monkey nuts, which could be roasted in some of the thick, red palm oil, pilfered from the docks. These rare treats were usually saved for our 'yasumé' days, when we could indulge in a bit of private cooking.

The library opened its 'doors' morning and evening on rest days, so that exchanges could be made.

Then being the seventh day, after 6 days of labour, a few of the many hundred men spared half an hour to attend church. Church was the same landing space as the library; hymn books not being available, we made use of the school blackboard and easel. We were fortunate to have at Chung Hwa, a Roman Catholic priest, Padre Rowles, and for those of us who were Church of England, we were led in our prayers and hopes, by a Naval Lieutenant, David Copley, who after the war took up Holy Orders.

The Emperor's birthday was also celebrated – by order – with an evening concert, and these were always well received and appreciated, relying absolutely on very amateur genius, and little or no props. It was strange that one tune common to both Guards, and Prisoners, was 'My Blue Heaven' and if we did not have it in the programme, it would certainly be requested, or ordered.

Of course, for us, Christmas was a common time for celebration, and I think that most Christmas days were marked, and we had at least a few hours in camp to do so.

All of us, stacked by something to make it a different day. There were secret stills, where a fluid from rice base, romantically called saké was produced, and there were various attempts to produce fruit wines principally from pineapple parings, which added dubious flavours to our intake.

When we had a few rice grains to spare, we ground them into flour, added a little gula, some peanuts, and some orange skin, and once this intriguing mixture had been thoroughly boiled in a piece of cloth for a couple of hours, kidded ourselves we were eating Christmas pud.

We circulated among closer friends, small snippets of card, with Xmas and birthday greetings. Among my treasured possessions is one piece of card, almost illegible, which just says

VERY BEST OF CHRISTMAS WISHES, AND HOPES
FULFILLED IN THE NEW YEAR. To Ray, from KIWI.

That was Christmas 1944, from New Zealand Navy Writer Kiwi Verry. His death is recorded by the War Graves Commission on July 13th, 1945,

To: *Donald*

FROM: *Ray*

Wishing you the sincerest
of birthday greetings, and
the fulfilment of all your
hopes in the very near
future.

LONDON TO US SEEMS SO FAR AWAY,

BUT IT REALLY DRAWS NEARER,

AS DAY PASSES DAY

SO SPEED ON THE TIME

WHEN THIS WHOLE BUSINESS ENDS,

AND WE'RE BACK ONCE MORE

WITH OUR FAMILIES AND FRIENDS.

Birthday Greetings to Marine Donald Brown
(ex-Prince of Wales) dated 8 August 1945.

MANY HAPPY RETURNS

WELL, PREPARE YOUR GEN. AND ALL YOUR DATA,
ON CHUNKEY REID AND THE LIBERATOR;
AND, ALLAN, LAD, I'LL SEE YOU LATER,
IN 'APPY 'AMPSTEAD WITH PA AND MATER.
SO FARE THEE WELL, MY GOOD OLD FRATER,
I'LL TOAST YOU SOON ON FISH AND TATER.

R. STUBBS. 31. 8. 45.

Birthday Card to Allan Anstead, LAC, 4 September, 1945.
(The outside had 3 pieces of cotton, red white and blue, and on the inside:
'WISHING YOU ALL THE VERY, VERY, VERY BEST,
NOW AND IN THE FUTURE)

aged 32, son of Thomas Herbert and Elise Luella Verry, of Palmerston North, Wellington, New Zealand. It was as well that our earnest expectations, and our minor celebrations were not marred by future knowledge.

Two other cards, which I sent, are also among my archives.

To Marine Donald Brown (ex Prince of Wales), dated August 8th, 1945, just before the end, and reads:

London to us seems so far away
But it really draws nearer as day passes day.
So speed on the time, when this whole business ends,
And we're back once more with our families and friends.

And three weeks later, on August 31st, when we were awaiting freedom, to Leading Aircraftsman Alan Anstead.

I'm glad to say that they both returned to marry and raise families, and to laugh over what we made of High Days and Holidays.

The Kempei Tai

"Ringa, Ringa." There was a loud shouting out in the play area of Chung Hwa.

"Ringa, Ringa, mari sini." There was a clattering of heavy boots, running across the concreted surface.

We peered out through the bars of the window, from which we could obtain an angled view, towards the camp entrance. There were six, or seven Japanese soldiers coming towards the building. We heard them pound up the wooden stairway, which led to the officers quarters on the first floor.

Again this peremptory demand

"Ringa, Ringa, lekas."

Captain Ringer, our English interpreter was often called for to add his abilities when the normal terms of broken communication failed. This, however, was obviously something different. Usually, it would be just the sergeant of the guard, together with perhaps one ordinary soldier, who had reached the limits of his patience, or his vocabulary, and wanted the assistance of our officer.

Frank Downing turned away from the bars, resignedly. "There were some strange faces among that lot," he said. "Takahashi was there, so was

Gladys, but I didn't recognise any of the others."

The rest of us still sat on the floor, carefully spooning our precious evening rice into our mouths.

"No point in letting me ration get cold," commented Harry Gosden.

"It's bad enough when it's hot, but it's like chaff when it's cold."

Charlie Tout appeared at the door, a dixie of hot tea, steaming in his hand.

"I was lucky," he said. "The Black Mamba has just been round kicking all the pots over, and putting the fires out. This had just come to the boil, and I managed to save it."

More shouting. The Master-at-Arms this time.

"OK then. Let's have you. Tenko. Tenko."

"Tenko," said Frank, "Can't be. We've only just got our rice, must only be about seven o'clock."

However, tenko it was, for very soon, there was a guard at the door.

"Lekas, tenko, tenko, all men."

"OK, OK, there's no need to shout," grumbled Charlie to himself.

"What's this in aid of?" queried Johnnie MacMillan, "they might have given us time to eat our wretched rice."

Out in the playground, it was clear that something special was afoot. All the officers were there. Commander Reid, Col. Hill, Col. Long, Lt. Cdr. Clark, Squ. Ldr. Clouston, Squ. Ldr. Howell, Subbie Bourke, Arkley, Lyle, Doc Reed, Doc Corcoran, Copley, Land, Stanton. They were all there – with serious faces.

By now, too, there was a formidable turn-out of guards, as well as the 'strange faces'. There was Gladys, Ito, Pig Eyes, Bungo, Crank handle, Leggings, Tor, together with the officers, Takahashi, the doctor, Nakai, the rations officer – Yamakawa. But it was the strange faces that were doing the talking. Agitatedly, urgently.

We were brusquely formed into fives, for the monotonous serial of the count. Takahashi saluted one of the strangers, and reported the full count.

With that, the stranger turned to his subordinates, who ran into the various parts of the building.

"So that's it then," whispered Johnnie, standing alongside me.

"Another count, another search. Wonder what they are after this time?"

The time seemed endless, our half eaten meals now cold and forgotten in the mess rooms. The tropical night had descended, bringing its inevitable chill. We shuffled and muttered among ourselves.

"No speak," screamed the venomous face of the stranger.

"All men, punish. All prisoner bad men."

Someone was rash enough to say something within hearing of a guard, and next minute, he had been felled by a blow with the butt of a rifle.

Our guards clearly stood in awe of the newcomers.

To demonstrate their allegiance, several of our guards then took it into their heads to pass through our ranks, finding any excuse to push, punch or kick, as they did so.

Outside, the native sounds had ceased. Inside, there was almost silence, and little movement.

"Benjo," asked a prisoner, obviously suffering from the onset of dysentery.

"Benjo, teda."

The poor chap stood there, unable to control any longer the ravages in his body. To add to his discomfort, he was slapped round the face as well.

The first light of dawn was showing in the sky, as one by one, the strange faces emerged from the buildings, and saluting their superior officer, rattled off some unintelligible Japanese.

Bland faced, he turned to Commander Reid, and Captain Ringer.

"You go now," was his curt order, as his own troops filed smartly out.

Commander Reid faced the Master-at-Arms.

"Please dismiss the men," he said.

Tired aching legs dragged themselves away. Back to the usual chaos which followed a search. Back to the tin plates, the dixies, the cold tea, the rice now offering hospitality to the cockroaches, which had, in our absence, been gratefully sampled by other four-legged creatures.

"Better get some sleep. Another two hours, and they'll have us up again." Poor old Frank. Despite the privations, his naval discipline always came to the top.

The rumour sped quickly round that natives in the town had been overheard telling news of the war, and clearly suspicions had grown that somewhere, perhaps in the prison camp, there were secret radios, or maybe there might be clues which might lead to the source of these outside truths.

However, the Nipponese authorities had considered it serious enough to call in the dreaded Kempei Tai – the Military Police of the Japanese invaders, whose reputation was on a par, if not worse, than the Gestapo.

It was our first brush with these ruthless, and all powerful men.

Our next meeting had more dire, and cruel, results.

That day, at the docks, had started quite ordinarily. A working party was struggling with the huge rice bags. Down from the deck of a small steamer came the line of carriers, wrestling with their loads, feeling with their feet, as they negotiated the steeply sloping gangplank. One by one, they thankfully dumped the bags in the store, and then slowly returned for the next.

Missing his footing, one man slipped, the bag came off his back, and as it struck the ground, burst, and rice spread quickly on the concrete jetty.

"Bakayaro. Engrisha soldya, fool."

To emphasise his words, he drew back his foot, and kicked the man hard on his unprotected leg.

In a split second, an unguarded moment, the man reacted. Quickly drawing himself up, he punched the guard in the face. Pandemonium ensued. Other guards came rushing forward, and held the prisoner, who by this time had realised the gravity of his 'crime'.

He, and we, regretfully, had to stay submissive, while one after the other, the brave soldiers of the Orient set about him with feet, rifles, battens of wood, and any weapon they could lay their hands on, until he sank virtually lifeless on the ground.

His limp body lay there, close to the broken bag, and pile of rice. We, now grimly reminded of our subservience, went back to our task.

Some time later, he was dragged away by the Kempei Tai. Who knows what he had to live through, at their hands. We never saw him again, but many weeks later the British Commander was notified that the Aircraftsman, Saunders, had died – of malaria!

I did hear that after the war, Squadron Leader Clouston went to great pains to try and uncover just what had befallen this unfortunate chap, but the trail had been too well hidden.

"What do you think of this then?" said one of the Scousers.

He was a big, brawny chap, even at this stage. He had a large, unkempt beard, but no hair. His tattooed arms sat on top of a lovely, flowery, sarong, which enveloped the rest of his body, as he pirouetted through the hut.

"Anyone for dancing?"

"Nice girl, only two dollar," said another, as he appeared in a bright red and yellow drape, tucked under his armpits.

The hut was in hysterics. Eventually, there must have been twenty or more male bodies, clad in these beautiful silk ensembles, parading up and down the hut, naturally to the wolf whistles of the onlookers.

It had been a good day for the working party in the town. How they had managed it is beyond belief, but somehow they had smuggled these articles back into the camp. What a godsend. Enough silk in those to protect the body at night from the spiteful mosquitos, and to provide some warmth and comfort on the bamboo slat beds.

The rest of us were envious of those who now treasured the long silk sarongs and we naturally hoped that there might be a chance for us to get one.

The appearance of two Indonesians at morning Tenko was hardly worth a comment, but when they were led round the ranks, peering into our faces, we knew something was on.

After the working parties had left and the few camp staff had gone about their duties, there was a sudden alarm. Everyone except the very sick in the hospital hut was turned out onto the parade ground whilst the guards and their two Indonesian informants ransacked all the huts.

It was inevitable that most of the sarongs were found.

That evening, as the outside workers dismounted from their lorries, they were herded onto the parade ground along with the rest of us. Several sarongs were produced as evidence and those guilty of the theft were ordered to step forward. Nobody moved.

Commander Reid was brought out in front of the lines, and instructed to tell us that unless the guilty men confessed there would be serious reprisals. Still, nobody moved.

We stood still in untidy ranks. Hungry, thirsty, and those who had laboured all day still grimed and tired from their efforts.

Sergeant Ito, raving now at our Commander and at Captain Ringer, the interpreter, repeated the order.

Here and there a man collapsed and lay where he fell. No aid, no water. The degree of pressure was stepped up. Men were punched, slapped and kicked.

Several more guards appeared on the scene. We were made to number off in fives. The fifth man was prodded forward. The tenth man was lined up with him, and the fifteenth, and the twentieth, and so on. They were led to the lower edge of the levelled ground and we were turned to face them.

The guards withdrew. There was a rattle of sound, as rifle bolts were cocked, and bayonets fixed. Was this the penalty for stealing a sarong? We were transfixed with horror.

Ito swaggered forward. He spoke.

"Ni ju san sarong. Ni ju san mati." (23 sarongs. 23 die).

He paused to prolong the agony. Through the interpreter, he made plain that the men 'selected' would stay there all night, and in the morning, the Kempei Tai would come to administer punishment.

The responsibility carried by Commander Reid, and the Senior Officers, must always have been a heavy burden, but never heavier than now. An impassioned plea for those who had taken the sarongs to step forward was acted upon promptly, despite what must have been in the minds of the culprits.

Ito watched. When the men were re-aligned, he slowly strolled along the line, scowling here, slapping there. Then he summoned the Master-at-Arms.

Through the interpreter, some short sentences were exchanged.

We stood silent, terror-stricken for our comrades, wondering what might happen to the rest of us, once the Kempei Tai were set loose. Another man fainted. One poor devil messed himself.

A guard was detached, and sent down to the guardhouse. He came back a few minutes later, swinging a bamboo stick, about three or four feet long.

The Master-at-Arms was made to step forward in front of the line of petrified men. The first of the guilty then was placed astraddle his back. Ito took the bamboo cane, and swished it hard over the man's buttocks. Then the next, and the next, until, all twenty three had received identical punishment.

Then suddenly, "Yasume." Dismiss.

That was the end of the sarong incident. We couldn't believe it. The men involved had very sore backsides, and all of us had endured many hours of fear. The anti climax was intense. Emotionally we burst out in song, some in tears.

Such was the reputation of the evil Kempei Tai, and the mysterious workings of the Japanese mind.

Sungei Geron

The rain came down incessantly. It rained, and rained, and rained. It was a deluge, day after sodden day. At times, when the sun beat down unmercifully on our bare heads and backs, we prayed for some respite. Now we had it. We squelched from place to place. Our unshod feet were always wet. The damp, humid air hung lifeless. Our few bits of clothes were moist with mould, and our rice sack bedding reeked with clammy inhospitality.

'Private cooking' in the yard was impossible, and we were reduced to the inadequate rice sweepings and the river weed supplied by our captors. We woke each day to the drumming of the water on the concrete surface outside the mess window. We dragged ourselves out to the uncovered oil drums which sufficed for our basic needs. We sat hunch-backed on the cold, unfriendly floor, to spoon the unappetising pap into our mouths, too dispirited to speak, as we faced the prospect of yet another day working in this hostile climate. I have read somewhere that the daily companions of prisoners in the Far East were silence and despair.

We were nearing the end of two years' captivity, and our physical and mental resources were near rock bottom. Reality was outside our comprehension. This must all be a bad dream. But the only dreams were of escape or release. The first was an impossibility, and the second a vain hope. But hope we must, for men without hope die. The struggle to survive must go on, for those who gave up that struggle, lost the very fight for life.

We were cold, damp, and miserable that evening, when Marine Donald Brown came into the room. Somehow, his young face, and cheery eyes caught my attention, diverting my glance from his shrunken chest, and bandaged, ulcerated legs.

"Hello, Don," I said, scarcely moving from the corner, where my bottom had warmed a small area of the hard floor.

Close behind him was another friend, Alan. Alan Anstead was a Leading Aircraftsman, he had been a member of the crew of PB 258, one of the Royal Air Force air/sea rescue service boats which had joined in the seaborne evacuation of Singapore, and like so many, met its Waterloo in the Bancka Straits. Alan was quite different in stature to Don. He was broad boned, and though the flesh on his frame was now ravished by our compulsory fasting, he dwarfed his sleek companion.

"What's this then – another gathering of the Cockneys?" asked Bristolian Charlie Tout.

"Wondered whether you had heard the latest buzz," said Alan.

"Well, it's not really a buzz," broke in Don. "We've just heard through Sergeant King that a new working party is going out tomorrow, to start building a new camp."

"New camp?" Bodies were sitting up and taking notice.

"What do you mean – we're leaving here then?"

"Sounds that way – the Marines have got to have ten men detailed off, and when Sarge asked which party they were wanted for, the only answer he got was that it was none of the existing working parties, but they would have to build huts."

The reaction was mixed.

Chung Hwa was bleak and bare, but we had got to know it. It was solid. It was reliable. We had made a home of it. Now it seems we were off into the unknown again.

"If we have got to build huts, then it will probably be like the aerodrome camp. Remember that dump. That seems an age ago – remember, we were there from May until August last year."

"Seemed like an age," broke in Harry. "At least here we've got tap water, and electric light."

"Tap water!" exclaimed Aston. "Most of the time the ruddy tap is dry, and when there is water, you've got to be right at the front of the queue to get any."

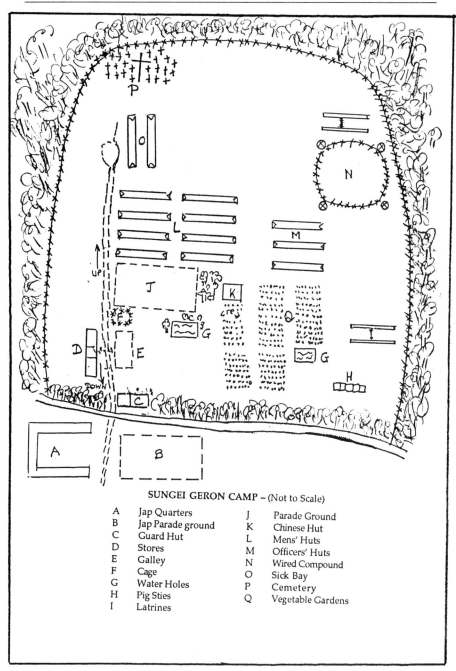

SUNGEI GERON CAMP – (Not to Scale)

A	Jap Quarters	J	Parade Ground
B	Jap Parade ground	K	Chinese Hut
C	Guard Hut	L	Mens' Huts
D	Stores	M	Officers' Huts
E	Galley	N	Wired Compound
F	Cage	O	Sick Bay
G	Water Holes	P	Cemetery
H	Pig Sties	Q	Vegetable Gardens
I	Latrines		

Sketch of Geron Camp.

"I should hold your horses," said Frank Downing. "Quite likely just another rumour, though Kingo is generally pretty clewed up, before he says anything. See what gives in the morning."

His words of caution did not still the speculation. A new topic had at least brought a little spark of life into our conversation.

It was true. The next morning contingents were sent from all the services to make up a jungle clearing party. Axes, chungkals, pick-axes, and saws were loaded on to the two lorries, and off we went.

It was no surprise that the lorries turned out of the town, and after a few miles down a rough earth road, eventually drew off to the right, where a track led down a short incline, before rising again, and then disappeared into the edge of the jungle. There was quite a large cleared space, several hundred yards, bounded by jungle on three sides and by the earth road on the other. The earth was hidden by weeds, but clearly at some time had been cultivated, as rough furrows ran over most of it.

"God, what a stench," bawled Blue Axton, one of the Australian soldiers.

"Hey, Shortie, is this where you bring the 'Benjo' cart?" asked Ernie James.

There was no mistaking the unsavoury odour.

Neither was there any denying the Jap guards, who were already screaming for us to unload the lorries, and to get working.

Almost at the same moment, the rain came down again.

Our Officers and NCOs were trying to get some order out of our unseemly rabble.

"Right, fall in in fives." It was 'Lofty' Claridge, with the Royal Navy party. Then further along Sergeant Bovingdon, with his army privates. Adjoining them were the few Royal Marines, and about an equal number of Royal Air Force.

The Jap guard shuffled along, peering through his spectacles, and flexing his fingers, as we had yet another 'Tenko' to make sure that all who left the Chung Hwa school, only a few minutes earlier, had not decamped somewhere along the road.

Charlie Tout waited until the guard had passed, and then out of the corner of his mouth, said, "That's where the smell is coming from. It's that guard. I don't reckon he has had a bath since war broke out." There were sniggers all round.

There was a Naval Sub Lieutenant in overall charge of the party, and when the Nippon sergeant was satisfied that the numbers were correct, he spoke briefly to his very wet audience.

"This place is called Sungei Geron. In the next few weeks, we have got to build huts to accommodate all the Service prisoners in Palembang. That is, from 'A' Camp (Mulo School), from 'B' Camp (Chung Hwa

School), and from the Officers' bungalows ('O' Camp). It is for ourselves, so it is up to us what we make of it. The Japs have promised that we shall be able to grow vegetables, and in due course, we shall have a pig farm. First we have to clear the ground for a storage hut, and a galley, and then we shall put up a series of long attap huts, each of which will take one hundred men. There won't be any problem with water, as we are going to sink two wells, and there is plenty of room to dig latrine trenches well away from the living quarters. Up to now, the site has been a Chinese farm – that was the Chinaman's house over there, that little palm thatched hut. As you can smell, we shouldn't have any difficulty growing things, as the earth has been well fertilised."

After that optimistic little speech, we were sorted out into small parties to commence the first task, which was to mark out a road, and convey all the stones which we could find to provide a hard core base so that lorries could drive in and out.

All Indonesian place names have a variety of spellings, and I have seen Sungei Geron shown as Sungai Gerong, and Sungei Ron – you pays your money and you takes your choice. Sungei means 'River' and as far as I have been able to trace, Geron means 'Thundery' or 'Growling', so we were to live in, or by, the 'Thundery River'. We never saw a river, but strangely, the large oil refinery, just outside Palembang, and which constituted the strategic importance of the town was known as Sungei Geron.

So that was our introduction to our new home. For days, and weeks, we slithered and slipped in the morass of mud, and excreta, as we worked in all weathers to transform this forest swamp into a habitation.

Three lines of barbed wire were slung round the outer perimeter, more to delineate a boundary, than to provide a barrier. The hardened track led eventually from the slough in the depression, up to long, low huts on either side. A small guard hut, which used all the best timbers, was constructed at the gated entrance, and the cookhouse or galley, was distinguished by having a concreted floor, on which to set the fires, a high attap roof, and no walls, except for a small area partitioned off to form a food store.

The huts were built of bamboo, and measured something like 100 feet, by 16 feet wide. A thin layer of folded palm leaf on split canes formed the roofs and the walls were similarly constructed, leaving a space of about a foot between the tops of the walls, and the roof slopes. Inside, on either side of a central walkway, were platforms of bamboo, raised about 2½ feet off the ground, and each man was allocated about 2½ feet width, or just sufficient to lay out straight.

The huts were up to a hundred feet long. They were constructed of bamboo poles with attap (palm leaf thatch) for the rooves and walls. The floors were bare earth. At each side of a central walkway of about four feet were bed spaces made of split canes, tied together with rattan binding. These were six feet deep, and each man had a space about two feet six inches wide. Light was provided by side flaps held open by canes. In construction, the Japanese only allowed us a limited amount of attap, and consequently the tropical rains penetrated all over the place. The bed spaces became infested with bugs, and rats scampered in the roof supports.

The advance party moved in in February, 1944, and the remainder, two months later, when all the 'Facilities' had been completed.

"Watch out," said Johnnie, "Gladys and Wolf are both out there watching the lorries being loaded. Better stick some of our personal gear in a rice sack, or cover it up somehow."

All our precious belongings were extremely vulnerable at this time. Our few private belongings had to be retrieved from their hiding places. The few remaining rings, or watches, or in my own case, photographs, necessarily had to be bundled with rags, eating utensils, and accumulated oddments, carried out under the eyes of the guards, and loaded into the lorry. My photos had been tied up in cloth and paper, and stashed away under the steps leading to the oil drum toilets. The Japs had a fear of disease, and since dysentery had been present from the very early days, they steered well clear of such a place. Now we individually had to run the gauntlet. 'Gladys' and 'Wolf' were two of the guard sergeants, and particularly officious when in the mood.

As we vacated Chung Hwa, the old school looked as if a swarm of locusts had descended. Walls were stripped of our drapings, and every removable piece of wood, likely to have a possible future use, was appropriated. Every shelf, every nail, every piece of wire or scrap of metal, found its way into somebody's kit. So, it was a strange looking array of men who mounted the lorries that day. We needed our hands to load, and climb on to the vehicle, and so, from every belt or rope waistband hung pots and pans, crude cloth bags, clogs, hats, drinking tins, and a dozen and one other articles. Everything was precious, and nothing was ever discarded. * See 'Truck Travel' (p.239)

The camp at Sungei Geron was taking shape, and it offered, perhaps, some improvements over Chung Hwa. At least, the Japs endeavoured to persuade us that this was to be so, and that the move was for our benefit. But over the next few months, we were to learn to our regrets of the very considerable disadvantages.

"It ain't bleeding right," said a voice outside the hut. "Them officers sat on their backsides, and all we get off is a bit of a day, once a week."

"Well, it's the same in the Andrew, isn't it? Upper Deck and Lower Deck, you shouldn't have joined."

"Not only that," came back the first voice, "You seen them mosquito nets, and fings they got, and their hut ain't crowded like our'n."

Surprisingly, an Australian voice joined in.

"Why don't you Pommies stop your whinging. Always moaning about something."

"Ark who's talking nar. Bloomin' Aussies landed us in this hole – scarpered down Malaya."

Frank Downing jumped to his feet inside the hut, and went out to face the group of men sat on the ground outside.

"Look," he said, "It's no good blaming each other, and working up a paddy. Thing is, we've got to make the best of it."

"I don't see why they should be treated better 'an us. Just because I was born in East 'Am, and they was born in Westminister, or some place."

"Trouble is, you were born on the wrong side of the sheet, like all of us, but there's nothing we can do about that now."

"Anyway, who'd like to be in Chunky Reid's shoes? Not me. You think of the responsibility he's got. Sooner 'im than me."

"It's not Chunky I'm on about, it's all them rubber planters. All they were good for was swilling gin slings in Raffles, wasn't it? Oh yes, sent us out to fight their war, but we wasn't allowed in Raffles, was we. Officers only in there."

"Oh, put a sock in it. You can't change the rules now. Remember before the war, it was always: 'Officers and their Ladies, NCOs and their Wives, and Ratings and their Women."

"I take my hat off to Chunky," interjected Harry Gosden, "Saved me from a right going over, the other day. 'Pineapple' was just lining up to give me a belting, and Chunky got himself in the middle, and stopped him, and called the Guard Sergeant."

"Yes, that's right, we're lucky to have him as Senior British Officer. Then Scottie, and Vic Clark, and some of the others. Damned good blokes. I don't envy them at all. Course, some of the Malayan Volunteer Forces should never have been Officers, but then there's good and bad in all ranks."

That more or less summed up, and brought to an end, this lingering argument.

While we had been at Chung Hwa, there were only a few officers, mainly regular, and I would think, hand picked, all of whom were highly respected. They all had their responsibilities, either in the camp, or in charge of the outside working parties. From the Royal Navy, there were several RNVR and RNR officers, including Lieut. David Christie, David Copley, Arkley, Lyle, Bourke, and McMullin, and Nagle. The senior Officers in the RAF were two Battle of Britain pilots, Squadron Leaders Howell, and Clouston, and the Army boasted several Lieut-Colonels.

However, within a few months of capture, the officers no longer had to do physical labour, and indeed, received what, by comparison with a man's working pay of ten cents a day, was a substantial allowance. This meant that a large number of officers at 'O' Camp lived a very different life to our own. They had money for food to supplement their diets, and to purchase, either from outside, or from the men, equipment and necessities for their comfort. Once in a single camp together, these differences were exaggerated, and the privileges resented. It is very much to the credit of Commander Reid, and some of his chosen officers, that this situation did not get out of hand. Indeed, it is on record that Cdr Reid imposed a contribution from the officers, towards adding something to the men's inadequate food, so that when for example, a small amount of fish, beans, or eggs became available, a proportion would be sent to the galley for the Other Ranks.

The topic which affected us all, however, was the treatment of the sick. Our lives in Chung Hwa had been isolated from the other camps, and from the Catholic Hospital of Charitas. Up to September of 1943, when men had succumbed to illness, or injury, which was likely to be of some duration, and the Japanese could be convinced of this, they were taken away to 'A' Camp, and even, in very exceptional cases, to Charitas. By that time also, because of our living conditions and lack of vitamins, our weakened bodies fell prey to more and more sickness, and injuries once sustained were difficult to mend or heal. Previously, we had been spared the harrowing sight of men fighting for their lives, against all odds, or worse, having to witness the last few days of surrender to inevitable death. The nuns and doctors of Charitas had used their remarkable skills, in the absence of much needed medicines and equipment, and had saved, or at least prolonged, many a life. Notwithstanding this, in September, the multinational staff of the hospital were accused of letter smuggling (which from all reports was probably true) and of supporting the Chinese and Ambonese underground movement (which almost certainly had no truth). In consequence, the hospital was closed, and many were severely punished, including Mother Alacoque, and Doctor Tekelenburg, who subsequently died. That meant that all the sick, serious and otherwise, had to be treated in Sungei Geron, and though a hut was allocated for this purpose, there was no sterile accommodation, or special provision whatever. It was fortunate indeed that we had three service doctors – Reed, Corcoran, and West, and a number of service medical orderlies – but to meet the increasing demands on their services, they had negligible apparatus, and even less in the way of drugs, or medication. The realities of our circumstances were now deeply underlined for us.

At night, when the sudden tropical dark descended on us, we would lie on the bamboo slats, keenly aware of the sounds all around us. The rain which pattered on the palm leaf roof, and all too often found its way through the insufficient cover, to drip, drip, drip, on the narrow bedspace. The creaking of the bamboo supports, as they swayed, and strained in the breeze. The scamper of a rat, or even a monkey, optimistically searching for some

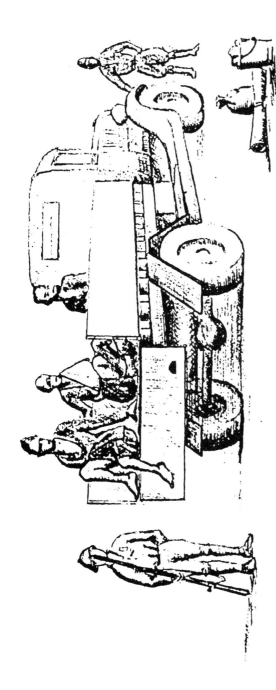

'Ambulance' – this was in use before the closing of 'Charitas'. It was probably the oldest lorry in the town, and was primarily the victuals supply lorry, consequently the sick frequently had to lie amongst the remains of squashed and rotten vegetables.

Courtesy of Lt J. Wallace Kemp, RN.

The Sisters of Charitas were teaching missionaries of a Roman Catholic Order who had nursing suddenly thrust upon them by the Japs. It was extremely laudable the way that these women turned to the work of nursing the filthy bodies, remnants of a beaten army, wrecks of men covered in sceptic wounds and riddled with dysentery. Only those who have experienced dysentery know how revolting the results can be.

Courtesy of Lt J. Wallace Kemp, RN.

morsel that had not been eaten – what a hope. The shout and clatter of a guard, quite oblivious of our total weariness – or perhaps noisier because of it. The grunts and snores of over one hundred men denied the space, and comfort, of a reasonable bed. Occasionally, the whispers of a conversation, the shuffle of bare feet, or the clack of clogs, as weakened bowels and bladders dragged men out into mosquito laden air, to seek the relief of the 'benjo'.

The affinities which had grown up in Chung Hwa were disturbed by these changes in routine, and breakdowns in relationships. It is a strange thing that resistance to the enemy brought forward a will not to give in, but the upheaval of the move, and the jarring of relationships, produced tensions, and strain, which were very difficult to subdue.

Life on the Farm

It really was quite surprising that within very few weeks we had adapted to our new surroundings. The main working parties were collected by lorry, as usual, but our captors had now decided that the light duty men – those who had minor injuries, such as tropical ulcers on their legs and feet, or those who were recovering from malaria, or dysentery – should form a 'Garden Party', and even if they could not stand, they could sit and weed, or hoe, and generally cultivate the quite extensive land around the huts. Their principle was simple – No work, no food, and rations for the camp were now measured on that basis. The 'light duty men' were then entitled to a reduced ration.

Before very long, we were all anxiously watching the small green shoots which promised something additional to our meagre and monotonous diets. The principal crop was the ubiquitous 'ubi kayu'. It grew something like sweet corn, having a stem some 5 feet high, with a bunch of leaves at the top, which were edible, but its main crop was the parsnip-like root, which grew downwards, perhaps 9 or 10 inches long, and between an inch or 2 in diameter. Just a small cutting of this root was sufficient to propagate a new plant. These roots when cut across had a similarity in texture to carrots, and could be boiled, roasted or fried.

In addition, we grew purslane, gondola, and portulacca – all a species of succulent, with high water content. In every small corner into which a tiny plant could be squeezed, there were chillies, tomatoes and onions – all very tiny by our standards, but nevertheless providing flavouring to our 'soup'.

Then dotted here and there over the camp area, were various fruit-bearing trees – strong smelling durians, with their thorny, spiky shells, rambutans, like hairy chestnuts, and occasionally small lime trees. It was a punishable offence to pick any of this fruit, but as we passed by, a mental note was made as the crop approached ripeness, and but rarely did any have the chance to reach that ultimate stage, before a clandestine raid would be mounted, and the spoils whipped away.

In accordance with their promise, the Japanese eventually supplied several tropical pigs. These were small, lean animals, and were put in the charge of an Australian contingent. It was said that the pigs were fed better than us.

Eventually came the time when some of the crops were ready to be reaped, and from acres of ubi kayu, and spinach, we expected our rations to be sharply improved. No such luck. They were loaded onto a cart, and taken across to the guard's camp, on the other side of the road. Only a small proportion was allowed to us, and these were the deformed, and broken roots.

My Australian friend, Kim Mendelsohn told me one day that the pigs were expecting a litter, and on the pretext of visiting the latrines in the far corner of the enclosure, we strayed over to the small range of sties. There was one large sow lying on her side, seeking what shade she could. I was sworn to secrecy that she had already produced five or six piglets, and even as I watched she lumbered to her feet, and produced two more. Tiny little bodies, only a few inches long, wrapped as if in cellophane, rolled in the dusty ground, as she unceremoniously kicked them away from her, and the 'cellophane' dried and split in the hot air. I had witnessed the miracle of birth for the first time in my life.

"Quick, Cobber, get 'em inside before the guard comes round again."

The two small parcels were promptly taken into the small feed hut, and immersed in a deep container of water. A tiny ration of pork was on the menu that night for some lucky ones, and the Japs were not to know that there had been eight piglets, and not six.

We soon realised that we had to play the guards at their own games, and in the dark of night, some of the plants would be lifted, their roots broken off, and the tops discarded. The Japs had their suspicions, and this operation posed extreme danger, which was countered by a very careful watch on the movements of each guard. After a time, they seemed to accept that it was the marauding monkeys from the adjacent jungle that came in at night and did the damage. Alas, we were not without fools, and one night, to speed his escape, someone used a knife.

When this criminal act of stealing the produce was discovered, the whole camp was paraded, and for nearly 24 hours, we stood, without food or

Producing a few vegetables of our own in little patches round the huts was the only method of supplementing our diet. To achieve the maximum results, the poor soil had to be manured, and liquid manure – mine – was the main source of supply. No one was allowed to move before reveille, but the gardeners were all ready for the whistle, and then there was a rush to the urine bucket, with whatever utensils could be spared to collect a pint or so of the precious fluid.

Courtesy of Lt J. Wallace Kemp, RN.

water, in the heat of the sun, and the chill of the night. The guards took it in turns to stroll along the lines, hitting out at random at whoever their malice lighted on. Many men collapsed – some never recovered, so impoverished were their bodies, and therefore their resistance to punishment.

"If I could lay my hands on that twit who used a knife," said someone when we were again in the shelter of our hut.

"Now we've got to pay for it," added Frank Downing.

"They've banned the use of lamps until further notice."

At Sungei Geron, we had no electricity, and so at night, we had contrived small oil lamps. These were made out of any container which would hold oil – tin can, small jar, length of bamboo, and through the lid we threaded a piece of plaited string, or rice sack binding, to form a wick. By these tiny, flickering lights, we passed the precious evening hours between work, and sleep. Now that temporary blessing was at an end.

"Wonder they ever let us use them at all, I suppose. Only needs one careless bod, and the whole hut would go up."

Next day, we learnt of an even further punishment. Between the galley, and the parade ground, for all men to see, a small barbed wire cage was taking shape. It measured something like 6 feet by 6 feet, and about 5 feet high.

At 'tenko' that evening, we were issued with a stern warning. If any man was found stealing, either on working parties, or in the camp, they would be incarcerated in the cage. What to do? We had to steal to live. But if caught, a day or two in the cage could mean a death sentence.

Commander Reid had the answer.

"We must let the present situation calm down. The guards are looking for trouble, and the innocent will suffer as well as the guilty. You all know what happened after the last parade. There are many men who are not in a fit state to cope with any form of punishment. I understand your feelings. Be patient, and hopefully things will ease."

By now, too, we had moved out of the rainy season, and the water holes, at one time overflowing, now contained only a few gallons of muddy water. Steps had to be cut in the slimy sides, so that even this precious fluid could be retrieved at the bottom of the 10 foot pit. We were rationed to one vegetable tin per man, per day. That to wash in, to cook with, to clean our teeth, to wash our bits of clothing. The galley received a daily water cart, but even that meant that our watery 'soup' was curtailed.

The months of 1944 passed inexorably by. The rains which greeted us on our move had been exchanged for humid heat, many days over 100 degrees. The mud was exchanged for arid dust.

Touch and Go

I was vaguely conscious of voices around me; voices that boomed to a crescendo, and then faded to nothingness. Meaningless sounds assaulted my mind. Then the voices were back louder than ever, vibrating, penetrating, piercing my eardrums. There was a huge brown face peering down at me. I tried hard to focus my eyes but the light and the movement sent my head reeling. I sank back again into near oblivion.

Now I could feel the touch of fingers on my arm, gripping my elbow. I could see the face again, this time bearded and close, only 2 feet or so above me. Dimly I watched his lips moving and felt a hand behind my head, lifting gently. "Good lad, good lad." The whisper sounded to me like thunder. "Here, try a sip of this." A mug was pressed to my mouth and several drops of sharp tasting fluid trickled over my tongue. I choked as I tried to swallow. My head clanged back and forward, filled with violent explosions.

"C'mon, try again. Just a drop more." This time it was better. It wasn't so acid, and I was pleased to swill it round my mouth before my parched throat again rejected it. A whistle sounded outside.

"Tenko. Tenko."

"Got to go now Stubbie. Just you lay there. I'll report that you're sick."

Sick. I was sick. How long had I been sick?

An unmeasurable time later the men returned.

"Oh, so you're with us again then?" said Johnnie MacMillan.

"Blimey, you gave us all a turn," commented Harry Gosden.

"I don't remember anything after I collapsed last night," I mumbled.

"Last night! That was three nights ago."

The throbbing of my head had now eased considerably, and I was reasonably able to follow the buzz of conversation going on down the hut. Good friends attended to my needs and I realised that this last attack of malaria had certainly drained me. The clack of utensils indicated that the evening rice was being distributed.

"Feel like some grub?" queried Harry.

The unappetising mound on the plate repulsed me, and there was a rush as others sought to share it amongst themselves.

Johnnie sat alongside me, at the edge of the bedding platform, his legs just resting over the side, as he ate his meal. He glanced towards me now and then.

"Oh, by the way, when the Doc was looking at you, he said that you'd have to have your foot looked at."

With the wandering consciousness of my malaria, I had forgotten the numerous cuts and scratches on the instep of my left foot. Not having to put it to the ground, I had become unaware of the spreading fester.

I eased myself up, and raised my knee so that I could assess the damage. The effort caused me to perspire again, and the giddiness in my head forced me to lie back again. But, I was conscious now of the throbbing ache which pulsed up my ankle and into my calf.

Several days later I hobbled onto the line of men attending sick parade. Line – it was more like a drunken 'S'. A straggle of fandushied bodies – the well dressed had some form of headwear, and most the hand carved clogs to protect their feet. Most men's bodies were now displaying the paucity of our diet, the effects of the climate, and the scars of our treatment. Protruding ribs, bony arms and legs, sunken jowls were all telling evidence of our physical deprivation, while the angry flush of inflamed ringworm, the suppurating blotches of skin diseases, and the stained coverings of tropical ulcers were outward indicators of the rapid deterioration of our bodies. Some had dragged themselves to the row of logs which formed make-do seats, and lolled, limp and uncaring until the next ferocious intestinal spasm forced them to clutch themselves, or creep away hopeful of reaching the latrines.

The hopeless task facing the doc and his assistants was met with understanding and patience.

Soon it was my turn, and I pointed down to my foot, resting gingerly on the ground, my weight almost entirely on my right leg. The orderly quickly removed the sticky strip of rag, to reveal five or six holes, the size of a farthing, each congealed with pus.

"OK, on the bench, and hold the tree."

By a small sapling was a roughly hewn seat. I knew the drill. I had seen others have the treatment. I sat on the seat, my left leg bent with my foot turned so that my instep was uppermost. I faced away, and gripped the tree. I felt my foot swabbed, and tensed myself as I waited for the probe. It was like a red hot iron, as one by one the cavities were scraped. Then, on the verge of passing out, I felt the relief of a binding being tightened round my foot.

"Try not to put weight on it for a while, and keep it covered. Next."

I knew without looking that the condition was worsening. The holes grew, they interlinked, until my foot from the heel to the arch was a honeycomb of pain. The throbbing, nawing, dragging intensity of the hurt grew until it was a relief to return again, and again, for the treatment.

Somehow, one day, it receded. A delicate covering of clean skin grew.

"Good – lucky chap," said the doc. I knew – I had seen the huge caverns on other men's legs. I knew that I was one of the lucky ones.

Me Christo

Able Seaman Shaw sat up sharply in his bed space. He swatted away madly at the bamboo slats. Johnnie MacMillan next to him was not well pleased.

"What the hell are you up to?" he shouted.

"It's these blasted ants," said Shaw. "Look at them – the size of wood lice."

True enough. Swarming up one of the bedding supports was an army of large red ants.

"They've got my gula," added Shaw, as he pulled back the covering of a tin, and disclosed some lumps of gula java, which was providing a tasty feast for these new invaders. "That lot took me two weeks to earn. A guilder's worth, and now these damned ants are eating it."

"More fool you for not putting it in something ant proof. Anyway, brush them off, and you won't know the difference." Johnnie, still not quite awake, was a bit gruff with his neighbour.

"What with ants, bugs, lice, rats – it's a wonder that we can preserve anything," broke in someone else, now the whole hut was rousing.

"It's not those things I'm concerned about," said Johnnie, "It's the two legged thieves that worry me. Someone said that in the army hut, there's a whole lot of pinching going on."

"Woe betide anyone that I find pinching in this hut," said the killick. "Bad enough with things as they are, without thieving from your own mates."

By now, steps were being taken to erase the long line of red ants, and clothes and rice sacks were being shaken off in the central alley of the hut. Strange how our moral outlook viewed these contemporary habits. Stealing from the Japs – that was fair dice, but stealing from each other was quite a different matter.

"Must be tenko soon now. Just as well it's yasumé day, with Shaw getting us all up."

Indeed within a few minutes, the Master-at-Arms was round with his familiar call, and we were trooping outside to muster on the hard-baked earth of the parade ground.

"Ray," it was Petty Officer Bolitho calling. "After tenko, Lieut. Christie wants to see you up at the officers' hut."

"Oh, what's that about?" I enquired.

"I don't honestly know, but I think it's something to do with the library books."

"OK Bill, I'll be there. Thanks."

So, in due course, I left the parade ground, and made my way up the

139

slope, past our hut, and to the officers' quarters. David Christie was standing outside the hut, chatting to Colonel Percy, his father-in-law.

"Ah, Stubbs," he said, as he saw me approach, "How's the foot?"

"It seems to be improving," I replied, "In fact, the ulcers on my instep have been less painful these last few days."

"Well, I've got a proposition to put to you – see what you think of it. I've been talking to the Commander about the books, and the library, and we have both thought that if the Chinese House could be repaired, it would make a good centre for that purpose."

"Yes, that's if it can be made weatherproof." I answered.

"That's not all," he carried on. "It could also be made into the Camp church, but that would require someone to keep it clean and tidy. What do you think?"

"Can we go and have a look at it, and then we'll get a better idea of what is needed. I suppose the guards won't object, you know, all this business of no meetings."

"I don't think so. I'll get Capt. Ringer to have a word with them, if it looks feasible."

We walked down to the small, palm thatched hut. It looked decidedly tatty inside, and there were several small holes in the roof, where the attap had rotted away, but it had a clear space of something like 16 feet by 20 feet, probably ample for the small number of men who congregated there on those occasions when a church service was practicable.

"I think that if we could get you on permanent light duty camp party, and possibly one other, between the two of you, you could knock this place into shape, and make good use of it."

"What do you mean – to live in it as well?" I interjected.

"Good idea – why not?"

"So long as it is someone I get on with. Be pretty miserable to be cut off from the other chaps, with a stranger."

"Right, leave it to me. I'll let you know."

It didn't take more than a few days for the project to become a fact. An army private, whom I knew reasonably well, Peter Bivand, was to join me in renovating the roof, and walls of the hut, and scraping and cleaning the hard packed earth floor. I suppose it was true to say that we were much of a muchness in character. He had been a school teacher before the war, and had much the same outlooks as my own. What I didn't know was that he was extremely practical, and he brought to bear his ample knowledge of arts and crafts. We were allowed a few extra bamboo poles, and several lengths of attap. These always reminded me of rows of kippers on a thin iron spike in the fishmongers shop, though they were palm leaves impaled on split lengths of bamboo. The holes in the roof were adequately covered,

CHINESE HOUSE
SUNGEI RON
PALS MARCH/45

Drawn by Peter Bivand.

and we were very pleased to find that, as compared with the newly built camp huts, the attap was overlapped several thicknesses. There was one entrance door, and three small windows, with large flaps, which could be closed down completely, or propped open at varying degrees. Here and there, the walls had been damaged, and with the aid of thin lengths of rattan, we were able to make them secure.

It was while we were doing this, that I made a fearful discovery. There, hidden in the attap was a long, narrow dagger. It must have been some 18 inches long, and only less than an inch wide, with a small carved handle.

"What shall I do with this?" I said to Peter. "It's a vicious looking weapon. If we are caught with that, we shall be for the high jump."

"Well we can hardly be blamed for finding it," said Peter.

"So, let's tuck it back where it was, and forget all about it."

There were already indications that one day, weapons might prove very useful articles, and that one would be readily available.

Once the floor was scraped, leaving a smooth dark brown surface, the two of us settled down to fitting this multi-purpose centre for its various uses.

We had an old trestle table, which had come from Chung Hwa, and

141

upon which the library books could be laid out. Another addition was a blackboard and easel, which also surely must have found its way from the school. Then Peter's skill, with my ready help, came into its own. By raking around the camp, we found several firm pieces of bough, and cut these to lengths of about 4 feet each. They were sunk into the earth, about half their length, until they were tight. Arranged in two pairs, some 6 feet apart, they formed the head and foot rests, of our beds. With suitably placed cross pieces, and two rice sacks slung between bamboo poles, like a stretcher, we now each had a relatively comfortable, individual bed, raised off the ground, and easily removable, when the space was required for other purposes. The real 'pièce de résistance', however, were the 'deck chairs'. For two years now, we had not sat on a chair. Generally we had to squat on the ground, and only very exceptionally had there been anything raised to rest upon. Now, with the ingenious use of pliant bamboo slats, connected by the supple rattan, we had each contrived a piece of furniture as nearly comparable as we could to a beach deck chair.

Religion, like politics, had proved to be a divisive topic, and although both cropped up now and again, neither had a great following. However, from the early days of imprisonment, attempts had been made to hold both Church of England, and Roman Catholic, services. In Chung Hwa, these had been spasmodic, and the venue was the upper floor of the school, in the vestibule which led to the officers' rooms. Now, with the table cleared, and a white covering contrived from somewhere, we had a suitable altar. A small, simple, bamboo cross completed the picture. There must have been at least one hymn book available, because Peter used this to chalk up on the blackboard, a couple of verses of the more popular hymns. I came into possession of a tiny bible, which I still have. This measures 2 inches by 3¼, and contains over 1200 pages of minuscule print. It was censored by the Japanese, and contains the Jap 'chop'. I wonder that my eyes then remained good enough to read it, for now I find it difficult to do so, even with spectacles.

With all the British prisoners now gathered together at Sungei Ron, we now had a Catholic Priest, Padre Rowles, and two other officers, Lieutenant David Copley, of the Royal Navy, and Flight Lieutenant Moore, of the Royal Air Force, who both acted as Chaplains, and I understand after the war was over, went into Holy Orders.

So we were now all ready to go, and on the first day of rest following the renovation of the Chinese House, we had two short services, one for each of the two main religions.

Since this structure was our 'home', Peter and I stayed quietly in the background for the RC service, and joined in the C of E service. We were both absolutely dumbstruck when Padre Rowles appeared with a parcel, from which he unwrapped, not only his ecclesiastical robes, but also a pair of candles. The other two officers conducted their services, mundanely clad in shorts and shirts, but perhaps because of this were more in one with the 'Congregation'.

Perhaps under orders, we had an ever present witness, a guard, with rifle across his knees, likely understanding little of our ceremonies.

These occasions were never very well attended, but those who did come joined in with enthusiasm, and I have no doubt that they provided some comfort, and even some guidance to help carry the cross with which we were burdened. It is certainly true that when men reached the last twilight hours of existence, they prayed to God, with the help of those ministering. And, when all was over, the final rites were observed, and appreciated, by all comers.

Of this aspect of camp life, I retain two notable memories.

The Catholic Padre was well supported by his flock, and they brought him many offerings – food, and miscellaneous pilferings, which of course, was common to us all. However, I felt outraged when, despite the Commander's very recent plea about stealing, and the effect of punishment not only on the thief, but on the sick, and the camp generally, the Padre referred to the fact that the candles were burning low, and if anyone could obtain replacements, he would be glad. There was only one possible means of replacement, and to even countenance this, in the circumstances, for such useless paraphernalia, was an affront to common sense.

Because the guard hut could be seen across the slight valley, from the Chinese House, it became a refuge for various of the guards, when they tired of patrolling around. Indeed, it was not uncommon for one to indicate that Peter, or I, should peep through a crack in the attap, and keep a look-out for the Sergeant, while the guard had forty winks.

On one occasion, Tor, who was the biggest Jap, or Korean, I ever saw, appeared at the door one day, rifle in one hand, and a small monkey, on a piece of rope, in the other. He sat in one of our chairs, tied the monkey to it, and placed his rifle on the floor.

"You, Christo?" he grunted in our general direction.

We nodded in assent.

"Me Christo, sama, sama. Christo bagus." (Me, too, very good).

First, he put his hands together in the form of prayer, nodding at us to follow suit. When we did so, he grinned, and repeated "Christo me' bagus" (Christian men, good).

Then he indicated that he wanted to go to sleep, and that we should keep a lookout for him. Unfortunately, the monkey did not want to go to sleep. It was only a tiny little thing, hardly more than a baby, and hopped round at the extent of its tether, squeaking and pulling.

Eventually, it jumped up on the semi conscious guard, and bit his hand.

Tor reacted by clouting it soundly. This only provoked the animal to be even more excited, and to nip Tor on the leg.

He struck out at it again, and realising that he was not going to get any rest, roughly pulled it up off the floor, and strode outside, with the now chattering, frightened little beast, suspended in the air.

Tor hesitated outside, then spotting two members of the garden working party nearby, burning up some rubbish, he dragged the monkey over to the fire, and held it hung over the edge of the flames. He laughed, chidingly, as the creature squealed, obviously intent on teaching it a lesson. He circled his suspended pet round over the burning embers, now lost in his rage, and eventually let the singed, still, body drop in to the heat.

Kobayashi Torao, alias 'Tor', or 'King Kong', also committed many crimes against the men, but I remember him most for this one against a little defenceless monkey.

On another occasion, he is said to have crushed the skull of a dog, and eaten its still warm brain.

He, who professed to be a Christian.

'Tor' finally paid the ultimate penalty himself, and was hanged on November 22nd, 1946 having been found guilty at the War Crimes Trials in Singapore after the war.

News, Rumour and Propaganda

By the middle of 1944, we had become so divorced from the outside world that it was impossible to know under which heading the titbits of information should be properly classified. The restraints on the dissemination of real news from the secret radio were so exacting that no factual source could be given, and in any case the spreading of messages by word of mouth led to distortion and misinterpretation. For this reason, there is no clear recollection of the invasion of Europe on 'D' Day, June 6th, 1944. After a while, the repeated references to French and Dutch towns, in particular, underlined that the sketchy facts which had reached us were based on fact, and with this important turn in the Allied fortunes, came a resurgence of hope.

Looking back now, and piecing together the diary, I am aware that my first card home arrived in the same week.

Also, as I have noted before, the local newspaper recorded that my family had news at last. These two events must have been a tremendous boost to the morale of the folks back home.

A colleague at my office wrote to my parents at the beginning of July.

Dear Mr & Mrs Stubbs,
I had the pleasure last night of telling the 'Shift' (Civil Defence Team) that our Stubbie was OK, and needless to say the news was received with great joy.

We would like to send him something, but I understand you cannot send parcels, and that only next-of-kin can write.

However, when you write please say that we all wish him good luck, and quick return home.

I'd like to offer you my congratulations. I am quite sure the world has been a different place for you these last few days.

Keep clear of the doodlebugs.
Yours very sincerely,

W. T. Fletcher.

Tucked away in remote Sumatra, there had been no warlike activity whatever for two years or more, but there had been a day of panic, when we were rushed back to camp, off outside working parties, and confined to our huts for many hours, and not allowed any freedom in the camp perimeter whatever. This seemed to correspond with a Fleet Air Arm attack on Sabang, off North Sumatra, about which I learned many years later.

All kinds of interpretations were put on the subsequent actions of the Japanese.

In the next few days, we had to dig air raid trenches, in various positions near to the huts, but most telling of all, was the erection of a barbed wire compound, within the outer wire, with dugouts for machine guns at each corner. This could have no value defensively, and we were not surprised when we were told that if one Allied soldier set foot on Sumatra, we were all to be executed. It was a grim reminder of our helplessness, but nevertheless, we felt it was a good sign.

Liddell Hart in his 'History of the Second World War' refers to a proposed attack on Sumatra, and a seaborne assault on Rangoon, in the dry season of 1943/44, being code named Operations 'Culverin' and 'Anakim', which were under discussion at the Casablanca Conference in January, 1943. It was again a matter of luck for us that these strategies were abandoned, since the needed air superiority and strong naval forces were not then available.

The warning of our fate did not go unheeded, however, and despite our vulnerability, we took steps to defend ourselves, or at least exact

145

some retribution should that day ever come.

I retrieved the deadly stiletto from its hiding place, and from that time on, it was slid into a crevice parallel to one of the posts which held my bed, so that night or day, I could retrieve it in a matter of seconds. I realised, too, that a similar hiding place on the other side would be a dry, and safe, repository for my remaining possessions, and my photographs and pen stayed hidden there until after the surrender.

In the event, of course, the rapid ending of the war in the East, brought about by the two atom bombs on Hiroshima and Nagasaki, meant that these dire circumstances never arose, but the book 'By Eastern Windows' written by William H. McDougall, refers to a forecast massacre on August 27th, 1945. Also, while unknown to the Other Ranks, Lieutenant Frank Brewer recorded that information was to hand on August 13th, 1945, that the air raid siren was to be the signal for the massacre of prisoners. (Lieut. Brewer was Army Orderly Officer, at Sungei Geron, in 1945).

Again, how lucky I was – otherwise this narrative could never have been written, over 40 years later.

And Many Did Not Return

Corporal Allan Jack Kirby, of the Royal Air Force, died on April 10th, 1944. I hadn't really known him well, but the paths of our destinies merged in that hurried exodus from Singapore, and now we were camp mates at Sungei Geron.

The details of that humiliating, and doomed, armada, have found scant reference in the pages of history, and there were many who then lost their lives, and who, to this day, have no known grave.

We, who through good fortune and the hazards of fate had survived, were still fighting for existence.

By the Spring of 1944, the casualty list numbered only about a further two dozen British subjects in the military camps of Palembang. Even these deaths had made little impact except to close friends, for the very ill were taken away to Charitas Hospital.

Now we were faced with grim reality.

"The funeral of Corporal Allan Kirby will take place at 10.00 am tomorrow," came the stark announcement.

It was clear that if conditions did not improve, there could be only one answer. Bodies which had been upright, and A1, were now bent and shrunken. Minds which had been active and alert, were now vague and lack-lustre. The senses were dulled, and intellects impaired. The main, and overriding interest, was to find enough to eat for another day.

Before the war, when I was about 18 years old, and on the lean side, my father had said I would probably put on weight, as he did, from about 21 onwards. Now at 24, I was nearly 6 feet tall, and weighed just over 8 stone. There were only a lucky few, on special working parties, or those who worked in the galley, whose physiques did not tell the story of our deprivation.

"Poor devil. What was wrong with him?" asked someone.

"Starvation, like the rest of us, I should think."

"We should have some representation from the Royal Navy huts," said Frank, "Those who can attend, should go. It is not a 'Yasumé' day, but there must be a few, surely."

Tuesday, April 11th was a dry, sultry day. The working parties had gone off for the day, leaving only the Camp Duty Party, the Garden Working Party, and the sick, around the huts. Yet, amazingly, there must have been at least three score men assembled outside the hospital hut that morning, and all of them turned out as tidily as our conditions allowed. Most had headwear of some sort, services issue in the main. Clean, patched shorts

Cemetery at rear of Sungei Geron POW Camp
(Photograph probably taken in mid-1944)

147

replaced the usual fandushi, and many had boots, sadly worn, but rubbed clean.

The bearer party of RAF men, each with a blue grey forage-cap, emerged. The plain coffin, made of planks, was covered with a Union flag. On top was a shallow basket of fruit – pineapples, bananas, oranges and limes – a mark of respect from our captors.

The word of command came from Squadron Leader Clouston. He stood there, grim faced, tanned by the tropic sun, dark bearded. The stripes of his epaulettes caught the light, as he drew himself upright.

"Attention. Slow march. Left, right. Left, right."

The procession marched slowly off up the incline. I could see my friend, Alan Anstead, up in front, with his Air Force colleagues. Behind came three lines of Army and Navy representatives.

We reached the small clearing, by the edge of the jungle. By the side of the solitary, newly dug grave, the small company were brought to a halt by quiet, but precise, orders. It was extraordinary how everyone stood erect, heads high, to give our comrade a fitting farewell.

"I am the resurrection and the life, saith the Lord; he that believeth in me, though he were dead, yet shall he live; and whosoever liveth and believeth in me shall never die." The RAF Chaplain softly recited the opening of the burial service, his eyes directed downward towards the crude oblong crate, which now rested on the ground. His words were carried on the slight breeze, which just moved the nearby trees, and caused the tall bamboo to bow perceptibly, as if in reverence.

As I listened, and watched, my mind went back to that day on the Aguila, way out in the Atlantic, as a shrouded body sped down a chute, into the depths of the ocean. The first service funeral I had witnessed.

"Forasmuch as it hath pleased Almighty God of His great mercy to take unto Himself the soul of our dear brother here departed; We therefore commit his body to the ground; earth to earth, ashes to ashes, dust to dust, in sure and certain hope of the Resurrection to eternal life."

Heads were bowed, as the Chaplain closed his book. The guard reached down, and recovered the basket of fruit. In the jungle, there was the sudden, harsh noise of wild birds.

Within a few moments, we were retracing our steps, back down towards the huts. Everyone was silent, pensive, reflective. How many would be carried along that same track. As things now stood, was it now a mercy to die? And what of our loved ones at home – no goodbyes, no obituary. Just a patch, scratched clean of entwining creepers. Just an end, seen only by a scattering of friends, a few comrades, and a Jap guard.

The guard shouted.

"Lekas." (hurry).

"Orang speedo, muchu worku."

Fifteen minutes or so of the day's labour must now be made good. For them, it was probably one less mouth to feed. For us, it was a pointer to the inevitable. A bleak milestone along a melancholy road.

The passing of the months of 1944 was marked only by the onset of the monsoon. In October, November and December of that year, over 32 inches of rain were registered, and Sungei Geron was awash; a dripping, squelching morass of mud and misery. And yet when the first rains came in August, after 92 days of drought, we had run outside, naked, to feel the blessed freshness of clean rainwater. We had larked, and sang, as it cleaned our bodies, and quickened our spirits.

Now we were approaching Christmas, and another New Year. Perhaps we should have a day's holiday, in celebration of our Christian feast. Feast – it was hardly likely to be a feast.

But there had been increasing signs of defensive measures by the Japanese. One occasion was noted by barrage balloons being hoisted, and another by the wail of air raid sirens. Perhaps 1945 would bring a change in our fortunes.

Most weeks now were punctuated by those solemn pilgrimages up the hill, to the jungle edge.

One of our London group, Lance Bombardier Wilfred George Groves passed away from us on December 15th, 1944.

A couple of days later, our Royal Navy killick, Frank Downing was taken into the hospital hut. With his ordered mind, and fierce spirit, he had fought hard. But now with the combined after effects of malaria and dysentery, beri-beri had worked its relentless way up from his swollen ankles, and his distended abdomen, until his whole frame was filled with the drowning fluid. Frank died on December 20th.

Lieutenant David Copley led the cortege up the hill. This time there were differences. There was no timber for a coffin, and even the long, narrow basket of bamboo was only a temporary bier to transport the body for that last few hundred yards. The shroud was two rice sacks, for the Japs had long since forbidden any use of our traditional flag. The six naval pall-bearers carried the corpse hip high, not because of the weight of the wasted body, although that was a consideration, but because of the frailty of the conveyance.

The single grave of Corporal Kirby had now been joined by 50 or more others, narrow ridged plots, bare and unadorned, except for the simple, plain cross at the head of each. There were three shallow pits, lying open to receive the mortal remains of three more prisoners, while a small party of grave-diggers stood ready to dig again once the solemn rites had been conducted over Frank.

149

"Attention. Off caps." A naval Petty Officer gave the subdued command, and David Copley softly uttered the now too familiar words. The heavy sky sped across the dominating symbol of our faith – a tree, shorn of its bark, the front face, scratched and scraped till it shone, with a simple, matching crosspiece, on which were beautifully carved the names of the men who rested below. There was no fruit, no flowers. There were just the solemn prayers and thoughts of men who had lost a good friend.

The Cage

The yasumé day started quietly enough.

Peter was putting the finishing touches to his sundial. It was his latest creation, and meant that on those days when we had sun – as opposed to those when we had nothing but rain – we could make a fairly accurate attempt at the time. It was a semi-circular piece of metal, set into a wooden base, and graduated across with lines to tell the hour. Set immediately above the noon line was a right-angled piece of stiff wire, whose shadow was thrown onto the graduations, producing the required answer.

I had spent an hour or two in the hospital huts, making sure that those who could read had something to occupy their minds in the endless hours, and chatting here and there to those still sufficiently aware to welcome a new voice and a new face. It was a necessary part of my function as camp librarian, and I was glad to do it. Nevertheless, it was a relief to get out again, into the air. The hut was little different to the others, being a long narrow structure, with beds of continuous bamboo slats down each side, but it did have two blocked off compartments. One housed the negligible amount of medical equipment and supplies, a few dixies adapted for their new use, and a number of pots of various descriptions, which served as bed pans and wash basins. My overriding memory is of the fearful odour, due to the lack of disinfectant, the absence of clean clothes and bed linen, and the inability of the hard pressed medical orderlies, with the shortage of water, to cope with bodies racked with fever and dysentery. The War Crimes trials, when dealing with Doctor Nakai, referred to the frightful conditions of filth and squalor which prevailed. The other separate compartment of the terminal hut was kept as a mortuary.

On my return, I passed Johnnie MacMillan, busy kindling a small fire into life with a piece of glass, concentrating the fitful sun onto a few dry shavings. From somewhere, he had conjured some small, dried fish, and a handful of green beans.

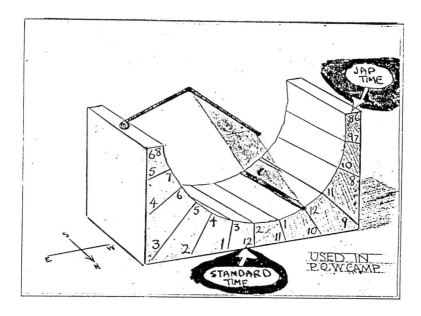

'Time-piece' by Peter Bivand.

"Salamat, tuan benjo besar," I greeted him. Ever since the lavatory party at Chung Hwa, he had been known as the Great White Lavatory Man – and still is to this day.

"Apa makan ada?" (What have you got there?) I enquired.

"Banyak makan." (Lots of food) replied Johnnie, looking ruefully at the two little piles beside him. I gathered that he had swapped a couple of cigarettes for his eats while he was out on a working party. I sat a while, quietly conversing, drinking in the appetising smell which rose from the glowing embers. Johnnie turned the fish over with a stick.

"Ikan bagus. Mau satu," (Fish good. Want one?)

He scooped up one little tiddler, like a sardine. It was crisp, and oily. I nibbled it slowly, savouring the salty, strong taste.

"Terima kaseh, tuan," (Thank you, master) I said, licking my lips at this unexpected treat.

At that moment, Tom Wannop came shuffling round the corner, the wood of his clogs clacking on the stony path.

"Bastards," he said. "They've got one of the Jocks."

"Which Jock?" said Johnnie, rising to his feet.

"One of the Argylls. I don't know his name."

151

He led us round the corner of the hut. Across the slight valley, up outside the guard hut, there was a knot of guards, surrounding a lone figure, clad only in a fandushi. The sound of angry voices carried across the incline.

"Poor devil. Gladys is on duty. That swine would murder his grandma."

By now, there was a subdued and scattered audience, helpless as always to intervene, as the words changed to blows, and the miscreant was punched, kicked and felled.

One of the British officers went hurrying down to the gate, to use his influence to stop the beating, but to no avail. In fact, it possibly prompted Gladys to new peaks of fury.

Eventually, Capt. Ringer was called for, and it was explained to him that this man had not bowed when the guard passed by.

"Awro me' bow. No bow. Punish."

The plea that the man did not see the guard was rejected out of hand. The prisoners must bow to the Japanese. Not to bow was the utmost discourtesy.

The prisoner was dragged to the 'cage', and left to nurse his bruises and lacerations. He was the first occupant of that open cell. Its dimensions were too small to allow a man to stand, too confined to hardly allow him to stretch out on the bare ground, and its wire barbs made it impossible to lean.

In fact, I think the captive was not a 'Jock', but one of the Northumbrians, who had graced the ranks of the Argyll and Sutherland Highlanders. He was tough. When we later passed the cage on our way to the galley, he was sitting with knees under his chin, still with only that diminutive piece of cloth to cover his loins. A discreet 'thumbs up' was met with fingers crossed, and an attempt to smile, through the swollen face.

The Japs had placed a bowl of water where he could see it, but not reach. When the evening rice came along, he was refused food.

During the day, it must have been purgatory in that den. As night came on, the mosquitoes filled the air, and ants and other insects covered the ground. It was sheer torture.

By the morning, the man was a coiled, shivering ball on the ground. He was left there for 3 days, despite any representations.

His mates carried him back to his hut. A cigarette (a whisp of tobacco in a piece of discarded paper) from one, a cup of tea (no milk, no sugar) from another. But above all, to be back among friends.

After that first incident, the new 'toy' became a common amusement for the guards, and was later almost permanently occupied, rain or sun, night or day, and was even occasionally used to house three or four men.

Somehow, though we were on the very edge of physical and mental breakdown, friendships brought relief. A small fish shared. A few whisps of tobacco given. A new day still brought some hope.

Cats, and Dogs, and Other Things

Peter and I sat silently in the Navy hut. Everywhere was quiet. We had been made to leave the Chinese Hut when the air raid had started. Only the occasional shout from one guard to another disturbed the eerie silence. We strained our ears for sounds of planes.

"Listen," said someone, "I'm sure I can hear something."

Tom Wannop eased the attap palm of the hut wall gently aside, and peeped out through the narrow crack he had made.

"What's going on?" asked Lofty Claridge.

"Can't see a thing," replied Tom.

"Maybe it's a false alarm. They're getting very jumpy lately," said Peter Robbins.

"I could swear I heard a low drone just now," added the first voice.

After a time, movement started round the hut. Men left their bedspaces, and wandered down the trodden earth corridor to speak to others. Some had now taken to mending clothes, or reading one of the now very worn books which were circulating in the hut.

A. B. Shaw sat on the end of the bamboo slats, knees drawn up, rubbing his ankles. Quietly he said, "Look, I think I've got it."

He pressed the flesh at the back of his calf. The impression stayed. His forefinger had left a small round crater at the back of his leg. While the rest of his frame was barely covered, his legs were bloated and puffy. It was no surprise that he, like most of us, had the only too obvious signs of beri-beri.

There was little sympathy. We were all in the same boat.

"Well maybe we'll be out of here by the end of the year. This can't be a false alarm, otherwise they would have sounded the 'All Clear' by now surely."

Thank the Lord, we still had some optimism.

"But where can the planes have come from?" asked someone.

"Does it matter," spoke Claridge. "The fact is that they're about, and that must be good."

Soon the 'All Clear' did sound. This was quickly followed by the Koreans hustling us all back to work. We had seen nothing. We really had heard nothing. Perhaps we were grasping at straws. It was nearly the end of August, 1944. Surely this war couldn't go on for ever. But the Japs said it would last 100 years.

Meanwhile at home, my family longed for other news. They travelled where they could. They wrote everywhere. They probed every corner.

The news that I was a prisoner of war had reached home in June, but of course that was only when my first postcards had been delivered, and there was nothing from official sources until October 13th, when a letter from the British Red Cross Society, was addressed to my mother:

The opening paragraph read:

> We have been officially advised that the above (Coder R. S. Stubbs, C/JX 205607) is a prisoner of war in Japanese hands. We are very glad that this news of his safety has been received.

The Hon. Secretary of my athletic club, Highgate Harriers, wrote on August 10th:

> Dear Miss Stubbs,
> I thank you for your letter of earlier this year respecting your brother. All Club members are very sorry indeed that you had had no news, and we are all hoping that one day, you will hear that he is safe and sound, when I know, you will let me know. I write this because only this week I have had news, the first for over two years, of a member of my Cricket Club, who was taken prisoner by the Japs, and whom nothing at all was heard of, until the postcard received by his parents this week.
> So we remain in hope,
> Yours sincerely,
> A. D. McSweeney.

Meanwhile, back at Sungei Geron, we were still counting the days, and hoping.

I was sitting in the Chinese Hut, doing the best I could to mend one or two books, which were falling to pieces, and I commented that it was now over 4 years since I had sailed from Liverpool, on October 10th, 1940, aboard SS Aguila.

Peter had been doing some running repairs to the hut roof, and came over to me, with a card in his hand.

"While you were sitting there earlier," he said, "I did a quick pencil sketch for you. How's that?"

Shaven head. Sunken collar bones. But a blessing – we both had something to occupy our minds.

A fortnight later a letter, or to be more accurate, the uncensored part of a letter, arrived from my mother.

November 9th was her birthday, and she was now in her early sixties. I suppose it would have been bleak and wintry in Southgate. In Palembang, on that day, we were aflood. The rain was incessant. It found every defect – I was glad that Peter had recently patched the roof. It flooded across the floor, and ran away down the slope at the front. The only sign of life outside was from the guardhouse, where we could just see the guards confined under their shelter.

Down from the hut, one of the water holes was overflowing, and the pathway was now a rushing stream.

Nearly 5 inches of rain fell that day in 2½ hours. It washed away our precious plants, but even the Japs had to concede that it was impossible to work in it.

The miracle was that the water hole, which in August had been a parched, cracked hole in the ground, now was inundated with frogs, and there were even tiny fish in its murky depths.

There was almost a mass exodus when the rain stopped.

"Woof, woof," shouted someone outside.

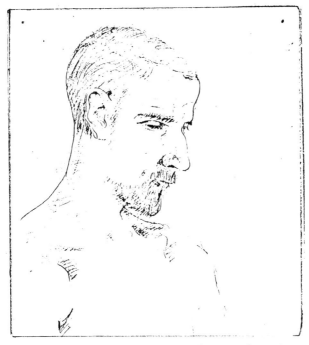

Ray Stubbs drawn by Peter Bivand 13 October, 1944.

I lifted the window flap. A knot of Navy chaps were picking their way through the mud down to the galley.

"Woof, woof," came the shout again.

A few yards away was an RAF corporal, with a cooking pot in his hand.

"Down boy," said the sailor, as he passed the corporal.

"Aw shuttup," growled the Air Force bod.

Peter joined me at the window.

"What's going on?" he asked.

"I don't know," I answered. "Looks like a bit of service banter. The Navy lads are chi-iking old Markham."

"It's been raining cats and dogs. Perhaps that's what it is all about."

It came out later. Round the camp were a number of mangy, skinny, dogs and cats. What they found to eat, I don't know, but they were useful in keeping down the rats and other rodents, which haunted the huts. One of the dogs had found its way into an RAF cooking pot – hence the catcalls. The pun was unintentional, but it wasn't long before a cat met the same end. This time in a Navy pot. From then on 'Woof woof' was met with 'Miaow miaow'. Having seen these scruffy, diseased animals, the pangs of hunger had not yet driven me to such lengths, but nevertheless, snakes, lizards, frogs, and the odd iguana had all now become ingredients in the camp stew.

Monsoon

Apart from darts, there was now little to offer in the way of recreation. After a day's hard labour on the sparse, starvation rations, physical sports had long since been abandoned. Our 'home made' darts and dart boards had now become works of art, particularly the wide variety of flights, ranging from card, to dried, hardened leaves, slivers of wood, and scraps of mica. There were a few packs of cards, but these were heavily thumbed, bent, and mostly incomplete. The officers had carved themselves an occasional chess set, and I believe, there was a Mah Jong set in existence.

Above all, we were almost entirely dependent on natural light to do anything. I say, almost, because with ingenuity, most men had equipped themselves with a small oil lamp, and at night each hut became a den of flickering wicks, in an otherwise dense gloom.

As usual with all things, the Japs waxed hot and cold over their use, sometimes turning a blind eye to them, and at others stomping through the huts, confiscating or destroying them, or at least ordering them to be extinguished, on the pretext of fire risk. There were also many tense moments when they demanded the source either of the raw materials, or more likely, the oil.

After the ritual sluicing at the water hole (there was certainly no shortage now), the rapid disposal of the evening meal (where the shortage was still sadly obvious) we converged on the Navy hut.

Around the end, some logs had been arranged to provide a few hard seats, as the ground was now very wet and muddy from the heavy, and prolonged downpours.

"Better get cracking," said Lofty Claridge, the skipper of the Navy side.

"Don't like the feel of that wind. I reckon we're in for another soaking before long."

"A bit black over Bill's mothers," added some wit.

"Right then," said the RAF umpire.

"Toss for starters. 601 up, and off with a double, finish on a double."

"Who's your first man," he addressed to the captain of the Argyll's side.

The first dart thudded into the circle of timber, which at a few feet, could not be distinguished from the manufactured article. It was just outside the circle delineating the edge of the double. The next found its mark, and a shout went up.

"Double five. Now we'll show these matelots a clean pair of heels."

The Scots were away, and it was not until Leading Seaman Bennett for the Royal Navy took his turn, that the sailors got their first double.

"It's this wretched wind, out in the open, that's doing it," complained George Byworth.

"Och awa'. It's the same wind for us, the noo," was a Scot retort.

"You're all ruddy wind. That's why you can cope with it."

The repartee continued as the excitement rose. After the first five games, the Argylls were leading three/two, and the third sailor took up the challenge.

"Blast. I felt a spot of rain."

In our concentration, we had all forgotten the darkening sky.

With a ferocious intensity, the rain lashed the flimsy side of the building. The wind was already lifting the insecure drapes of the attap leaves, and there was a hurried sight of the foreboding sky, now deep with anger.

"Oh God, I must get to the Heads." It was Bagsy Baker, his face contorted in agony, as his stomach writhed with the tearing pain of the dysentery within him. He kicked off his wooden clogs, pulled a rice sack around his withered frame, and wrestled to open the bamboo door out into the night. As he did so, a fierce blast swept through the hut. The flickering lamps nearest the door were immediately extinguished, and those further away bent to the force of the wind, casting strange flickering shadows in the obscure murkiness.

"Poor devil. Bagsy must be in a bad way to have to go out in this downpour."

The wind was now at gale intensity, and the wall timbers were creaking as the sheets of rain hurtled into the soaking attap. Conversation had virtually stopped. It was almost impossible to hear anything above the noises of the storm as the huge jungle trees fought with the forces of nature. The water cascading down the hut walls, was now relentlessly forcing its way across the floor.

The palm leaf door was opened again, and there, clutching the pole at the side was Bagsy, rain pouring off his crumpled figure, his bare feet and legs now covered in mud, and down one side muck and filth stuck to him where clearly he had fallen over in the darkness. Several pairs of helping hands reached out for him. He was half carried, half lifted onto the slatted platform while others tried to achieve the impossible by drying him whilst keeping him clear of the constant flow of water now coming through the roof in many places.

The fury of the blast was steadily worsening and the walls of the hut, now saturated, were bowing and sagging with the impact. In the impossible light, men were pulling their bits of bedding towards the centre aisle, away from the rain-laden tornado. Others were vainly trying to escape the deluges which were virtually now making a colander of the roof.

There was now a perceptible lean to the hut, and the attap on the windward side was, in places, standing out horizontally, like many small pennants straining for their freedom. The noise grew yet louder, and above the thunder of the storm we all heard the first creaking splitting of one of the bamboo struts.

"Look out," shouted Lofty Claridge. "The blasted hut's coming down!"

As if to give it strength, we all leaned as best we could against the soddened leaf, pushing hard with what strength we had against the framework.

There was another sharp crack and, like a greenstick fracture, one of the poles suddenly leaned dangerously from about two feet above the ground. Splinters of bamboo quivered upright from the stump.

"Good God, mind those! They'll cut like a razor! Abandon the hut! It's coming down!"

The prophesy was only too accurate. Within a few minutes the poles collapsed, one by one, over our heads.

I slithered down what used to be a path to the Chinese Hut. Fortunately, that Chinaman had built it to a better specification than the guards had allowed for the prisoners. I was pleased to share my refuge with many

During one night a terrific storm swept over the camp, in the course of which several huts were battered down by weight of wind and rain, destroying the few belongings of many of the inmates. Amongst the huts destroyed was that belonging to the Royal Marines. I caught several of our gallant allies looting the damaged huts the next day, such were the frailties of nature under these conditions.

Storm damage to Royal Marines' Hut.

Courtesy of Lt J. Wallace Kemp, RN.

other soaking disconsolate prisoners. We dug a narrow channel across the floor to direct the rivulets of water.

The frenzy seemed to go on for hour after hour, until I am sure we all wondered whether even this hut might collapse. When dawn broke, all we could see was mud and water. Our crops had been flattened. The paths had been obliterated. The toilet trenches were discharging their foul content down the slope – fortunately away from where the huts were built.

The forest animals were strangely quiet. The guards were non-existent.

The rain had slowed to a steady patter as the daylight came with its tropical suddenness.

A party of naval officers with the Master-at-Arms in the lead were inspecting the fallen hut.

There was an announcement.

"The breakfast rice will be late this morning. The wood in the galley is soaking wet, and the cooks can't get the fires going. Working parties will fall in for work as usual, immediately after Tenko."

"Oh, get stuffed," was the only reply.

Hopes and Fears

And so the year 1944 ended. We did have a day's 'resto' for Christmas, but there was little in the way of extra food to mark the celebration. Morale was now very low. We had been nearly 3 years in captivity, and the resilience and humour which had been the mainstays of the earlier weeks and months, had been eaten away by the depressing weather, the starvation diet, and the steadily rising incidence of sickness, and almost inevitably, death.

We knew, without any doubt at all, that the Allied Forces were progressing well in Europe, but even there, there was a long way to go. The news in the Far East was thin, and even the rumours had little impact, as we laboured and endured one long day after another.

The morning of January 24th dawned as usual. It was a dry, but dull day. The working parties were paraded, and set off for their various locations. There was nothing untoward.

Peter and I had downed our 'breakfast'. I went down the hill to the galley, and collected a ladle of thin rice paste to repair the binding of one of the library books, and carry out some renovations to others, which were now very little more than a bunch of loose pages.

As I left the galley, I heard the Jap guard at the camp entrance shout to his companion, and point excitedly to the sky. Following his pointing finger, just over the tips of the jungle trees, I could see a small object rising into the sky. It was shaped rather like a lemon. It was either patched, or it was camouflaged in green and brown. As I watched, this thing rose slowly into the morning grey. Then close by there was another, and another. Barrage balloons.

I hurried back up the camp road, across the parade ground, and ran into the Chinese House.

"Peter, quickly. Come and look at this."

Peter, who had been immersed in his task of lettering the new spines of some library books, looked up in his quizzical way, and rather slowly came over to the hut door.

We did not have to comment. By now there were about six or seven of these strange shaped balloons, hovering a few hundred feet up in the direction of the River Moesi.

I thought of that September day when, in 1939, I had driven with Arthur Walker through the green of Finsbury Park, and saw the silver shapes of London's barrage raised seriously, for the first time.

*'Avenger' of 849 Squadron, from HMS Victorious, crossing West coast of
Sumatra, en route to Palembang.
(Photograph taken by Petty Officer Harry Copping).*

161

Over in the guards' camp, a whistle sounded, and there was frantic activity in the guard house. Before long, Japs and Koreans were running through the camp, hustling men into the huts.

"Lekas, speedo, no worku."

The garden party were urged to quickly drop their tools, and run into the nearest attap shelter.

From our vantage point in the Chinese Hut, we could see the guards, with bayonets fixed, and glinting, taking up positions around the boundary wire, and at certain main points throughout the camp.

Presently, the rotund, bespectacled figure of Lieut. Takahashi appeared, hurrying down the road, shouting orders to the guard commander, as he passed the gate.

Within a few minutes, a lorry came out of the distance. It was crammed with prisoners, all rapidly collected, and returned from their work places.

This must be the real thing at last.

More shouting. Capt. Ringer was in urgent discussion with Takahashi and the interpreter. Ringer was pointing to the air raid trenches, and gesticulating towards the mens' huts. Takahashi was waving both hands in denial, and then beckoned Ringer away.

"Whatever is going on, they're not going to let us out of the huts," I said to Peter.

In the distance, we could now hear the sound of heavy gunfire, and a few tell tale puffs of grey smoke pockmarked the clearing sky.

We assumed that the guards had only got us in the huts so that we could not see what was going on. Certainly the attap leaves would provide no protection whatever.

"Damn fools. They make us dig shelters, then they don't let us use them," commented my companion.

We both took up positions on different sides of the hut, and gradually opened cracks in the leaves to peer out. The guard commander, our hated Gladys, was walking smartly along one of the long huts, rapping on the props which held up the window flaps, and forcing them all to be closed.

Now added to the sounds of the ground defences, there were several low crumps, and the staccato rattle of small arms, or machine gun fire. The guard I could see by the wire on the jungle edge was straining his eyes up into the sky. Because of the overhanging attap, I couldn't see what he was watching, but there was no doubt now. There were aerial battles going on in the near vicinity.

Peter beckoned me over. From his vantage point, he could see a guard taking off his soft peaked cap, and donning a metal helmet.

"Look," he whispered. "They've been caught with their trousers down, and now they must know it's a real raid."

162

*Air attack by 150 planes of the BPF on Palembang, Sumatra, January 24 1945
from 'Alarm Starboard' by Geoffrey Brooke.*

I felt my heart leap. For 35 solid months, our forces had been at the receiving end, and now before our eyes, they were hitting back.

"They are too high to see anything. What do you think they are – Yanks?" I queried.

"God knows, but it obviously is not just a reccy. There must be quite a lot of them up there judging by the spread of the anti-aircraft fire."

We heard 'Gladys' shouting to another guard.

"Keirei, Kanemoto." Then again, louder "Keirei, Kanemoto."

Kanemoto came running round the corner. Bowed abruptly to his superior officer, and was then dispatched with a message, across to the guards' quarters.

Then, a frightening, but exhilarating noise. The scream of several aircraft, as they swept virtually from one side of the camp to the other.

"Could you see those?" I asked, as Peter with his eyes now glued to the split in the attap, was gazing out to the right of the hut.

"Only just. By the time I had spotted them, they were disappearing over the trees."

"I counted five or six. They must have been below the height of the balloons. Couldn't make out any markings – they were travelling so fast."

"What do you reckon they were?"

"No idea. Don't forget we've been shut up for three years."

That is something we couldn't, and probably never would, forget, but it made us realise that time hadn't stood still, and the strange shapes we were seeing in the air were a tremendous advance on the Brewster Buffaloes we had seen in Singapore, and the Fairey Swordfish and Fulmars of the Navy Fleet Air Arm.

"Crikey, look at that!" Peter almost shouted in his excitement.

Now over the tree line, we could see a column of black smoke rising.

"That must be the oil tanks. Surely that is the direction of Pladjoe."

"Here comes another lot. Cor. Good-ho."

For the moment, our personal safety was forgotten in the excitement. To think that just up there, within sight, were friends.

There was no marking to the prison-of-war camp to indicate what it was, and from the air, it could be taken as a military camp.

"I should think they must be after the oil installations," mused Peter.

"That, or the railway, or both," I answered.

Suddenly there was a series of shrill noises. I had heard similar before in Liverpool, in London, in Malta, at sea, in Singapore.

"Get down," I shouted instinctively, and we both fell to the ground.

We found later that two stray bombs had dropped just inside the camp perimeter. Fortunately for us, they landed in soft ground, and didn't damage any buildings, or harm any of the prisoners. It was said that one of the guards was slightly injured, but we had no proof of that.

Then, as quickly as it had started, it was over. There was silence.

The only indication that it had not just been a dream was the thick smoke rising into the sky.

It seemed an age before the guards allowed us to leave the huts, and there was a rush for the latrines, a queue at the water hole, and many enquiries as to when we might get our midday rice.

But all of these things, pressing as they might be, were lost in the overall feeling of new hopes, almost an uncontrolled animation. Everywhere small groups of men were gathered talking, calling to each other, laughing, almost crying.

Then the guards. They turned out in strength. Swaggering round, still with their helmets on, and bayonets still fixed. They broke up any gathering they found. Kicking, shouting, flailing about with rifle butts.

"All men, worku."

We didn't mind that. This was a shot in the arm.

The next day or two, the stories went round. The oil installations have been devastated. The airfield has been wiped out. There are great big bomb craters in the town. The Allies have landed on the West Coast.

But Tenkos and working parties became purgatory. At the least excuse, men would be beaten. The sadism of some of the guards was shown in their retaliation.

Yet we had new strength. New determination. New courage.

Five days later we heard the air raid alarm again. Barely had it sounded than the air was filled with planes weaving and diving. There were dog fights, there were explosions. There was the unmistakeable sound of gunfire, light and heavy.

The camp site was chaos, as we were all driven back into the huts. Once more we were treated to the sight of aerial battles, even more intense than the previous occasion.

And then the silent aftermath.

"Tenko. All men tenko."

It was nearing midday again. Not the usual time for tenko.

There was no argument though. We hadn't misheard. The guards were clearing the huts. Fit men, sick men, working men, camp duty men. All were summoned, and pushed and shoved onto the parade ground.

Captains and Commanders, Lieutenant-Commanders, Majors – all the British and Dutch officers were there. Commander Reid was in serious discussion with his Dutch counterpart.

"Kiotsuke."

We were drawn to attention in our services.

"Royal Navy. Attention."

"Army, Army, 'shun"

"Royal Air Force, stand at ease. Royal Air Force, attention."

We stood in our serried ranks. Out in the heat. Few had hats. Fewer had shirts.

The Japs counted us in fives.

"Ichi, ni, san, shi, go, roku."

Someone fainted. The guard lost count. Started again.

"Ichi, ni, san . . ." – the tedium mounted.

There was a mumble of discontent. The guard kicked out savagely at the bare legs of the culprit.

The individual guards reported to the guard commander, who totted up the numbers on a piece of paper. He said something, and waved his hand vaguely in the direction of the Dutch contingent, the Army ranks and the Royal Air Force. Then "Navee, ni."

The order to dismiss was barked out in Dutch, and the Hollanders trooped away. Then on instruction from the guard, we heard Squadron Leader Clouston.

"Royal Air Force. Royal Air Force, turn right, dismiss."

The Army also fell out, and with puzzled looks in our direction, gradually left the parade ground.

Sergeant Kurata Takeo then took the stage.

In bits of broken English, laced with bits of Malay, and Japanese, punctuated with snorts, and the typical hisses of indrawn breath, he explained that all naval men from the Royal Navy were bad men. They had tried to wreak havoc in Palembang, but the brave Japanese airmen had repelled them, and had shot down many planes. The rest had fled. Now Navy men would be punished. He also wished to remind us that if one soldier landed on Sumatra, then all prisoners would be shot.

"Must have been successful," whispered Johnnie, by my side.

The ordinary guards wandered along our ranks, throwing a punch here, and landing a kick there. I sensed, rather than saw the Black Mamba in front of me. It wasn't exactly eyeball to eyeball. As I stood as upright as I could, he just about reached my Adam's Apple. He grunted, and stabbed his rifle butt down on my bare feet. I flinched, and bit my lip hard. The pain was excruciating. Fortunately, it was not the ulcerated foot that took the worst of it. The little yellow swine passed further on.

About two hours later, when several men had been quite badly beaten, and others collapsed, we were dismissed.

I went straight back to the Chinese Hut, and bathed my feet. Fortunately there was only bruising. The skin was unbroken.

I lifted the support to my rice sacking bed. The stiletto was still there. I might need it one day – and that day may be soon.

It was not until long after the war had ended that I chanced upon various accounts of those raids on Palembang.

The attacks were made by the British Pacific Fleet, steaming off the West coast of Sumatra, necessitating a long flight over jungle, and enemy held territory. They were the largest Fleet Air Arm strikes during the whole of the war.

Palembang was considered to be of great strategic importance, being an important road and rail centre. Pladjoe was the largest oil refinery in the Far East, and Sungei Geron, the second largest.

By early 1945, Japan was crucially short of oil and tankers, and the refineries at Palembang were capable of supplying two thirds of her requirement of aviation fuel.

The Fleet, including four aircraft carriers, Indomitable, Victorious, Illustrious and Indefatigable, were en route to Australia.

Two hundred and forty four aircraft were embarked, including Avengers, Corsairs and Hellcats. In nearly 400 sorties, 41 aircraft were lost, and 68 enemy aircraft destroyed.

The refineries at Pladjoe and Sungei Geron were put completely out of action for 1, and 3 months respectively, and neither was in full flow for the remainder of the war.

Special arrangements had been made to recover pilots who were forced down, by means of a submarine patrolling off the coast, and a Walrus seaplane. Nine airmen were captured by the Japanese. These brave men were taken to Singapore. They were later beheaded on a beach near Changi jail, after the end of the war.

Apart from the strategic benefits of these raids, Rear Admiral Sir Philip Vian, and his pilots and men, would not have known of the tremendous boost to morale that they brought to the British prisoners of war.

(See Appendix X – Memorial Stone to "Palembang Nine").

Twenty-Fifth Birthday

I have no idea why, but all my friends decided that we should have a 'party' on my birthday.

'Party' might give the impression that there would be wine, food, singing, and celebrations of all sorts. Yes, to an extent there was. Perhaps the fact that we had an ideal venue in the Chinese House, led to the idea. Possibly the fact that we had had no excitement since the bombing raids at the end of January, meant that morale was on the downgrade again. I would like to think that never ever did friends and friendship mean as much as it did in those days. I hope that running through this saga there may be a thread to indicate that without friends a man was lost; with friends, good staunch friends, a man could better face the future with courage, with hope, and even with some humour.

The great day was to be March 23rd, 1945.

The Chinese House being used for religious services, for the library, and occasionally for small meetings, was well suited and although the guards seemed to have forgotten their edict that there should be no gathering of more than a few men, this could well be disguised.

Every one of the guests was exhorted to save, hoard, pinch, cook, produce some little tasty titbit, and really this must have been the original 'Serve Yourself' food counter!

When the working day had ended, and the rice ration and watery soup allocated in the huts, the invitees gathered in the hut, with Peter and myself.

There was Johnnie MacMillan and Tom Wannop, Harry Gosden and Stan Orton, Peter Bivand and Ted Evans. There was Sick Bay Tiffie Tickner, Donald Brown and Kim Mendelsohn. From the RAF were Alan Anstead and Bert Weaver. In all about a dozen.

We ate our rice amid reminiscences of birthdays past. With it we had what Peter describes as 'Super Stew'. It contained Purslane, Gondola and Anastasia – I can't recall (perhaps fortunately) what these tropical vegetables tasted like, and certainly no-one dared to seek their origins. In addition there were Ubi manis (sweet potatoes), Ubi kayu (wooden potatoes), Ubi Kayu tops (coarse green leaves) and spinach. There was salt, a few chillies, and two tiny tomatoes. To wash it down there was a secret recipe, optimistically named 'Citronella'. Basically it contained a couple of limes, an orange or two, complete with rinds, a few chunks of pineapple, some coconut milk, and was laced with rice which had been fermented in brown sugar.

For the first time in many weeks, we sat back, moderately replete. We savoured not only the food, but the company. We grinned, and joked as the stories came out, as to how the various ingredients had been garnered.

"Going round the buoy?" asked Johnnie, proffering some more of the hooch.

"I haven't heard that since I was on Encounter," I replied. "Ada lagi." Nowadays there was never the chance of seconds. For a time, we used to say to the Indonesians 'Mau Lagi' when we wanted some more, but the natives themselves were suffering from the rampant inflation that had hit the Dutch East Indies, and the fact that convoys were not getting through meant that even rice was in short supply, and all kinds of food were very, very expensive.

Johnnie gave me about half a cupful of the frothy, yellowish

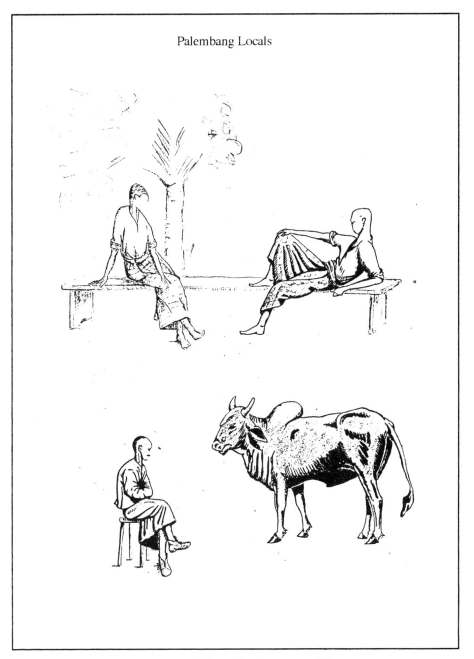

Palembang Locals

Courtesy of Lt J. Wallace Kemp, RN.

liquid. Today was my birthday, and if I had a headache tomorrow, so what!

It was too dark to play darts, and everyone seemed happy enough to just sprawl on the earth floor, and yarn.

"Did you see our new camp mate?" asked Tom Wannop.

"No, who's he?" queried Harry Gosden.

"It's not a he, it's a she," said Tom.

"We don't even see the German woman these days. I wonder what has happened to her?"

"So come on then, who is this new female?"

"Well, she's very well built, and got a lovely swing as she walks," added Tom.

"Don't keep us in suspense then. What was she doing in the camp?"

"She came in with the rations, and I believe they're going to keep her down near the galley. I should think she'll be very useful on the working parties."

"With the working parties. She'll be slaughtered."

"Don't you kid yourself. Nobody has got the energy."

"Well, she has I can tell you," grinned Tom. "There she was pulling the cart, all by herself. Mind she did hum a bit, and her rear needed a bit of a clean up."

"Sling something at him," exploded Stan. "Twit's talking about the ox."

"That's not an ox, it's a yak."

"It's a turn up for the books, anyway, isn't it. It used to take six of us to pull the benjo cart up the hill, now the Japs out of the goodness of their hearts have provided a yak."

"Goodness of their hearts. Probably pinched it off some native."

"So what's the odds. Certainly do us a good turn."

Covetous eyes were often focussed on that filthy swinging oxtail, and there was a mad rush every time the animal performed, and the fresh dung was washed round our little growing plants, in the hopes that overnight they would be nurtured into producing something worth eating.

It really was surprising how that little celebration provided an uplift. A bit of extra food. The clandestine drinking of a concoction of fizzy fluid. For me it was something to remember my 25th birthday. Those precious bits of grub, which had carefully been hoarded, had been generously contributed. Despite everything, there was a oneness, a sharing.

"Lights out." The Master-at-Arms was on his final rounds.

"Cheerio, Raymond. It's been a good party."

"All the best. Happy birthday."
"Goodnight."
"Goodnight."
It had been a good day.

And Now it was May

"Nippong Solja ada kichil makan." (Japanese soldier has little food).

All 6 foot plus of 'Tor' stood looking down at the scant dollops of rice which were being carefully measured out to each individual in the hut.

Lofty Claridge held up his metal plate in disbelief.

"We're expected to work all day in this heat, on that?" he said.

Tor shrugged, and grinned.

"Engrish no good. Engrish prisona, Nippong Solja sama sama makan." (English prisoner, and Japanese soldier have same food.)

It was unbelieveable. It was, of course, also untrue.

Our rice ration had been cut, and meat, eggs, and fruit had all but disappeared. The rice ration for a 'heavy duty' man was now officially 400 grams a day. 'Light duty' men received 200 grams, and 'sick' 150 grams. From these amounts must be allowed about a fifth for short weight sacks, and loss when the cement dust, rat's droppings, and other foreign bodies had been sieved out. Clearly, no-one could exist on 150 grams, or even 200, so the Commander had decided that the bulk ration must be more evenly distributed between the three categories. Hence the pitiful ration that each now received.

Tor swaggered off.

"Lying bastard," mumbled someone.

The scraping of empty plates closed the episode.

We couldn't believe that the guards' ration was as low as our own. Indeed we saw the supplementary food that went into their enclosure, and the vegetables that we laboured to produce, and which were then confiscated by them. Only one grain of hope stemmed from this – the convoys simply were not getting through. That didn't do us much good!!

The months of 1945 wore slowly by.

The optimism kindled earlier by the naval air raids had long since evaporated. Perhaps the only positive signs of change were that the guards had become even more sullen, the hut searches were more frequent and ruthless, and tortures, under the guise of punishment, were relentless and commonplace.

The 'cage' continued to be well used, and it was unusual to pass the Jap guardhouse when there was not one, or more, prisoner, being lashed verbally, and physically, or standing in the unbearable sun, holding high a chungkal, or lump of rock, literally dropping with fatigue.

In this climate, it is not surprising that the capitulation of Germany, when whispered as 'camp gen' was not believed. Our hopes had been raised, and dashed, too often.

News of the Italian surrender, 20 months previously, had taken months to seep through to us, and seemed to have had little effect, if any, on our existence.

All this time later, our chances of survival were pathetically remote. In any case, we were on the other side of the world from Europe.

But the rumour was insistent. It had started on May 10th, only about 30 hours after what we later knew to be fact.

Even the cryptic notes which were secretly kept by the few who had scraps of paper, wisely did not chronicle this event.

My own mind did not accept this moment of history, and personally, I have no recollection of how long it was before it *was* believed.

There certainly was no outward sign from the Japanese that they had now lost the assistance of their major ally.

Despite this tremendous turn in the fortunes of war, our immediate concern was food. Any sort of food. Just food. Simply something to fill those aching voids. Something to stave off the increasing effects of vitamin deficiency.

Shrunken skeletons cruelly distorted by the oedemas of beri-beri, were all around. Brains and senses were afflicted by the wasting processes. Eyesight and taste suffered from the lack of nutrients. Teeth decayed from lack of attention, and our skins were blotched and broken from physical hurts, and the constant war with bugs and lice.

The 'fit' men dragged their swollen legs from place to place, ever hopeful that that day's labour would bring some reward in pilfered goodies.

The 'light duty men' sat resting their ulcerated feet and legs, as they scratched another narrow crevice, waiting for the next body to be carried up the hill, or hoed and weeded the vegetable patches.

In the hospital huts, the darkened silence was broken only by the demented sounds of someone who was no longer rational, or the subdued sobs of a soul who knew his end was near.

The combination of slow starvation, lack of vitamins, tropical diseases and the bestialities of the guards were now taking a daily toll. The sick bay artificers moved silently around. A word of comfort here, a damp cloth there. There was nothing else.

The month of May that had brought joy and deliverance in Europe, brought only despair and despondency to us in Sumatra.

But there was something else. A bombshell that was to upset even further the limbo between life and death of our ghetto.

We were told that men from another camp were to be transported in. Our already cramped conditions were to be invaded by men from Pankalan Balai. This camp, which we had vaguely heard of as Dai Ichi, was some considerable distance from Palembang, but was also under the overall command of Captain Hachisuka.

This intake was to be balanced by the draft out of a large contingent of men who were to be sent away from Palembang, their destination unknown. This draft was to include all the Senior Officers (all those of army field rank and above, and their equivalent in the other services). These numbered approximately one hundred. In addition, there were to be about one thousand other ranks, officially described as 'light duty', meaning 'unfit for heavy work', but not actually hospital cases. In fact, this term might well be extended to cover all those who weren't bedridden.

This dramatic development meant that those selected to go faced the uncertainties of a journey to an uncertain destination. Those who remained would be left without the benefit of any Senior Officer representation.

Some of us had experienced the gross discomforts of long overland travel through the jungle roads, but the prospect of a sea journey posed even greater fears.

Friendships which had formed the bedrock of our miserable existence were to be severed.

Above all, we were to lose our respected Commander, and those officers who had taken the brunt of the responsibilities in the Camp organisation, arguing in the most difficult circumstances for our rights, and stoically resisting the pressures put upon them.

We couldn't fathom the Japanese mind. What connected the higher ranking officers, and the light duty men? If the enemy were on the retreat, taking their captives with them, then why were the supposedly fit men to be left. Nothing made sense. What new plan lay behind this?

When the die was cast, my very good friend Johnnie MacMillan went, and Tom Wannop, Peter Bivand, and I stayed.

The Senior British Officer, Commander Reid, together with Wing Commander Wills Sandford, RAF, various Lieutenant-Colonels, Captains in the Army, Squadron Leaders in the RAF, and Commanders and Lieutenant Commanders in the Royal Navy, all went.

We were left under the command of an Army Officer, Captain Corrie.

A young Lieutenant, A. M. Nagle assumed charge of the Royal Navy and Royal Marine personnel.

As things turned out, those that went fared best. Those of us who stayed in Sumatra were starting a grim period of even more deliberate deprivation.

I believe that of those that went there were no further casualties among the British. Of the 'fit' that stayed, the mortality rates speak for themselves.

Commander P. H. S. Reid, (later Captain Reid, OBE) in a post-war affidavit stated as follows:

'After a meal in camp at about 1600 on May 25th, we marched to the docks about 2½ miles away, carrying all our kit. This was a severe strain on most of the party. Ten minutes stand easy was allowed half way. We all embarked that evening in a four hold cargo vessel of approx 1200 tons, which was loaded with coal. POWs remained on the two well decks for the voyage without awnings or other shelter. All the officers were on one hatch. There was no room for all to lie down at one time. Latrines were wooden gratings slung over the side. There were no doctors, or arrangements for the sick. There were no washing arrangements. . . . I think that we were on board for 4 nights, arriving at Singapore on the afternoon of May 29th, but it may have been 5 nights.

The food on board was plentiful, compared to camp conditions, though of very poor quality. Boiled, sliced green bananas, rice and fish. One Dutch POW died and was buried at sea. Most of the POWs suffered in health from the strain of the move, and a large proportion were hospital cases at Singapore, until release in September. They were lucky however, to have got away from Palembang, where conditions became terribly bad after our departure.

Life saving apparatus would have been hopelessly deficient. There were no attacks, or sinkings (there were two other vessels, and two escorts). The ships carried no special marking, that we could see.'

Johnnie, in a subsequent letter, gave a more graphic description from an 'Other Rank' viewpoint:

'About 1000 men crammed into a small coaster, and made to stand – could do nothing else, as there was no room – and during the voyage several prisoners went mad and jumped over the side. One meal per day of boiled, green bananas – filth and stench with no sanitation – voyage lasted I think, 2 or 3 days, and after docking in Singapore, I lay down on the dockside, and fell fast asleep out of sheer exhaustion.'

The Bitter End

It was about mid-morning, as I made my way back down the hill from the hospital huts. I gulped in the air, glad to be away from the putrid stench where pitiful creatures lay, racked by the fluctuating pains of dysentery, the stealthy development of beri-beri, or the rigours of malaria. It was a poor service I was able to give – to take them a tatty book, which in their lighter moments they could try to read, or sometimes I would spend a short time reading aloud a few paragraphs to those whose eyes could no longer focus.

I made my way towards the main huts where I knew there were a few other casualties. The half dozen books I had under my arm all badly needed repair but they might serve a need here or there. 'The Invisible Man' by H. G.Wells, 'Four Feathers' by A. E. W. Mason should find takers, though most prisoners had read them at least once. The Navy hut should appreciate 'Three Men in a Boat' by Jerome K. Jerome, and certainly 'I was Graf Spee's Prisoner' by Captain P. Dove would find a ready taker. There was an Edgar Wallace too, and 'Shakespeare to Swinburne', but everyone knew the endings of the mysteries, and Shakespeare had a limited appeal in these circumstances.

In the other direction, a small cortege passed. Just six men, and the corpse, partially covered by a rice sack. The padre led the quiet group, then an Army sergeant. I assumed the bare-footed bearers were friends of the dead man.

No longer were funerals widely attended – they were too frequent, or close friends had already passed that same way. There had been several deaths each day over the last week of June, and from what I had seen this morning, there would be quite a few more.

I pushed open the attap door of the Navy hut, trying to accustom my eyes to the gloom after the brightness of the sun outside. What the hell was going on?

I could hear voices shouting at each other, making accusations of pilfering other people's belongings. It was bedlam, but the noise quickly abated with the arrival of the Master-at-Arms and two other Petty Officers.

"Look, you lot. For Heaven's sake, calm it. Whoever has stolen what, if this row goes on we shall have the guards in and then it won't be a punch up among yourselves but a thumping in the guard room and a few days in the cage to cool off. And believe me, if I find anyone thieving from his own mates, it will be half rations for a good few days."

Whatever the truth of the matter, whether someone had stolen, or whether the owner had forgotten that he had eaten his 'hoard', personal attitudes were soured. Distrust was added to the pernicious atmosphere of camp life. Except among very strong friendships, the law of the jungle was asserting itself.

Every day, there was a desperate search for anything that could possibly be turned into food. There was no doubt in anyone's mind that the Japs were pursuing a deliberate policy of eliminating the service prisoners by a systematic reduction in rations. They had taken away the Senior Officers, and left the so-called fit men to provide a necessary labour force for their garrison. Now these were expendable.

I suppose that statistically the number of tortures, as opposed to simply beatings and bruisings, was comparatively small and, above all, very few men were committed to the hands of the Kempei Tai. But there were some individual guards who took great delight in inflicting pain, purely to people who did not bow to them. Men were made to kneel for long periods on rough edges of wood, so that the timber dug in to the fleshless shins, or as a variation to impose the wood at the back of the knee joints. A similar practice was to wedge slivers between the fingers, and tighten the hand. Where there was not callous indifference, there was active spite. I remember an occasion when Kaneyama (Black Mamba) suddenly appeared round the corner of a hut, where four of us were sat chatting. Before we could rise to our feet, there was the stupid soliloquy of

"Kiotsuke." (Stand to attention)

"Engrish solja bow."

"Why Engrish solja not bow?"

Then an unmerciful bashing for each of us. Fortunately, we were able to stand together, which not only reduced the guard's individual targets but gave us support when collapse on the ground would have brought into play the inevitable boots. That incident cemented still further the friendship and trust of Johnnie MacMillan, Andrew Galbraith, Tom Wannop, and myself.

Mass punishments became the norm, and not many weeks went by without a whole parade being kept at attention for hours in the heat of the sun, or the chill of the night, with little cause, or no cause at all, other than to satisfy the pique of an individual guard commander. On occasion this treatment resulted in the deaths of several men, who had become too weak to stand such privations.

It must have been soon after the arrival of the Dai Ichi contingent that one of the infrequent medical checks took place. As I have mentioned earlier, these were usually because of the fear of the Japs of epidemics spreading to themselves, and never ever resulted in anything beneficial to us, apart from one inoculation (against what we were never told) with one needle to over 1000 men. At this particular time, we were weighed on a set of very antiquated balance scales. My weight was just a fraction over 6½ stones.

I can't say I was surprised, but it is one thing to feel emaciated, and another to have it confirmed.

"Never mind, Stubbie, have some of these," said Charlie Tout, that same evening in the Navy hut.

"Ruddy hell. Six and a half stone," I repeated.

Charlie held out his Army type dixie. In the bottom was a mass of yellowish, brown, crispy looking things.

"What on earth's that?" I asked.

"Go on, tell him, Charlie."

Without any enlightenment, Charlie merely held out the dixie again, shaking the 'things' so that they rolled into the corner of the receptacle.

"C'mon, what is it?" I asked again.

"Maggots, that's what they are, maggots."

I nearly puked on the spot. I think I had eaten very nearly everything – snakes, frogs, leaves, bad fruit and vegetables, boiled banana skin, meat from very dubious origins. But maggots. They could only have one source. The latrine trenches were full of these pale yellow, writhing larvae. These squirming, wriggling things had been dredged from the pits of mucus, blood and excreta.

"Go on, taste one. They've been cooked. And they was washed first."

I couldn't.

When I got back to the Chinese Hut, I told Peter of this latest addition to the menu.

"Something must give soon," he said quietly.

"We can't go on much longer," I said.

"There have been 15 deaths among the British in the last 3 days. At that rate, there's not much time left for the rest of us."

We were consumed with our own private thoughts. So far from home. Perhaps as well our loved ones did not know these things.

One thing we (mercifully) didn't know. One of the Korean guards had informed one of our Officers that at a given signal, on August 27th, we were to be herded into the specially built stockade, and massacred.

Dobrovolski

Could it really now be mid-August? Could have been the 12th, 13th, or 14th. We had no calendars, and each day was the same as the next. It didn't matter.

But now the huts at Sungei Geron were agog with buzzing conversations. Why this sudden turn of events? All outside working parties had been stopped. In fact, those which had been out 3 days before, had been rounded up in the middle of the afternoon and brought back into camp.

The Jap guards, in their quarters across the road, were strangely silent. Yesterday, when they had paraded to the usual shouts of command, there had been a long emphatic address. This morning, another. It wasn't followed by the customary drilling and bayonet practice. We saw them, at attention then solemnly turn, and heard the roar 'Banzai'.

There was now no conversation with them as they inspected our huts. They had no wish to communicate. No longer were we cursed and mocked. No more were we kicked and punched.

Several days of speculation went by. Apart from the absence of outside working parties, camp routine was unchanged. Newly erected double strands of barbed wire were visible from the huts. Hastily dug machine gun nests within the new inner perimeter now baked in the heat.

What was in the wind?

"If one enemy soldier lands in Sumatra, all prisoners will be shot."

Was that it then? Were they only waiting for the order from higher authority?

Perhaps this was the crunch. The vague signs were that the allies were now on the offensive. Surely they must land in Sumatra before we could be freed.

There was the usual Tenko at 8.00 am, but no assembly for working parties.

The only party to go outside the wire was the one to collect rations. We hoped that they might bring back some news. What was going on in the town?

We hoped, as always, that they also might bring us in some more food. Always, like Oliver Twist, we hoped for 'more'.

The endless procession to the camp cemetery continued. One of my 'townies' from North London, Private Donald Richardson RASC, had died at the end of July. He knew it was the end, and I had promised to see his mum and dad, if (and it was a big 'if') I got home. Already this month there had been Gunner Dodd, Private Grant, Marine Lomax, Sergeant Smith – more than a couple of dozen – some familiar names, some not well known to me. There would be a lot more if something didn't happen soon.

The shrill whistle made me sit up and take notice.

"All services are to parade at 3 pm this afternoon. This is not a Tenko. Sick men will be excused." It was the familiar voice of the Master-at-Arms. Then again:

"By order of the Japanese Commander. All fit men will parade by services at 3 pm this afternoon."

"What the hell's that all about?" enquired Peter.

"Search me. Haven't seen that sod Takahashi for a few days. Wonder what he wants?"

At a few minutes to the hour we crouched, passive, in our ranks. We had no clocks or watches, but the word had soon passed round and we had dragged ourselves down to the jungle clearance which served as a parade ground.

Captain Corrie stood silent, waiting with a group of other officers.

Across the dip in the access road, past the guard hut, we could see in the mirage of the tropical heat the tops of the Jap quarters, from which Takahashi would come.

Suddenly, a guard appeared. He was carrying a wooden box. He placed it carefully on the ground, right in front of us. A few yards behind was the rotund figure of Takahashi, the doctor Nakai, the interpreter, then Ito, and in the rear, the mincing gait of Gladys.

"Royal Navy. Attention.

"Army. Shun.

"Royal Air Force. Attention."

The commands broke the silence around. They seemed to echo from the jungle trees.

Takahashi, perspiring in full uniform, polished high brown boots, the yellow and red stripes and stars of his rank shining on his revers, mounted the box. He adjusted his spectacles, bent down towards the interpreter and exchanged a few words.

His high pitched voice was incongruous from such a well filled frame.

Strange how those words, probably the most important I have heard throughout my life, for they signalled the end of our purgatory, have gone from my mind.

They were brief, and strangely couched, but something like–

"Today, I greet you as friends. I am glad to call you my friends. Now all men are the same – Japanese, English, Dutch."

No mention of the war being over. No mention of surrender. No explanation whatever.

I don't know the date. I'm told it was August 22nd. My thoughts were confused – I wasn't alone. All I know is that August was nearly over. Our bodies were worn, our spirits were low, and our knowledge of the outside world was negligible.

Was this the end? Was this the freedom we had hoped and prayed for?

Takahashi saluted the company, and stood down. He turned and slowly walked away with the two sergeants. Captain Corrie stepped forward, and spoke to the interpreter.

We looked at each other, still unable to grasp the import of the situation.

Captain Corrie mounted the 'rostrum'. He told us that the interpreter had now briefly explained that the Nippon Government had agreed terms for ending the war. There had been two horrific bombs on the Japanese mainland. The local command were not able to judge the reaction of the various Military Commanders, and since we were unarmed and defenceless, it would be wise for us to remain quietly in our camp. We should not go out and forage for food, and we should do nothing to incite the guards.

Instructions were given for us to display 'H' shaped pieces of white cloth, large enough to be identified by aircraft, and which the Japanese had been instructed to supply, together with radio equipment.

August 22nd, 1945. What was it Dobro had said? I cast my mind back to that day early in 1943.

Dobro was sat haunched on the ground. His knees drawn up under his gaunt face and greying beard. We were silent in the tropical evening. We were spent following the day's slavery. Even conversation had waned, as we sat out in the open of the Chung Hwa recreation area.

Dobrovolski – I never knew his first name – had fled as a child with his family, at the end of World War One, from Russia to Bulgaria, then later on to Java. There, he eventually became a cinema proprietor, and took Dutch nationality. Consequently, when hostilities were imminent in South East Asia, he was a volunteer in the Royal Netherlands East Indies Army.

His wisdom and philosophies were magnets which drew me to him, and even after our physical energies were exhausted, we could still exercise our minds on any manner of subjects.

After a year in captivity, our thoughts were projecting forward to the day of freedom.

Scant, unsupported news, rumour and malicious Jap propaganda – these all played havoc with our appreciation of the progress of the war, and our prospects of release.

That day someone had happened upon a quotation from the Bible. I have never found it since, but it made reference to the moon's phases and seemed to indicate that a miracle was just a few months away.

I told Dobro of it. What would he make of it?

"No," he said. "I'm afraid not. It won't be until 1945. Some time in August," he added almost as an afterthought. His tone was positive. It brooked no argument.

"We shall never survive until then," I commented. He reinforced his view.

"Yes, you will, my friend," he said. "Mark my words. Our friends will come in August 1945 – the end of August."

Our conversation ended. We trudged to our respective messes, hardly able to contemplate a further 2½ years of this dreadful existence. But he seemed so certain, and at least he was confident of our survival. But we were certain that his assertion was as ridiculous as the Bible quotation.

Now it *was* August 1945! I looked across at the Dutch lines. Dobro was still there. Tall, but bent, his Dutch green uniform jacket barely concealing his pinched frame. Below his tattered trousers both legs were bound tight with stained and discoloured rough bandages.

"Well Dobro," I said, with a new-found cheer. "Remember what you said about the end of the war? You were only a few days out – you said the end of August. Only just over a week now."

"My friend," he replied. "You have forgotten my words."

"No," I responded adamantly, "you said that the war would be over at the end of August 1945. Here we are, almost at the end of the month, and there is peace."

"You have forgotten my words," he quietly repeated. "What I said to you was that our friends will come at the end of August. You will see in just a few days."

I smiled in acceptance of his firm statement.

One day followed another. The ration lorry came in – fully loaded. The rice ration was virtually doubled overnight. Eggs and meat, vegetables and fish, were miraculously 'found' by our captors. Some clothing was sent in.

The drugs for which our doctors had pleaded for the relief of dysentery and malaria were located in a warehouse, and rushed in.

But sadly more men died.

What sixth sense did Dobro enjoy? How could he be so definite over the arrival of 'our friends'? He was so sure. Well, he would be, wouldn't he? Now the war was ended, some Allied representatives must come soon. Maybe it would be the Red Cross, who would send officers to find us, and sort out our destiny.

Yes, that could be it. The Red Cross.

But we were tucked away in the jungle, many miles from the nearest Friendly territory. Whoever it was would have to come from India, or Australia. It could be months.

Dobro had said 'the end of August'. That was only days.

I hoped he was right, because even with the luxury of our comparatively new status, our trials were not yet over.

Please God let him be right.

23 August 1945

On the eve of our release from a Japanese Prisoner-of-War Camp in Palembang, Sumatra, I wish to place on record, as 1st Lieutenant, Royal Naval Detachment, the extremely high opinion I have formed of the character of Coder R. Stubbs, R.N.

Prior to our finding ourselves in the same Prisoner-of-War Camp, Stubbs served with me in Singapore, and both then and since he has proved himself to be a young man of the highest personal integrity and reliability. In whatever capacity I employed him, most especially in the Library and Canteen in this camp, the almost insuperable difficulties placed in our way by the Japanese authorities, have been only equalled by his invariable cheerfulness, initiative and resource in surmounting them under the most trying and dispiriting circumstances. Above all he is full of sound practical common sense, and will I feel sure make a success of whatever career he should choose to pursue. He has my very best wishes.

(D. Hamilton Christie,
Lieut., RNVR, MATCD)
Collonial Education Service

University Club, DUBLIN

Why Are We Waiting?

The attap door to the Chinese Hut was open, and it was only the shadow blocking the sunlight which announced the figure at the door.

It was Lieutenant David Christie.

"Ah, Stubbs," he said as I looked up. "I hoped that I would find you here. No, don't get up."

He motioned with his hand, as I started to my feet.

"Any news yet, sir?" Peter and I both chorused, in the hope that this visit was connected to some fresh development.

"Nope." He pursed his lips. "Afraid not. It's a question of being patient a bit longer. No, I came to give you this. When we were talking a couple of days ago about getting back to civvy street, you said that you had a job to go back to, but I thought this testimonial might be useful at some time in the future. You might want to make a change, and for what it's worth, you're very welcome. We may well all be split up any day now, and I wanted to let you know how much I appreciated your loyalty."

As he spoke, he handed me a single sheet of rather rough paper. It was typewritten, and signed.

Strange. The war had only been over a few days. Yes, now we must start planning for what lies ahead.

I glanced at the paper.

I felt a little embarrassed by the words. Many of the officers had lived a life apart during these traumatic years. It was good to feel that the First Lieutenant of the Naval Detachment had shown his appreciation.

I stood up, wondering whether any employer would want to take on this scruffy, skinny, bearded, individual.

To cover my feelings, I quipped – "I suppose I could turn my hand to being a librarian. I've learnt a lot handling the books, though I doubt whether they stick them together with rice paste in England."

"Well, there you are. None of us knows what the future holds. I don't know whether I shall go back to the UK, or return to Malaya. There's a lot to sort out."

Then suddenly changing the subject.

"Have you seen the new Air Force chaps that have been brought in?"

"Yes, we saw them being taken up to the officers' hut. Four or five of them, weren't there?"

"That's right. Two officers, and three sergeants. They were in a plane attacking a Jap convoy in the Sunda Straits. They sank a sub-chaser and a tanker, then a stray shot set one of their engines on fire, and their Liberator crashed in the jungle, down in the south of the island."

"Liberator? What a smashing name. Could do with a few of those round here."

"Too true. Anyway, that must have been ten or eleven days ago. Something like that. But they were lucky. Apparently, where they were first imprisoned, there was some scribbling on the cell wall, showing that earlier airmen who had crashed, had been executed. It was only the atom bomb that saved these – and us."

"Atom bomb? What's an atom bomb?"

"These chaps have been telling us. We don't know much about it. It's a bomb much more powerful than tons and tons of high explosives. The Yanks dropped two on two Japanese cities. Completely wiped them out apparently, demolished the whole area. Must have taken a few thousand Japs with them."

"That must be what the interpreter was talking about then. Serves the little yellow swines right."

"Yes, it could be, I suppose. Now, if you'll excuse me, I've got to see about getting some of the Navy chaps down to the Fort. The Japs are clearing beds there to take the worst of our sick. Hope it's not too late for some of them."

As David Christie made his departure, we had new topics to talk about. Cut off for so long, we yearned for news.

The next day, some of the desperately sick, those who were able to be moved, were stretchered out to the Jap hospital. Perhaps something could be done for the likes of Able Seaman Mogridge, Petty Officer Devis, Lieutenant Partridge, Aircraftsman Twiddle, Ordinary Seaman Bibbings.

"Hope someone knows we are here," said Peter. "Otherwise, there'll be a few more joining those poor devils."

Despite these developments, our spirits needed constant reminders that this was not all a dream. When would *real* relief come? When should we see some friendly faces? Why were we waiting?

The next day, Friday August 24th, Captain Corrie was told to expect aircraft, and to make sure that ground identification signals were ready. But nothing happened.

Perhaps our saviours would come up the river. There was even a strong rumour that the aircraft carrier, HMS Illustrious, was moored at the mouth of the River Moesi.

What we didn't know then was that there was a possibility that some Japanese Commandants would be unwilling to admit defeat, and ignore their Government's decision to surrender, and because of the overwhelming numbers of the enemy, small Allied parties going to help prisoners might be in considerable danger. As a result, Lord Mountbatten ordered that no prisoner-of-war camp should be approached until there was certainty that the surrender terms were being upheld. This ban applied until August 26th.

Arrangements were made for leaflets to be dropped to camp authorities, the local population, and the guard troops, informing them all of the present situation, and requiring their compliance.

We hadn't any knowledge of these things, or of the immensity of the task then being planned. To us, the end of the war had spelled freedom, relief from all our sufferings, and a speedy return to our native country and our loved ones. Why were we waiting?

Interminable days passed.

The dawn came bright and clear on that marvellous day, August 28th. Our new, gleaming, metal plates had been scraped clean. Each grain of pure, white rice, with brown sugar, and condensed milk, had been consumed, and washed down with mugs of steaming hot, sweet tea. This was luxury!

The only work to do was the necessary camp chores, and to attend, as best we could, to our personal hygiene. Most of us now boasted a pair of highly coloured, cotton shorts. There was even soap, and clean bandages for our tropical ulcers.

Our attention was largely directed at the gate, for that was where the arrival of a lorry signalled either a welcome addition to our diet or to our wardrobe, or medical welfare.

The drone of a single plane went almost unnoticed until it was near enough to see that it had four engines. We had never seen a four-engined plane before. It seemed colossal!

By now, everyone except the bedridden, was outside. Faces lifted upwards, eyes straining.

The plane flew by. Then it returned. It came lower. It circled. It made a run over the camp. It was enormous. It was beautiful.

Then over the tops of the jungle trees, came another. We could plainly see the camouflage. It had wonderful roundels on its wings. It dipped in recognition.

It made another, slower, run over the camp. We waved like mad things. Some said they could see the crew waving back.

We watched as the two aircraft climbed rapidly away. We gazed breathless, hands raised, reaching out, until they disappeared from view.

Our friends had come. It was unbelievable.

Our friends had come. How could Dobro have known, so precisely, well over 2 years before?

'The end of August, 1945' he had said. It was the 28th day.

'You will survive' he had said. I had.

The RAF Operational Records briefly detail this flight of 99 and 356

ORDERS TO ALL JAPANESE GUARD TROOPS

All Japanese land, sea and air forces have surrendered. His Imperial Majesty the Emperor has been graciously pleased to sign the surrender document and with this the Pacific War is ended.

During the next few days Allied Aircraft will drop leaflets written in English, Dutch and Indian languages where Allied soldiers and civilians are held by Japanese guards telling them to remain calm and composed, and to stay in their present positions.

Where such leaflets come into the possession of Japanese guards they are immediately to pass them politely to Allied soldiers or civilians. After handing over the leaflets all guards are to return to their own billets.

Japanese guard troops are responsible for providing Allied prisoners and internees with food and for their correct treatment. In the next few days Allied officers carrying wireless sets will come to places where Allied soldiers are held by the Japanese. Their principal task will be to make contact with Allied soldiers and to communicate their requirements to the Allied Supreme Command. Japanese guard troops are not to obstruct them and are to assist them when possible.

Orders issued by the Japanese High Command, following surrender.

Squadrons as 'Operation Birdcage'. 'To operate in pairs of aircraft, the first to drop leaflets to Japanese guards, and the second to drop other leaflets to British and Indian internees in Sumatra and Malaya.' To us, that brief sight of those massive planes, was salvation.

We danced in the huts. We danced in the open. We talked incessantly. We cavorted around in our new shorts. We fondled the softness of the newly issued blankets. Our palates were tickled with the taste of fresh fish, eggs, bananas, pineapple, and soup in which we could even see little pieces of meat.

Tears were shed unashamedly as men talked of their families, but these were tears of joy. These were tears of hopeful expectation. Thoughts now raced forward to the imminent homecoming. We pictured our home countryside in the autumn. An evening, listening peacefully to the wireless. The scent of an English rose. The shrill of a blackbird at dusk.

Trysts were made to meet up again.

"You will come over to Golders Green, and meet Anne," invited Alan

Anstead. "I expect we shall get married as soon as we can." Temporarily forgotten was the fact that he had shed 6 stones in weight, and beri-beri and colitis were still wreaking havoc. He made me promise this before he too was carried away, and down to the fort, where he fought for his life, and won.

"We shall have to meet up at the Spurs," I said to Private Tickner.

"Yes, that's right. Do that. You'll have to pass my house, from where you live in Southgate. It's on your way."

What an age it was since I had stood in the schoolboys' enclosure of the new stand, and cheered on the Lillywhites.

With much spare time on our hands now, we wandered from hut to hut, chatting and passing the time of day.

Petty Officer Telegraphist Ainsworth, and Yeoman of Signals Jones came over to tell us of the latest news gleaned from the three new RAF sergeants.

"They've been telling us all about 'D' Day."

" 'D' day? What's 'D' day?"

"Oh, sorry, that's what they called invasion day, when our troops, and the Americans landed in Normandy. Got some catching up to do, haven't we?"

"Yes," said Pots. "That must have been some operation – think of the organisation."

"And what do you think. There's been a General Election, and poor old Churchill has been thrown out. Some chap called Attlee is Prime Minister. There's a Socialist Government."

"Good Lord. After winning the war. Is that the treatment they've given poor old Winnie?"

"Yes. Apparently quite an overwhelming majority too."

"Oh, and another thing. Those two planes that came over the other day. They were dropping leaflets. The interpreter brought one in to Captain Corrie. They're printed in several languages, confirming that the Japanese forces have surrendered, and telling the Japs that they will be held responsible for providing prisoners, and internees with food, and for their proper treatment. There was something about wireless sets too. I'm not sure whether they're going to drop sets, or whether the Japs have got to supply them."

"Well let's hope they don't sit too long on their backsides. Now that they know there is a prison camp here, surely it shouldn't be long before things are moving."

187

Triumph And Tragedy

"The stupid twits. They must be out of their tiny little minds."

It had just been revealed that a small group of three or four men had slipped under the wire, and out of the camp, and Lofty Claridge, the Leading Seaman in charge of that hut was clearly very annoyed.

"Of all the daft things to do, particularly when we had been warned not to upset a delicate situation. They'll all be on charges when they get back – if they get back. It's that little Scouse clique – they've been a damned menace. Now the war is over, they think they can do what they like. They'll learn differently."

Amid uproar they did come back, later that night. They were all the worse for drink – probably some native hooch they had drunk – and one loudly boasting of his conquest of a native girl.

The odd voice looked on them as heroes, but the overwhelming opinion was that they could have brought down dire consequences on us (and themselves!)

What was outside our knowledge then, was that General Itagaki, the Japanese Commander at Singapore had notified Field-Marshal Terauchi, the Imperial Commander in the South East Asia area, that the Japanese armies were undefeated in battle, and he intended to fight on. Fortunately for us, Terauchi convinced his subordinate that unconditional surrender was the only way out.

We were also unaware of the smouldering fires of Indonesian Nationalism. Even in our role of prisoners-of-war, we had generally retained a degree of friendliness with the local population, and even a small measure of respect, once the yellow 'liberators' had been shown in their true colours. It was not unusual to be told that 'When war finish, English come', almost as an unsaid prayer. The natives certainly did not want the Dutch back, and as the Americans had not been involved in Sumatra, to the ordinary citizens, the British probably appeared to be a reasonable option. It was to be only a matter of a few weeks, until an uprising would spread throughout Indonesia.

In the midst of the euphoria of our freedom, we were skating on the thin ice of tragedy, which might well have been triggered by the thoughtless acts of a few.

Inside the camp, there were other developments. Wood lorries were a frequent sight. No longer did we have to labour in the jungle to fell green trees. Now loads of cut, dry wood were deposited regularly outside the cookhouse.

A consignment of European tinned food was received. It must have been stacked away in a warehouse for at least 4 years, and many of the tins were rusted and bent, but 'Sell by', or 'Best before' dates had not then been inscribed on labels, and I doubt whether they would have made any difference to our appetites. We tucked into chicken soup, salmon, corned beef, and many of those things which had for so long been only memories, or dreams.

As my friend, Johnnie, would have said, 'Banyak makan' (Lots to eat).

But Johnnie had gone – we thought to Singapore, months ago – I wondered how he was. What we really wanted now was people – our people. Our first priority, which for so long had been food, had now switched to friends, our liberators, whoever they might be, to get us out of Palembang.

Over in the Dutch huts there were sounds of music and singing. With a few special exceptions, our living in close proximity to the Hollanders had not been a happy experience. Petty differences in our outlooks and attitudes had caused a definable rift to grow between Allies. We found them often more morose and sullen, even than we were ourselves.

Now, however, there were the pleasant noises of celebrations.

"What are the Gottvordommers up to?" asked Tom Wannop.

"Search me," said Charlie Tout.

Parachutes falling on 'Sungei Geron'.
(Photograph taken from Liberator).

189

"From the row that's going on, they've probably got hold of drink of some sort."

This proved to be not far short of the mark. Some of their countrymen, who had served in Sumatra, had managed to establish contact with natives, and a flourishing black market through the wire had been established.

We didn't appreciate that this particular day, August 31st, was Queen Wilhelmina's birthday, and that now for the first time in 4 years, they were able to feast their Queen.

And none of us were to know what Saturday, the first day of September had in store.

It was well into the afternoon that the first Liberator flew over. As before, it was closely followed by a second. They made two or three circuits, coming lower and lower. What had been two small specks in the sky were now huge, pulsating machines.

Once again, the huts had emptied. Once again, all thoughts of chores were forgotten. There wasn't a pair of seeing eyes that weren't focussed on this tremendous sight.

Then, even as we watched, there were puffs of white from the underbelly of the first plane. Small, white balls, which abruptly opened into mushroom like 'chutes.

The cheers rang round our jungle home. They even drowned the thunderous roar of the quadruple engines.

"Here they come, they're dropping parachutists."

"Ah, beautiful, he's coming right on target."

Another, then another, and another. A dozen or more silk shrouds floating slowly, so slowly down, drifting very slightly, in an unnoticed breeze.

But wait. That's not a man. It's a cylinder.

The first chute, now only a matter of hundreds of feet high, with its load steady underneath, moved hesitantly across the camp perimeter.

The canister struck the ground just short of the galley block. It caused a heavy tremor as it bit into the sun hardened ground, a few yards away from the camp store.

From the parade ground, it was only a matter of 100 yards to the landing spot, and we ran down the camp road towards the gently fluttering silk. Before we got there, there was an angry buzz, and a gust of hornets, disturbed from their nest in the bamboos of the store, swept across the road.

"Right, back you chaps. Keep clear for a moment." It was Lieut. McMullin, who had come round from the galley, and with a weather eye on the hornets, walked slowly round the torpedo like object, now sat cantwise, partly covered by its drape.

"Better stay well away until these wretched hornets have settled. Don't

190

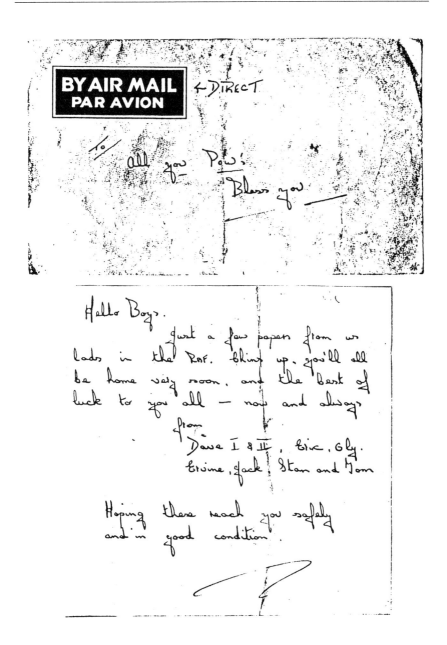

The handwritten message dropped by RAF boys, with magazines, they had in the Liberator – the one that crashed after dropping its load to us.

want to run the risk of pretty nasty stings at this stage. In any case, we'd be far better to spot the fall of the other chutes, in case any of them go into the trees."

It was a case of so near, yet so far. I wondered what was in these manna-like objects. Maybe cigarettes, maybe food, maybe clothes?

We wandered slowly back to the parade ground – a good spotting viewpoint. It was like watching a firework display.

"There's another just gone down behind the trees."

"Yep, and there's another heading for the pig sties. Poor little porkers will get a shock."

Somewhat impatiently, a knot of us stood waiting for instructions to go and gather whatever harvest had come. Nearby stood two guards, awestruck, like ourselves, at the immense size of the two Liberators.

Again they traversed our enclosure, this time so low we really could see the crews. We exchanged wild waves, and cheered, as if they might hear us.

Now we saw small packets and bundles, spreading like confetti, as they dispersed.

"It's papers, fags, chocolate." We ran and recovered those nearest to us.

The planes droned away to the south. The first tilted onto its starboard side, and nose up climbed away.

The second plane followed suit, veering away in the path of its leader. The port wing rose until the plane appeared to be almost vertical as it turned very steeply.

Even from where we watched, perhaps a mile away, we heard the breaking of boughs, and the sheering of metal. The great tail of the plane seemed to somersault in the air, and then there was a tremendous crash.

We stood momentarily, stunned.

At our side, one of the guards laughed.

Someone turned, delivered such a tremendous punch to his little, yellow face, that Kanemoto ('Cats eyes') was laid out cold. For a split second, I thought of Aircraftsman Saunders. He was the last man to strike a Jap, and for his 'crime' was dragged away, and died in the hands of the Kempei Tai. Now the circumstances were different.

Then, in a flash, we ran blindly, forcing our neglected limbs forward, under the boundary wire, through the jungle undergrowth.

But even as we ran, we heard the muffled explosions, as petrol tanks blew up. We saw the dark pillar of smoke climb into the air, and when we reached the scene, we knew there was nothing we could do. The intense heat of that funeral pyre forced us back, to stand mute, near to tears that such a dreadful tragedy should have been the culmination of this day of triumph.

We who had dreamed for many months of the coming of our saviours, were struck silent, and they, who had waved in joy, were hushed forever.

It was a subdued camp that evening. We feasted on new goodies. We devoured even more the English and American newspapers that had been dropped. But our rejoicing was at the expense of all eight crew of that Liberator, and that shadow lay heavy.

To the hundreds of Allied dead in Palembang were added the names of Flying Officer Steele, P/O Pearson, F/O Manktelow, F/S Newton, Sgt Martin, FS Parkes, Sgt Bowden, and F/S Ryalls.

Among the bundles of newspapers which were dropped that day was an Air Mail envelope. In handwriting was inscribed *TO* All you POWs. Bless you.

Lady Edwina

It was only when extreme fatigue overtook us that evening, that anyone thought of turning in. We built an enormous bonfire, with the two-fold object that the smoke would keep the mosquitoes at bay, and the warmth would take the chill off the tropical night. It also served to warm soup, and boil water for the many helpings of tea and coffee.

In the glow, we relived the events of the day, relieved now that firm contact had been established with the outside world. In the remaining day-light hours, there had been a hurried distribution of newspapers – American, Australian and British.

It is said that there is nothing as stale as yesterday's news. These papers had obviously been quickly gathered together by the RAF lads, and the most up to date was at least a week old. But as we were 3½ years behind the times, they were read from cover to cover, and then passed on and exchanged.

Lieutenant David Copley had looked into the Chinese Hut during the evening.

"Would you and Peter make sure that the hut is tidy for a church service in the morning please? We shall have a special thanksgiving service, combining all denominations. I'll let you have the hymn numbers, and the hymn book in the morning."

True to his word, David was along early the next day. He had even found a fresh stick of chalk for Peter to print the words up on the blackboard.

"Do you reckon that we'll get them all in the hut?" I asked.

"The Catholics usually have about two dozen, and we're lucky if there's

193

THE SERVICES NEWSPAPER OF

SOUTH EAST ASIA COMMAND

Special Edition For Our Liberated Comrades, August 1945.

Printed by Courtesy of

THE STATESMAN in Calcutta.

Admiral Lord Louis Mountbatten, Supreme Allied Commander, SE Asia, sends this personal message to all Allied prisoners of war and internees :

I have given instructions that as the surrender of all the Japanese forces in South East Asia has been accomplished, first priority must be given to bringing you the help that you need.

As soon as we can reach your camps, arrangements will be made to get you home. But you must remember that many camps are so far away that it will be some time before we can reach you.

Until we do, and until our shipping, designed for the invasion of Malaya can be re-deployed, I shall see that you get all possible help, supplies, and news from home.

Arrangements are being made to inform your relatives at once that you are safe and at liberty. This has been a long war. But from the time when you fell into enemy hands you have never been forgotten, either in England or among the armies that have defeated the Japanese.

I hope that it will now be only a matter of a few weeks at most before you are on your way home.

The two Supremos meet. Left, Admiral Mountbatten, S. E. Asia and right, General of the Army Douglas MacArthur, Pacific. This picture was taken at their meeting last month in Manila, before Lord Louis left for Potsdam and London.

Good Morning . . .

Let us introduce ourselves. SEAC is the 7-day-a-week newspaper of the soldiers, sailors and airmen of South East Asia Command.

It was founded by Supreme Commander Admiral Lord Louis Mountbatten to tell the men in the Burma jungle and in the eastern skies and seas what was going on in the rest of the world, especially at home. It voices their opinions.

This morning, we salute you, our newest readers tho' our oldest comrades in the war against the Japanese, and hope that you will be among our firmest friends.

*

What gave the Japs initial victory?

Treachery certainly ensured them a long start. Terror exploited it.

Their seamanship rated high, and they had long explored the waters which surrounded their intended conquests. Once they had crippled the US Pacific Fleet at Pearl Harbour and sunk Britain's *Repulse* and *Prince of Wales* off the Malayan coast the eastern seas lay open, for Britain was stretched to the limit in the Battle of the Atlantic.

In the sky also Japan had numerical superiority. The Battle of Europe had not yet resolved air mastery for

Extracts from Newspapers dropped from Liberators at the end of August, 1945.

ATOLL GREETINGS
99 and 356 SQUADRONS
COCOS ISLANDS 30:8:45

Hello there! All ranks of all services,

This is a greeting from your comrades in arms in the R.A.F. and R.C.A.F. and with it we send you a few of the odd comforts without which you have been so long. We also send you our best wishes for a speedy return home, and our sincere thanks for the part you have played in defeating the common enemy – the Jap.

These small tokens of our appreciation have been donated by every man in every Army and Air Force unit on these islands. We intend to continue these supplies as long as our stocks hold out.

If you receive these goods in good condition put out a + (plus sign) in white strips when our aircraft fly over: if you do not receive them in good condition put out a – (minus sign). We shall be on the look-out for your signals.

As you probably know by this time, the war is over and we have won. Till the next time - the very best of luck.

THE BOYS OF 99 and 356 SQUADRON

Letter from Boys of 99 and 356 Squadron.

more than fifteen, but that makes about forty, and that will be a tight squeeze," commented Peter.

"Well, we'll see. Since we don't have to bother about the guards any more, we can leave the door and window flaps open, and any overflow can stand outside."

It was a fairly short form of matins, and I don't know who had chosen the hymns, but one I remember was 'Now thank we all our God', and even now when I see the German phraseology 'Nun danke alles Gott' I have a wry feeling that this should have marked the end of a terrible war with Japan, and her major ally, Germany.

For once, the hut did overflow, and as was now customary, our gatherings ended with a spirited rendition of 'Land of Hope and Glory'. How amazing that after our captors had banned the National Anthem, they never tumbled to the fact that this was a very suitable substitute.

But still the deaths went on. Even well into September, there were those whose stricken bodies had gone past the stage of recovery, and we said our farewells to Aircraftsman W. Twiddle, Lieut. E. Partridge, MRNVR, and a very much respected naval Petty Officer Devis, and several others.

Our joys and gladness were also conditioned by names like Belsen and Buchenwald, and the stories of the heavy losses at Arnhem, and Okinawa. Those of us from the south of England in particular were concerned to hear of the rockets and buzz-bombs, the V1s and V2s. It must have been a terrible and tragic era for many people.

The first 'friend' I spoke to maybe added a little light relief, and caused some distorted stories to circulate around the Navy huts. Now having a clean fandushi, a pair of Japanese khaki shorts, a very colourful shirt, and some soft, Jap jungle boots, I had taken myself off, down to the water-hole, complete with soap and flannel, to have a really good cleanup.

I wasn't unduly alarmed when I heard the Japanese on the gate shout a command, and looked up to see a smart uniformed person speaking there, before proceeding down the camp road. I carried on with my ablutions, enjoying the feel of the warm sun on my naked, sudsy body, expecting this slight figure to be another Jap, and to be visiting the galley, or the stores.

Suddenly, a female voice, with a slight accent, said "Good morning." Startled, I looked up to see this smiling, white face, only a few paces away. I reached to grab my towel, slipped on the muddy surface, and finished on my stomach – fortunately – on the ground. There was a rich peel of female laughter.

"Pardon," she said, and was away.

The first white woman I had spoken to for over 3 years, and I had nothing to cover my embarrassment, proved to be one of several Dutch nurses, who had been dropped in to Sumatra.

However, better was to come.

It must have been about mid-September that we were told that in a day or two there would be a visit by a very important person, and we were all requested to be ready to parade, and to be as neat and tidy as we possibly could be.

Two days later, it was confirmed that this was to be the great day, and as soon as breakfast (now including bread rolls, and fruit) was out of the way, we were all sat around in our 'Sunday best' awaiting our visitor.

I don't think we were told who it was to be, possibly because there might have been a change of plan, or personnel, but when a Jap Army car drew up at the gate, we were surprised to see a lady alight, followed by another, and then an Army officer.

Lady Edwina Mountbatten.

Quickly, we lined the camp road, craning our heads for a better view, as the small delegation, flanked by several of our own officers, and with Takahashi at the rear, made their way, slowly, into the camp.

The mystery of who this leading personality was, bending her head, and listening attentively to Captain Corrie, was soon solved. It was Lady Edwina Mountbatten, wife of the Supreme Allied Commander, SE Asia, Admiral Lord Louis Mountbatten. She was accompanied by Captain Elizabeth Ward, an officer of the First Aid Nursing Yeomanry, attached to Lord Louis' headquarters staff, and Major Abhey Singh.

Lady Edwina was wearing a soft, peaked cap, and a safari suit, or uniform, on which were Red Cross and St John badges.

As she walked, stopping now and then to speak briefly to one of the men along the roadside, she half lifted her hand in acknowledgement of the cheers, and smiled, or responded with a word or two to the shouted remarks.

As the visitors progressed up the slight hill towards the main huts, we fell in behind, anxious not to miss anything.

Despite her cheerful response to the ex-prisoners, her face also reflected the gravity of what she was seeing – our camp conditions, the shrunken frames, and despite our new found clothing, the poverty of our dress.

In due time, she reached the rear of the camp, by the jungle's edge. She stood, silent, contemplating the large cross, itself rough hewn from a forest tree, and now overscribed with names, and the small wooden markers, in their uneven lines. She spoke a few quiet, questioning words to her companions. As she did so, she brushed the uneven ground gently, with the sole of her shoe. It was an involuntary movement, almost to bring a little tidiness to this hallowed ground. The dry, dusty ground, crumbled away, to reveal the extremity of a knee, or an elbow.

Takahashi, who was by her side now, spoke. Presumably, words of apology, or vindication.

She rounded on him, very much in command, yet her composure temporarily broken by this horror.

She spoke but one word. It was an order, an absolute directive.

"Pigi." she said. (Go).

Takahashi half lifted his arms, as if to say something. He must have seen the imperative expression on her face. He turned and slunk away. We never saw him again.

Before she left, Lady Edwina addressed us on the parade ground. She told us she was appalled at what she had found in Palembang. In all her travels thus far, Sungei Geron was among the worst she had come across in the Far East. She promised that she would do her utmost to have us flown out as soon as humanly possible, hopefully in a few days.

She was true to her word.

I am informed by Broadlands Archives that her diary for September 18th records that she visited Palembang on that day, and states that there were Naval and Royal Marine survivors, and also that the men in these camps were in worse physical condition than anywhere.

Elsewhere, I have read that Lady Edwina made countless calls in 16 countries, and travelled over 33000 miles, much of it where travel was hazardous, and conditions primitive. She told her husband of the almost unbelievable tortures and horrors the prisoners had suffered. Auschwitz and Belsen were mere kindergartens by contrast with some of the camps in Sumatra and Malaysia.

Her strength of will, and remarkable endurance are a living testimony to this marvellous lady.

When she was in Sumatra, she is reported as saying: 'I came here to see the prisoners, and the internees and not the Japanese. I will have nothing to do with them.'

Return Journey Paid

"Well, what do you think?" asked Peter that evening, as we mulled over the day's events.

"She was absolutely incredible," I responded.

"Mind from what I saw of Lord Louis at Malta, they are birds of a feather. Fantastic couple."

"But, I mean do you reckon we shall be out in a few days?"

"She did say that she would do her utmost, and with her husband being the Supreme Allied Commander, I should think there is a jolly good chance."

It must have been nearly a month since I had carefully uncovered my few precious photographs, and my fountain pen, from where they had been buried under the hut. The bits of cloth, and newspaper, in which they were wrapped had preserved them well, and only one had touches of mildew on it.

I had also lifted the bed leg, and revealed the deadly stiletto in its hiding place. Thank God, I had not been called upon to use that.

"One thing," I said to my companion. "It won't take long to pack, will it?"

I still had my green Dutch haversack, rather the worse for wear now, but the strong canvas was unholed, and comfortably held all my wordly possessions.

Peter was relaxed in his self-made 'deck chair', thumbing through some more newspapers. There was so much to try and take in. The items ranged far and wide. We learned of the execution of Mussolini and his mistress, of General McArthur's return to the Philippines, of the recapture of Rangoon, and the SuperFortress attacks on Japan from the Marianas. There were pictures of the Japanese surrender delegation arriving at Manila, of the homeless and displaced persons from mid-Europe, and nearer to our own situation, of the Burma/Thailand Railway, which had cost the lives of so many of our comrades. But there was also the luxury of reading, despite rationing, of recipes for tasty dishes, of easing of war-time restrictions at home, of messages of cheer, and looking forward.

Within a week of Lady Mountbatten's visit the great day came.

The worst of the sick had all been taken into Charitas Hospital, or the Fort, and those that could face an air journey had been flown away.

Those that remained – the lucky ones – those that were fit, or to be more accurate, those that could walk, were assembled in batches, mainly by Services, and driven in lorries along that familiar road to the aerodrome, where 3 years earlier we had toiled incessantly. On the runway fashioned by our blood and sweat, stood an unfamiliar looking plane.

There were no procedures to hold us up, no regulations with which we had to comply. We had been counted on to the lorries, and now we were counted off, as a double check, and then in an eager, but apprehensive, line, walked the 100 yards or so towards the steps.

"Here y'are, Cobber."

"Gimme that," said another, taking our bags.

Rich, welcome Aussie voices. Big, strapping, bronzed bodies. Hands which crushed our feeble fingers in warm handshakes.

We moved slowly towards the ascent which would mean the end of our stay in Sumatra.

I had gone only four or five steps upward, when my legs refused to move further. I hadn't realised that it must have been 2 years or more since last I had climbed stairs. Pushed, and pulled, I made it into the plane's cabin, my knees, and thighs reacting strongly to the unaccustomed movement.

But here we were, in the plane's rough, metalled belly, lined against the fuselage, for what was my first air flight.

The engines roared into life, and we could feel the whole metal frame of the Dakota tremble and vibrate as the wheels began turning, and the plane slowly rolled to the end of the runway.

One of the aircrew passed quickly down the length of the craft, making sure we were all settled in our seats, facing inwards. Then came the surging rush, and we were off.

There had been no sight of Palembang, left behind us with its memories, only below the mass of green jungle.

I can remember a moment's consternation as an air mechanic hastened through to the cockpit, carrying a large oil-can, quipping as he went.

"Sorry, you Poms, the elastic's broke."

We weren't so sure. We could see the rust smudges on the wings, and the tears of black oil, eddying in the slipstream, around the engine cowling. Neither were we to know that these dauntless old war-horses would be in service for many years to come.

It was no time at all until someone announced that we were over the sea, and then shortly after, we were above Keppel Harbour, and there nestling into the blue water, was clearly defined a Royal Navy cruiser, proudly displaying the White Ensign.

That did cause a panic, as being all Navy on the plane, we moved over to the starboard side to get a better view. With all the weight suddenly on one side, the plane lurched dramatically, causing an anxious Aussie voice to shout from the cockpit to regain our seats 'Bloody Sharp'.

Then, with a crunching, rattling series of jolts, we were down.

Within minutes, we were being led off across the tarmac, seemingly surrounded by British uniforms.

Perhaps that is why my memory is a bit hazy about the next few days. We did not have to think for ourselves. We were bussed away to nearby quarters. I recall a comfortable bed, clean, white sheets, soft pillow. I recall strolling outside, gazing out on the sea, and taking in gulps of air. I remember the exhortations over diet, not to be too impatient to cram ourselves with good things, and to go easy on our suffering digestive systems.

We were kitted out with tropical shorts and shirts, and all the other necessary bits and pieces. We were medically examined. We were interviewed. And yet, all these things were so unobtrusive. RAPWI (The organisation for the Repatriation of Allied POWs and Internees) had swung into efficient action. Its well-drilled, well-oiled mechanism functioned without fuss or bother.

About this time, on September 21st, 1945, the Post Office were delivering a Telegram to my parents in Southgate:

'Information received that your son Raymond S. Stubbs, C/JX 205607 was in Palembang Camp, Sumatra on September 15th, 1945. Further reports will be communicated as received.
Commodore RN Barracks, Chatham.'

And then from the Prisoner of War Relatives' Association, a couple of days later:

"Each day brings our boys from the Far-East nearer, at least 24 of them are on the Right Road to Home – and the Grand Welcome that awaits them.
To the Next of Kin of those that have not yet heard from their man, we extend hopes of speedy news, and I eagerly look forward to receiving the card enclosed to them with this notice, and share the pleasure of knowing of their safe delivery.
Sincerely yours
W. S. Beardow

PS Glad to hear the good news. We share your joy.

Our brief stay in Singapore flashed by. Only those needing urgent medical treatment, were flown on. The rest of us were advised that it would be better to become gradually acclimatised on a sea journey back to the United Kingdom. Furthermore, it was hoped to clothe our bones with a little more flesh, and make us rather more presentable to our folks at home.

At the end of the third week of September, a month from the day when we had been informed that the world was at peace, we were among friends. We were being fed, and clothed, and properly tended. Already, my weight was showing a substantial increase.

A few days later, I was mounting the gangway of SS Antenor, bound for Ceylon, Suez, and the Mediterranean.

SS Antenor

As she stood by the quayside, Antenor looked positively huge, as indeed she was by comparison with my memories of Encounter. Her 11,000 gross tonnage dwarfed Encounter's 1,300, and promised a comfortable journey home.

She had been built in 1925, as a cargo liner for the China Mutual Steam

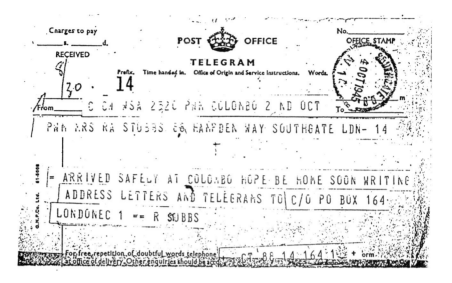

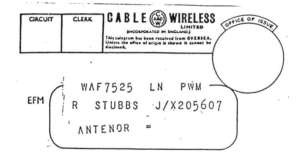

WONDERFUL NEWS SO THANKFUL
COME HOME SOON LOVE FROM US
ALL = MOTHER

MARK YOUR REPLY "Via Imperial"

ANY ENQUIRY RESPECTING THIS TELEGRAM MAY BE MADE AT ANY OF THE COMPANY'S OFFICES
AND SHOULD BE ACCOMPANIED BY THIS FORM.

Navigation Company, a subsidiary of the Blue Funnel Line.

From her role of carrying 180 first class passengers in the Far East, she had been refitted for service as an Armed Merchant Cruiser, but later was converted to a troopship.

There were many, many more than 180 passengers aboard, as we sailed from Singapore's Keppel Harbour, and by no means could the accommodation be described as 'first class', but to us, this was the height of luxury.

In the warmth of the sun, tempered by the cooling breezes in the Malacca Straits, we lazed on the open decks, barely conscious of the passing of the distant greenery, which marked our last view of the coast of Sumatra.

Our first port of call was Colombo. We anchored out, and there was no opportunity to go ashore but while we were there, we had an opportunity to send a telegram home.

That was absolutely terrific. A distant, but personal contact had now been established. Fears of what may have happened in London, and in Sumatra had now been set aside. They knew I was coming home, and I knew I had a home to come home to.

On Antenor, our diet was rapidly widening. There was fruit and vegetables in abundance. Our palates and digestive systems were learning, once more, to cope with eggs, and meat, and fish. I can't remember that my stomach rebelled at all, certainly not at the variety, perhaps only we were conditioned as to quantity.

On most days something was arranged to interest us. There were talks on a variety of subjects. Moderate exercises became a daily habit.

Necessarily, there was a series of medical examinations. We were, quite rightly, put through the mill.

The past history of malaria, dysentery, and beri-beri, followed the words 'Not complaining of anything at Present.' My spleen, liver and colon showed NAD (no apparent disease), and I was shown as Free From Infection. My eyesight was given as normal, my heart regular, but my breathing was harsh, I had tender reflexes, and skin serrations, and dental treatment was required. The debilitating weakness in my legs was noted. It was indicated that all of these things would be followed up soon after arrival in the UK.

A series of interrogations by Intelligence Officers was arranged, and Confidential statements were taken. These possibly formed the basis of subsequent action leading to War Crimes Trials.

We were emphatically warned that we were not to communicate to the Press, Red Cross Society, Welfare organisation, or any other unauthorised person, any accounts of escapes or experiences in POW camps prior to repatriation, which concerned the existence of an official Escape Organisation.

Meanwhile, Antenor had made her way north-westwards across the Indian Ocean, and up the Red Sea, heading for our next port of call – Adabiya in Suez Bay. It wasn't long before this was translated to Abdabs – the serviceman's unaffectionate name for a dose of the runs.

At the Port of Adabiya, we went alongside the docks, and there, on the quay, was a military band to welcome us. I have a vague recollection that one of the tunes they played was 'Don't fence me in'.

The object of our stop south of Suez was to kit us up with warm clothing, which we would need on our return to England, at the end of October.

The arrangements for dealing with ship after ship, carrying ex-prisoners and internees, in their thousands, was quite superb. At Adabiya, there were all kinds of recreational facilities, such as a restaurant, cinema, swimming pool. There was a post office, and there were arrangements to deal with welfare, financial, and immediate medical matters.

The morning after we docked, following breakfast, we were mustered in our Services, and led off down the long gangplank to the dockside. The scene there was reminiscent of that which greeted us when we stopped at Simonstown, on our way round the Cape in the spring of 1941. There were all manner of people there, some civilian, but mostly uniformed service personnel. There were cars, and Jeeps, and all kinds of vehicles, and a small single line railway, which ran past the dock buildings.

Pots Ainsworth and Yeoman Jones, Tom Wannop and myself kept together among the comparatively few of the naval squad. We stood waiting in the pleasant, warm sun, while various other parties were led away.

Out from one of the buildings came two young women. It was only when they were comparatively close, that we were able to recognise that they were both members of the WRNS. One had a clip board in her hand. She looked down.

"Signalman Wannop, and Writer Stubbs?" she said queryingly.

Pots had to give me a push. I was taken by surprise at hearing my name. We both stepped forward.

"Actually," I said, "I am not a Writer, I am a Coder, but I was advised to change my Rating when we were captured."

"Okay, that's alright. You two lads come with us."

Tom and I grinned. Lads! We felt like a couple of pieces of salvage. Lads! That was a boost to our ego.

The second girl took the inside of my arm, to lead us in the direction of one of the naval vehicles. I had a short sleeved shirt on. The touch of her fingers on my skin was electric. This casual gesture was the first physical contact I had had with a white female since we had been in Durban in March, over three years before.

I looked down at her. Clean, brown hair fell neatly from under her service cap. She had a slightly freckled complexion, with no make-up, and no lipstick to accentuate her smiling lips. Her immaculate, white blouse and navy blue skirt hid a slight, trim figure.

Tom was off ahead, already chatting away to his escort.

"Where are you from?" queried my companion.

"Er, London, north London."

"And when were you last home?"

"Five years ago – September, 1940."

"That's a long time. Have you heard from home yet?"

"Yes, I had a telegram from my mother in Colombo."

"She'll be pleased to see you then. You'll have some celebrating to do. Wish you luck. I've not been here long, so I expect it will be a while before I get back. Here we are. You sit up there, and we'll take you off to the stores."

The four of us now seated in the truck, which rumbled off along the shore line. The second girl was now making the conversation, in quite a broad, Scottish accent. I was aware of a fresh, sweet fragrance. I could see my guide's small, manicured fingers, folded in her lap.

"Nice hands," I thought to myself.

Subconsciously I rubbed the inside of my left arm, where she had gripped me. She turned her head and smiled again.

"That's the clothing shed over there," she said, pointing to a building just coming into view.

"Oh, good," said the Scottish lass, "There's no queue yet, so we should be in and out fairly quickly. They've got it pretty well organised."

Indeed they had. We were passed along a high counter, where first we were supplied with a naval kit-bag. Then everything else but the kitchen sink. Soap, toothbrushes, toothpaste, medal bars, Pacific Stars and Burma Star medal ribbons, jerseys, shirts, collars, boots, shoe brushes, underwear, socks, arm badges, gloves, razor blades.

Two things struck me. How did they know our sizes by just looking. And fancy thinking of medal ribbons, good conduct stripes, and such like.

We dragged our kitbags into changing rooms – they were far too heavy for us to lift, and both Tom and I were well pleased with our fits.

After a short while, a Royal Marine sergeant came through.

"You chaps alright," he asked. "As soon as you're OK, label your bags – name, number, SS Antenor, and leave them here, and then rejoin your escorts outside."

Outside, the two girls were waiting in the sun.

"All fixed up, alright. No queries?" said the Scot. She seemed to be the senior, and in charge.

"Yes, fine," I managed to stammer. I couldn't get over how young they looked. And fresh, and clean.

"Come on then. We'll go and have some refreshments."

Eventually back the short distance to Adabiya, we were led into an enclosed compound. There were small tables, each to seat four, laid out, with white table cloths, under huge umbrellas. There were already a number occupied, and our guides led us across to a vacant table on the extreme edge.

"You just sit there, and we'll see what's going," said the leader.

"What do you prefer?" asked my companion. "We can offer you tea, coffee, lime juice, probably milk. And how about a nice sandwich, and some cakes."

"Yes, please, that sounds grand. Lime juice for me."

She turned, and steered her way through the tables, up two steps, and into the open door of an adjacent building.

"Nice," said Tom.

"Yes, smashing," I half replied, my eyes tracing that attractive rear view. "I wonder how long it will be before we feel normal again."

"Strikes me, it won't be long. I'm quite enjoying this."

"Yes, but I don't know what to say."

"Never mind, just enjoy the view – and the weather." Tom was quite soon at ease.

The girls re-appeared. They both carried small metal trays.

One had a large jug of pale green lime juice, with glasses, and the other a plate of small, white sandwiches, and a plate of the most delicious looking pastries.

"There you are. That's the best we can offer. Hope you like the corned dog. Not much choice, I'm afraid."

"They look delicious, and the company's better," quipped Tom.

The girl on my right put her hand on my wrist.

"How long since you had a corned beef sandwich, Raymond – it is Raymond, isn't it?"

I don't know whether I replied. I was stuck for conversation, but my stomach certainly welcomed the thought of those sandwiches.

"Good," she said, as she approved of my taking two, and gently took her hand away.

The sandwiches soon disappeared, and I was first to be offered the plate of cakes. I remember wondering how they had conjured up such an attractive, and varied dish in this far corner of the world. I set my eye on a large, oblong pastry. I suppose it would fall under the heading of cream slice. It was an inch and a half thick, with delicious puff pastry, interspersed with cream and jam.

It was quite an art to convey it to my mouth. I opened my lips, and took a huge bite. In one fell movement, it disintegrated into my lap. There were crumbs, cream and jam all over my bare knees. My escort moved quickly with a small handkerchief. I think I must have blanched. A female touch on my arm was one thing. To grip my wrist was another. But when she started dabbing at my knees and thighs, all the embarrassment within me welled up. I stood up, quickly brushed myself down, and with a quick apology, disappeared into the canteen, or restaurant building, where I was able to have a quick wash, and to recover my composure.

After that, we had a leisurely stroll, down to the water's edge, and back to Antenor. I never did know the names of those two lassies. They were 'ships that passed in the night'. It was a splendid idea to provide each serviceman with an escort, and to assist with our kitting up. Tom and I had been especially lucky to have two charming, and attentive young girls, but I, for one, had experienced one of the first problems of resettlement.

Homecoming

Antenor cruised slowly through the Suez Canal, into the blue Mediterranean, on past the towering Rock of Gibraltar, and now we were on our last stretch, northwards, in the grey water.

She was but one of the long line of craft, all trekking homeward from South East Asia. Famous names among them – the Georgic, Chitral, Empress of Australia, Queen Elizabeth, Ile de France, Queen Mary, and the P & O liner Corfu. Despite the tragic losses during captivity, I believe there were something like 80,000 ex-prisoners now making their way homewards on that epic journey.

On Tuesday, October 23rd, there was a huge celebration dinner aboard Antenor. Arrangements for this had been made by Captain J. E. Cooper, OBE, his Officers and Crew, and Lt. Col. J. H. C. Lawlor, OC Troops. We all sat down to a Menu of tomato soup, salmon in hollandaise sauce, roast beef with all its trimmings, followed by plum pudding, or fruit salad. The long mess table was the scene of a happy feasting. The autographed menu card carries the names of twenty of my then close companions, soon to be scattered throughout England, Scotland and Wales.

I think that the 23rd had been chosen because we were due to arrive in Liverpool on October 24th, but as we came up the Irish Sea, the wind whipped up, the ocean erupted, and for the next 24 hours, Antenor became

The longest two days of my life.

a cork, tossed from side to side, and most certainly not the ideal spot for any kind of revelry.

On the evening of Thursday, 25th, we could dimly see land away to our south, and turned in that night confident of landfall the next morning. It was not to be. Daylight revealed the north Wales coast a few miles off, but 70 miles an hour gales had forced the Captain to anchor, and ride out the storm, before attempting to enter the Mersey Estuary.

The next 48 hours were spent so near, and yet so far. The waiting must have been equally as frustrating at home, for my mother had kept the newspaper cuttings:

'REPATS' HELD UP read the News Chronicle.
The giant Cunard liner, Queen Mary, heaving and straining at her anchors as great seas crashed against her sides and swept her superstructure, spent another night riding out the storm off the Isle of Wight.

Despite the lashing gale, we gazed across the storm tossed waters. Yeoman Jones peered through the rain endeavouring to pinpoint the various landmarks.

"That'll be Rhyl just over there, and just further along, on the port side is Prestatyn, and I live just inshore of those. Should be indoors there tomorrow."

In fact, by Saturday morning, the storm had abated sufficiently for Antenor to make its way slowly into Liverpool Bay, round the familiar point of New Brighton, and up the Mersey.

It was a sodden morning, heavy and bleak, but every man jack was on deck as the Liver Building hove into sight, among cheers and shouts. Vessels tied up alongside the docks sounded their sirens, and there were hooters and whistles, and noises of all descriptions, as we edged our way slowly to our berth.

The pipe for 'Hands to Dinner' went absolutely unheeded. No-one wanted to miss the excitement on the dockside. Bunting and flags hung forlornly from the buildings, but the many Union flags held by the crowds ashore were waving enthusiastically, and here and there was a more personal notice – 'WELCOME BACK, JIM'. 'GOD BLESS YOU, LADS'.

Faces were being scanned from ship, and from shore. Searching for dear ones. Eyes, many clouded with tears of joy, and emotion, scrutinising the decks, and the milling throng. Occasionally, there was recognition, and people ran along, trying to keep abreast with Antenor, as she now closed the last few yards.

Tom, next to me, thought that he had spotted his father. Then fell silent,

211

when the man held up a strange, small child to wave, and he realised it was mistaken identity.

Moments after docking, the gangways were in position, and after a few preliminaries, people swarmed on board. Arrangements had already been made for the various services to look after their own men, and we were warned to have our kit ready to be offloaded.

There were just a couple of hours of the early afternoon to get our things together, to say our goodbyes to our former companions in distress, and then we were filing slowly down the narrow aisle, which led to the solid earth of England. Or more truthfully perhaps, the dank, stained, concrete of a Liverpool landing stage. In the gusty, drizzly climate of that Saturday afternoon, nevertheless, we all felt like stepping into Paradise.

A willing band of helpers manhandled our cases, and our kitbags, as we stepped forward to pats, and hugs, and kisses, mostly from complete strangers.

And there *was* Tom's dad, and closely behind, his mum.

"Tom, Tom, it's wonderful to see you. How are you. Where are you going now?"

A mumbled introduction, and then "How are you, Ray. Lovely to see you boys home."

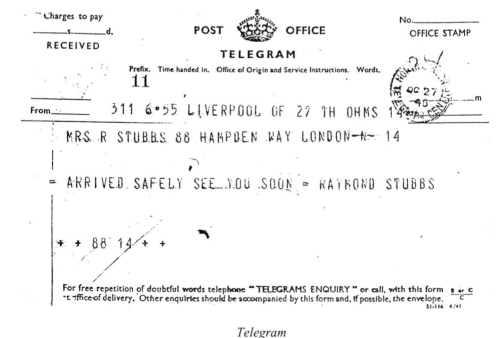

Telegram

There were tears, there were fond, and silent embraces. Each little knot of beings wrapped in their own personal thoughts. Quiet appraisal of the changes that had been wrought in the four years, or more, of separation.

"Right, Royal Navy, over here please." Not a command, but a reluctant request, to break up the intimate greetings.

"Royal Navy ratings will go first to HMS Wellesley, where all the necessary preliminaries will be carried out, as quickly as possible, and then you will be given pay, identity cards, rail passes, and so on, and then you are free to join your families and friends."

"Cheerio Tom, cheerio Ray. See you then in a couple of hours. Let's have a meal, and a long chat together." It was hello, and goodbye.

'HMS Wellesley,' I thought to myself. That brought memories. Life-saving exercises. Lancashire hot-pot. Marching through the streets of Liverpool. The early bombing raids. The overground railway. That was Autumn, 1940. Now it was Autumn, 1945. Leave wouldn't be counted in days, but in months. Hopefully, home in London, tomorrow.

The Last Lap

The portals of HMS Wellesley had never before signalled such a warm reception. The Royal Navy had certainly done their homework, and while there necessarily was a heap of routine to surmount, it was highly organised.

After being allocated to messes, we assembled in the cinema – that was certainly something new – a cinema 'on board ship'.

King George VI and the Queen sent a message to each one of us, bidding a very warm welcome home. Duplicated, of course, but nevertheless, a nice touch.

Again, we were allocated guides, and each had a pro forma to make sure that we went through all the necessary channels.

First, a telegram home

Then all the trappings of wartime Britain. We received an identity card, clothing coupons, ration book, and a railway warrant. We handed in surplus enemy currency, and received our first pay.

There was a small parcel for each man from the British Red Cross, and a carefully contrived bag meal and mug to tide us over the remainder of the afternoon.

We had to check out with a doctor, and a dentist, but nobody wanted to delay on that score. The notice board showing times of trains was besieged, as each person sought for the earliest possible journey home.

BUCKINGHAM PALACE

The Queen and I bid you a very warm welcome home.

Through all the great trials and sufferings which you have undergone at the hands of the Japanese, you and your comrades have been constantly in our thoughts. We know from the accounts we have already received how heavy those sufferings have been. We know also that these have been endured by you with the highest courage.

We mourn with you the deaths of so many of your gallant comrades.

With all our hearts, we hope that your return from captivity will bring you and your families a full measure of happiness, which you may long enjoy together.

George R.I.

September 1945.

214

Tom's parents were collecting him that evening, but for me, there wasn't a train to London until after midday on Sunday.

We made our way to the canteen, where our enamel mugs were topped up with sweet, hot tea, and we sat down and ate the packed meal, consisting of two kinds of sandwiches (cheese and meat), two slabs of cake, and an apple. It all sounds so mundane now, but these were heady days, and bread, with fillings, was still a luxury.

All the routines being completed, we waited around in the large entrance hall, until Mr & Mrs Wannop came for us.

"We had a nice meal just up the road, at lunchtime," said Tom's dad.

"I expect there's something on the menu that you will like. The proprietor has reserved a table for us. Promised us something good," chipped in his mum.

From outside the restaurant looked an ordinary kind of place, but once inside, we were struck by the warmth.

As soon as we were in the door, the owner came out from the back of a small bar.

"Here you are, I've kept this table for you in the corner."

He extended a large hand to each of us.

"Welcome back, boys. Make yourselves comfortable. There's the menu, but if you like it, I've got a nice steak and kidney pie, for you." The rich generosity I had found earlier in the Liverpool folk was still there.

"Steak and kidney pie!" exclaimed Mrs W.

"Well it is a special day," said the restaurateur. He touched the side of his nose, and grinned. "I can generally find something for a celebration," he grinned, once more.

Tom and I looked at each other, and with one accord said: "Good old English steak and kidney pie. Yes please."

Sunday morning came, still wet and miserable. I looked in the mirror. I had had second thoughts over my beard. Perhaps I should have shaved it off. No. I changed my mind again. My skin was very sallow, and my cheeks still a bit sunken. No, I'd leave it on.

My hair was better. Must be over half an inch long now. Bit of Brylcream, and I almost had a parting.

I polished my new boots until they shone. Brushed my serge jersey, and trousers – they mustn't have a scrap of dust, or hair on them. The sailor's collar and silk felt strange, but apart from the traditional creases, sat well enough.

My small brown ditty case was packed and unpacked numerous times. Had I got my travel warrant? What had I done with my identity card? I was unused to these bits of civilised paraphernalia. The morning dragged. Wellesley was emptying rapidly. There had been a regular stream of people calling to collect their long lost sons, and husbands, interspersed with the Royal Navy truck which ran a shuttle service to the Liverpool trains.

Then eventually, over the Tannoy!

"Hear ye, hear ye. The London train is due to leave Lime Street in just over an hour. All ratings travelling on that train should be at the main entrance no later than 1200 hours."

We didn't need any urging. This was the best 'liberty-boat' we had ever wanted to catch.

A trio of Naval Police waited at the station, with a Master-at-Arms. They helped with our bags, and soon we were watching the English countryside flashing past, through the dripping and steamy windows. Most of the familiar faces had now gone, but the passengers were mainly service men.

We chatted in a desultory kind of way, being very much more interested in marking our progress as station names hurtled by. We picked at the meal bags which had been provided. I thought of that steak and kidney pie. I would ask my mum to make a steak and kidney pudding – that was my favourite. She would probably suggest boiled fish. Easy to digest, she would say.

The same Master-at-Arms came round, through the carriages.

"When you get to Euston, just get out onto the platform, with your luggage. We've arranged for everyone of you to be met, so please don't wander off. There'll be all kinds of volunteers with cars, and vans to take you to your homes, or across to other termini, so bear with us, and we'll get you away as soon as we can."

So, at last, there I was on the platform of Euston. I had dumped my bags on the ground, one of many small piles scattered among the hurrying feet. A few minutes later I heard a voice ask, "Three chaps for North London?" Two others joined us and in no time we were following him off the platform and being bundled into the back of his waiting van. We pulled out into Euston Road, swung right into Camden Road past Holloway Prison, more and more familiar sights flashing by. We dropped off the other two first, then we were drawing to a halt outside No 88 Hampden Way. A white ensign was flapping over the porch; the front iron gate had gone, but the sloping crazy-paved path still led to the front door . . . I leapt out, down the path, and rang the bell. Then I realised I hadn't got my small brown case so I went back to the van to fetch it. As I came back down the path I saw the door open, and the light from the hallway flood out. My dog ran to me, barking and squealing. The driver was ahead carrying my kitbag and my mother, in the excitement, was hugging him, crying "My boy, my boy," until I said quietly, "Well, don't I get a kiss?" and she turned to me, realising her mistake. "You've got a beard. Son, son, you're just like your Maker. I didn't think you might have a beard. Come in out of the rain." My dad and sister were now in the hall and the dog was rushing up and down. Chaos! I was home . . .

My father stoked the sitting room fire. He said little, but I could feel him looking. Perhaps his thoughts parallelled my own. He'd been a big man. All of six feet tall. Now he seemed to have shrunken. He'd been athletic – always striding out in front when we went off for a walk. Now he was a little bowed. He coughed, and as he did so, I noticed his hand move to his groin. Had he still got that hernia?

Bess was lying down at my feet. I spoke to her, and her little black tail beat a staccato on the floor.

There was a ring at the doorbell, and my younger brother appeared in the doorway.

"Good to see you. Brought you some eggs, from one of my customers."

"What about Dick?" (my elder brother) I asked. "Where is he now?"

"He's still in Germany. He's a Flight Lieutenant now, you know."

Mother's voice was full of pride. She still had the Royal Navy brooch I had brought her in 1940 on one lapel of her blouse. And on the other side she had a small encrusted pair of Air Force wings. Her face was creased, but her hair was still jet black. Suddenly, it was out.

"What about you, boy? Did they treat you badly? Did they do anything to you?" The pent up questions came pouring out. She couldn't restrain her emotions any longer.

"You know what I mean. We've heard such awful things. Was it that bad?"

"Perhaps he doesn't want to talk about it – tonight, anyway," butted in my brother.

"There's a lot of letters waiting for you. There's news of some of the other Encounter boys. And the neighbours have been so kind. They've put flags up all down the road, you know."

"I told Dr Collingwood you were due home any day now, so if you need to see him, it will be all right." My mother's half-hidden fears continued to rise to the surface.

How they had fared at home. Coped with air raids. Managed on the rations. All these things were temporarily forgotten. This was a red letter day!

"Have you heard from any of my pals? I expect most of them are home by now. Pete Young, Des Ball, Ron Hassell, Ron Reed – anything of them?"

"Oh yes," cut in my sister. "Ron Reed has been round enquiring after you. He lives with his parents just by Oakhill Park now. He was a prisoner in Germany, you know. Captured in Crete. He says Peter Young is home. He's married. Pretty girl. There's so much to tell you. Yes, and you wouldn't have known, both Ron Hassell and Des Ball were reported missing a long time ago. Dare-devil, that Des, wasn't he?"

"I'll have a lot of catching up to do."

Dad poked the fire into life again. "You sure you're warm enough," he said quietly.

"There are two families I must go and see in Enfield. We had a little group of us in the camp from North London. We promised to call. Is it still the 29 bus to Enfield?"

"Better see how you are in a week or two. There's no rush, surely?"

"Yes, these two are fairly urgent. You see we promised that those of us that got home would call and see the relatives of those who didn't."

"Oh dear oh dear, poor souls. Yes, you must do that. Surely you can get a taxi one day later in the week?"

"I must write first, otherwise it will be too much of a shock for them. We spent many hours talking about our homes and families you know. Donald lived in Monastery Gardens in Enfield. I think that's just past St Andrew's Church. He was single and lived with his mum and dad. I think he had a brother."

"What about the other one?" asked my sister.

"He was a married chap. I don't think he had any family. Worshipped his wife. I don't think they had been married long before he was sent off East."

"That will be very difficult. They'll be very upset. Perhaps it would be better to leave it a while?"

"Yes, it won't be easy, but I promised them both."

My brother took another tack. "You know, we don't know how you were captured. The telegrams and letters from the Admiralty were very confusing. They thought you were still on Encounter when she was sunk. Then, by the time they had sorted that out of course, Singapore had fallen. Sounded a right shambles out there."

"It's a long story. You don't want to hear it all tonight. Another time," I said.

It was well into the early hours of the next day that I climbed the stairs to my small bedroom. My legs still rebelled against this unusual exercise, and it was heavenly to sink into my own single bed and to revel in

218

24 Monastery Gardens
Enfield
3/11/45

Dear Mr Willis

My wife, & family tender our very
greatful thanks for your extreme kindness
in writing to us and we deeply
appreciate the thought which prompted
you to send us the Xmas Card which
our dear Son gave to you; we certainly
will cherish this as a lasting
remembrance of Donald's spirit; thank
you ever so much

Do please call to see us, as we
feel it will help us to bear our grief
somewhat to be able to talk with
someone who had met Don whilst captive,
more so, one who had been a friend of
his

I, myself will arrange to leave
my work on Wednesday afternoon to
see you, and meanwhile take this
opportunity of expressing our sincere
hope that your terrible experience has
not left its mark too heavily upon you.

Thanking you for your kind sympathy
Yours very sincerely
J. P. Richardson

From Father of Don Richardson, POW, Palembang.

comfortable privacy. Privacy. I had forgotten that word.

I was to find out in a few days how many friends I had lost in my long absence, but also how many folk there were who were to be so kind and helpful in my resettlement.

I did write to Donald Richardson's mother and father. They were so grateful to hear.

I also wrote to the wife of the other chappie who had lived nearby, but whose resting place was a grave by the jungle edge. I had no reply.

The call at Monastery Gardens was a harrowing affair for us all. Stan Richardson begged of me to tell of his son's last hours, and all I could honestly tell was that he had had a proper service burial. Not that his emaciated body was just temporarily covered with a rice sack, as we trudged up the hill. Not that his early end was hastened by bites from the rats which thronged the putrid atmosphere of that hut from which we all knew there was no return. His mother, her hands twisted and deformed by arthritis, squeezed a small handkerchief, and constantly tried to halt the flow of tears.

A ring at the doorbell forecast the arrival of their other son, and his wife.

"Let's put the kettle on, Mother. I'm sure we could all do with a cup of tea. Where did you put the biscuits?" This universal panacea proved effective.

"Have you parents? How are they? Were they in London all through the war? What will you do now? Have you a job to go back to?"

After about an hour, I rose to go on my way.

"I must go now. I promised to call on another lady in Enfield. Lost her husband. I did write, but strangely, there wasn't a reply."

"Where does she live? Oh, in Enfield, too. Where? Off Lancaster Road?"

Strange looks passed round the room. I didn't understand.

"You're wasting your time. She won't be in. Always out. Americans. Canadians. All sorts. Sorry, we shouldn't have said that."

Mr Richardson walked to the door with me.

Hand on my shoulder, he said, "I do apologise. Mother was so upset. We couldn't imagine how a young woman could carry on like that. Particularly with her husband out there. Please come again. We do hope you will. Do you know the way to go?"

I walked slowly along the main road. Turned left at the main 'T' junction. I scanned the names of the turnings, as I passed. Ah yes, this is it. What was the number? No, there wasn't a reply. Perhaps the bell didn't work. I tried the knocker. The front garden was uncared for. A flurry of wind disturbed the dead leaves, and scraps of paper, which had heaped themselves in the shallow porch. I knocked again. No. There was nobody in. I popped a note through the letter box.

It must have been more than a week later. I had managed to walk up to the local shops. I was hardly in the front door.

"That woman called. That woman you went to see in Enfield. She said she had been away. Sorry she had missed you. Left these tickets for the theatre. Thought you might like to go with her one evening. Didn't seem at all upset about her poor husband. It's up to you, but I didn't like her type."

I thought I should call again, and form my own opinion. I wrote and returned the tickets, with the apology that I was not yet fit enough to enjoy such an evening out. I heard no more.

Some didn't come back. Some came home to find more tribulations, and tragedies awaiting them. I came home to warmth and comfort. I was one of the lucky ones.

And What Now

To add to the pile of post awaiting my return, the postman daily brought new tidings. Most, I am glad to say, good.

From Argyllshire came the wonderful news that Johnnie MacMillan was safely home.

"I am extremely happy to know that Tom and you are now on your way home to the UK, and that Palembang had at last been relieved. Words cannot express the welcome I received when I entered again the portals of Argyll House and believe me it was the happiest moment of my life. I know the same welcome awaits you. I certainly missed you all when I left Palembang for Singapore, but the camp at Changi Gaol was 100% better than the conditions in Sumatra. Fortunately there, we were able to get the news daily from a secret wireless set.

I was fortunate enough to wangle on board SS Monowai, the first ship to leave Singapore . . . the Corfu beat us to it for the honours of being the first ship to arrive in UK containing the war-worn exiles . . .

I was delighted to know that both you and Tom came through alright, for while at Singapore, I heard that the death rate at Sungei Ron was heavy . . .

. . . believe me our people at home certainly stood up to as awful an ordeal as ourselves and only the greatest fortitude and faith pulled them through . . .

I will write later . . . till then all the very best from the bottom
of my heart, Your old pal, Johnnie.

This letter, dated October 10th, 1945, enclosed a cutting from The
Bulletin and Scots Pictorial, with the banner headline 'SCOTTISH POW
IS FIRST TO LAND.' 'Bronzed and smiling and looking remarkably fit,
a 27 year old Scot, Telegraphist John MacMillan of Tarbert, Argyll, was
the first ex-prisoner of war from Singapore to step ashore at Liverpool
yesterday'.*

The newspaper article goes on to say that closer inspection revealed
evidence of the ordeals the men had undergone – gaunt faces, staring eyes,
and unhealthy pallor.

However, that was now all in the past. Perhaps one day, we could renew
our strong bond of friendship. We did, in fact, and it still is strong today.

Also from Scotland came news of my friends on HMS Encounter. Robert
Steel wrote from Glasgow to report his arrival home. Although a clerk, he
had been transferred from Macassar to Nagasaki, for being a Glaswegian,
the Japanese were convinced he must have a knowledge of ship-building,
and would be useful working in the docks of that town. He had witnessed
the atomic explosion from only a distance of about three or four miles, had
survived, and returned to his native town. He sent to me his account of the
sinking of Encounter in the Java Sea on March 1st, 1942, a fortnight after
I was captured.

One of our benefactors in South Africa, Mrs Zeederberg wrote from
Kalk Bay, to say how delighted she had been to see Sid Lillywhite, who
had survived captivity, and had called in to see her, while taking passage
home, from the East. He had told her of the death of Leading Telegraphist
Peter Denham – our mutual great friend, Horse, – while prisoner in
Macassar. Obviously he had not been able to tell of myself, since his last
contact was by letter early in 1942. Sid and I, and many other members of
the ship's crew, met at a grand reunion, during that first post-war winter. I
can so clearly remember the hall echoing to the tune of 'My Old Dutch' as
Sid and his family celebrated his homecoming. Strange to relate, his
daughter married a 'Ray Stubbs'.

Alan Anstead wrote from his parents' flat at Golders Green. He had
been re-united with his fiancee, Anne, and wedding bells were imminent
on the Isle of Man.

Nostalgia of pre-war days was unbounded, as earlier friendships were
rekindled. The ships' lamps swung, the tanks rumbled, the shells exploded,
the dusky maids surrendered, as we swopped our stories.

*See Appendix VIII.

The Palmers Green & Southgate Gazette reporter called for a story, and later carried a short paragraph 'TWICE REPORTED MISSING' Now Raymond Stubbs is home.

The Southgate branch of the British Prisoners of War Relatives Association held a magnificent party, and each one of the Far East prisoners was presented with a fountain pen. It was black, it was a Waterman. It was simply engraved 'From Southgate POWRA – In Appreciation'. I thought of that other pen. It too was a black Waterman. Torn from my grasp by a thieving Korean guard, then discarded in anger when he found it did not work. This one too has now lost its perished rubber sac, but its shell is kept in gratitude to those who kept the home fires burning.

There was news from relatives. There was word of schoolfellows. There was an invitation from my office. Wanted to discuss my future. I might need some form of testimonial. I would ask Commander Reid. I met an old girlfriend. The past had gone. Now was the present, and we must look to the future. It was to be a good future. Yes, I was one of the lucky ones.

Old Schoolfriends

It was a strange feeling to be going back into the old school again. To be turning the clock back nearly ten years. Mrs Hassell thought it might be a good idea to pick up some of the missing links.

"Probably there'll be some of your contemporaries there, Tubby."

Funny that family had always known me as, 'Tubby'. I never had been, and I was far from it now.

"Certain to be someone you know. I should go if I were you."

TWICE REPORTED MISSING

NOW RAYMOND STUBBS IS HOME

The last Sunday in October, 1945, is a date which Mr. and Mrs. R. A. Stubbs and family at 88 Hampden Way, Southgate, will long remember. On that day the youngest member of the family, Coder Raymond Stubbs, who had twice been reported missing, came home.

Mrs. Stubbs was informed that Raymond was missing in the battle of the Java Seas, but later—after she had received a letter from him with a Singapore address—she was told that a mistake had been made because of his transfer.

LONG AND ANXIOUS PERIOD.

But sad news once again reached 88 Hampden Way, when Raymond was reported missing for the second time. On this occasion the information was correct and two and a-half years elapsed before the family heard from him to say that he was a prisoner of war in the Far East.

During that trying period, however, the family never lost hope and their faith was rewarded by his safe return after perilous adventures at sea.

Raymond was first at Banka Island camp and then Palembang Camp. Two Enfield West soldiers were among his comrades there: unhappily they died of malnutrition.

THEY KNEW!

Owing to the ingenuity of one of his companions our boys in the camp learned of the German and Japanese surrenders before the Jap guards! Mr. and Mrs. Stubbs wish to express their sincere thanks for the solicitude and help of many neighbours and Raymond, too, thanks POWRA for their help.

This 26-year-old sailor has been in the Royal Navy since 1940, and before joining up was in the Town Clerk's office at Shoreditch Town Hall. He has three brothers and two sisters.

Reprinted from 'Palmers Green & Southgate Gazette.' November 16th, 1945.

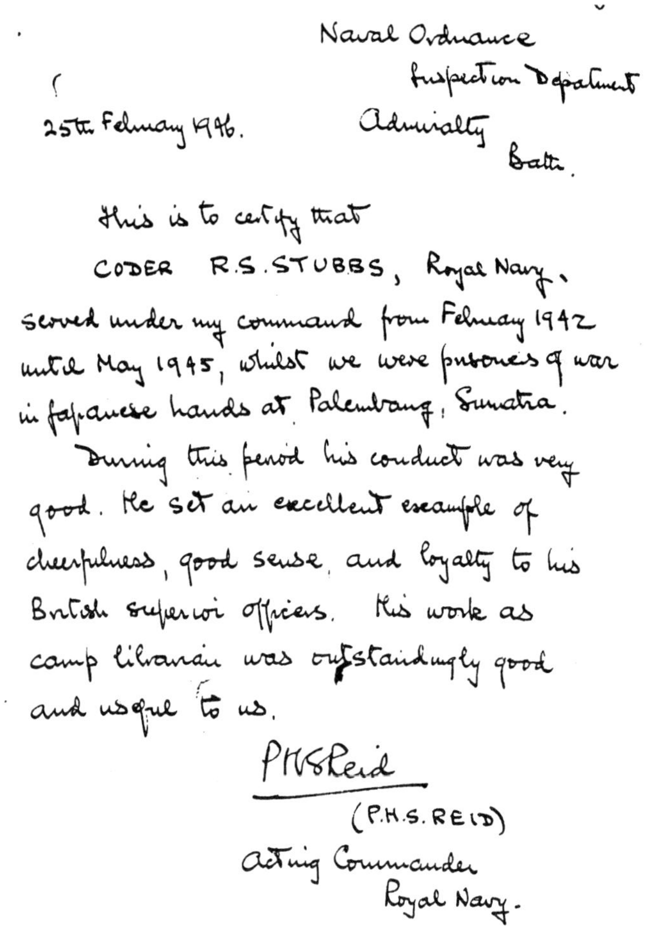

Naval Ordnance
Inspection Department
Admiralty
Bath.

25th February 1946.

This is to certify that

CODER R.S. STUBBS, Royal Navy,
served under my command from February 1942
until May 1945, whilst we were prisoners of war
in Japanese hands at Palembang, Sumatra.

During this period his conduct was very
good. He set an excellent example of
cheerfulness, good sense, and loyalty to his
British superior officers. His work as
camp librarian was outstandingly good
and useful to us.

P.H.S.Reid

(P.H.S. REID)
Acting Commander
Royal Navy.

"What about you, Eileen? Will you come?"

"Sure. That would be nice. Don't forget then. Saturday week. Shall we say just after seven? You call for me, and we'll go along together."

"Oh, I'm so pleased," said Mrs H. "Do you both good. I'm sure you'll both enjoy the County School Reunion."

Poor Mrs H. The war had robbed her of husband and son. And, she was clearly now worried about her young son-in-law, who was serving with the Red Devils in Palestine. Yet there was still that warmth of welcome in the Hassell household.

BRITISH PRISONERS OF WAR RELATIVES
ASSOCIATION
(SOUTHGATE BRANCH)
5 Farm Road, N.14

We members of this Relatives Association, have constantly admired your splendid morale whilst in captivity, and we have tried to realise the immense privation and suffering that you have endured for us so cheerfully.

Your letters home have been a source of great comfort, considerably helping us, and inspired us to assist you as far as possible.

In asking you to accept this Presentation Pen, subscribed for by the members, we do so as an appreciation for the help given us and as a memento of the wonderful spirit of comradeship which exists between your Next-of-Kin, brought together in unity during the times of great anxiety.

May this pen give you good service and always be kept in remembrance of the great love and kindred companionship that the Relatives have given each other during your absence.

For and on behalf of all the Members,

Sincerely yours,

H.S. Beardow. Hon. Sec.

"Bye for now. Do please pop in and see us when you like."

Ron Hassell's first letter after he had been called up for the Royal Navy, had been written from HMS Royal Arthur, and had reached me at home, in the early summer of 1940. Being just a few months older than myself, he had preceded me on his call-up, despite my personal efforts to 'jump the gun' by enlisting the name of Admiral Sir Edward Evans (of the 'Broke', of First World War fame) to get me into the Royal Navy.

"The life's absolutely grand," he had said, proceeding to give some tempting details of his early experiences on the shore-based 'ship' at Skegness (formerly Butlin's Holiday Camp).

It had only been a few weeks after receiving that letter, that I left behind my dad, and my girl friend, Joan, on the platform, at King's Cross Station, and found myself following in his footsteps, by which time, he was 'Somewhere at Sea', as the Censor would have it.

Then only three months more, to the day, on October 10th, after that very elementary training, and kitting out at Skegness, Liverpool, and Chatham, and I was on board SS Aguila, heading for Gibraltar, to join HMS Encounter.

More than five years passed, before I was home again, trying to establish communication, to pick up the strings, and to renew the friendships that had been severed by distance, and circumstance.

Alas, many were never to be continued.

225

Ron had perished in the English Channel later in 1940. His dad had never got over the shock. His sister Eileen, who I remembered as a lean, gangling, kid, in her early teens, unbelievably, was now a young married woman.

The anti-malarial 'mepacrine' had given me a jaundiced look. My new crop of hair was about ¾'' long, and just about covered my scalp. My weight was soaring rapidly towards 9 stones, covering my nigh on six foot frame with a little more flesh. I was beginning to look forward to some social life.

The hall of Hornsey County School was, as I remembered it a decade earlier, when I had ended my schooldays. The tall, square pillars were clad with oak panelling, the brain child of our craft master, Frank Large. The walls recited, in gold lettering, the school and house honours, in academics, and in sports. Some Christmas decorations partly obscured the windows on the north side. To the east, was the small stage, or platform.

I mused, half anticipating the swing doors to open, and waited for the 'new' Headmaster, Mr Bannister, to lead in the masters and mistresses, filing on to the platform.

I wondered if the former head, Dr Piggott was still alive.

I thought then of those revered persons, in their black academic gowns, the hoods dressed with various coloured silks and furs, and topped with mortar boards, the individual angles of which demonstrated their wearer's innermost character.

My mind drifted to Friday afternoon assembly, and the words of that familiar hymn – the last one in the school hymn book – 'The day thou gavest, Lord, is ended . . .'

My recollections were disturbed by a young fellow in pristine naval sub-lieutenant's uniform, with the economy half gold stripe on his cuff. He was shaking my hand, and virtually repeating Ron Hassell's words.

"What do you think of life in the Andrew?"

Before I could reply, he said: "Great, isn't it."

I felt somewhat annoyed at his intrusion into my thoughts. What did he know about it? A couple of MTB trips off the Suffolk coast, in an English summer, long after the war in Europe was at an end, seemed to be the highlights of his experience.

My returning vitality did allow me to attempt a couple of jigs around the dance floor, and I think I was lucky enough to win a spot prize, or something.

Musical Knees, and Pass the Parcel, provoked a bit of harmless fun, though any physical contact with the other sex was still strangely embarrassing.

After a short refreshment break, the Head welcomed the assembled company, and expressed his pleasure at seeing so many of the pre-war faces.

He said he had some announcements to make, mostly about forthcoming fixtures. Firstly, sadly, he was compiling a list of persons from the school, who had made the supreme sacrifice. The School War Memorial was to be suitably engraved.

My gaze went casually to the House Honours – Brackenbury, Hodgson, Kelland and Greaves. I had been in Greaves House – it always seemed to be last, in everything.

I thought of the names of that Class of 1931.

"Des Ball, Madeleine Cavell, Dorothy Dunsford, Doris Dubery, Doris Ellman, Dorothy Gluckstein, Eddie Hutt, Ron Hassell, Gwylam Hughes, Irene Lane, Ralph Loly, Ray Martin, Ray Nicholls, Denis Pettit, Aubrey Sampson, Dick Salmon, Bob Tanner, Harry Ward, Joan Watkis, Joan East, Florrie Wilson, Enid Winchester, Peter Young . . ."

. . . but the Head was reading out his own list.

"Desmond Ball (RAF Pathfinder Squadron, killed attacking rocket installations in Northern Europe.)

Ronald Hassell (Royal Navy, killed English Channel.)

Raymond Nicholls (killed on flying duties, RAF.)

Raymond Martin (Eighth Army, killed Western Desert.)

Raymond Stubbs (Royal Navy, Missing, Java Sea, 1942.)
. . ."

Strange, I thought, three Raymonds in a row. But, wait a minute, I am here, I am alive. Surely it was all a dream. Probably my mental faculties had not fully adjusted from the extreme indigence they had undergone.

Nevertheless, when a little while later, I presented myself to him, in the flesh, he was clearly very pleased to correct the record, which had probably originated from the time I was reported missing following the sinking of HMS Encounter. In view of the fact that until June, 1944, there had been no news, this was understandable.

The Headmaster was obviously delighted to report this good news to the assembled company.

It seemed only a matter of months afterwards, that the school ceased to be a Grammar School, and was swallowed up by the intake of the Greek and Cypriot population, which in the early post-war years, congregated in that part of London.

It was the end of that era, and I have not been back again.

Pilgrimage

I suppose that in my mind I had always had a feeling that I might go back. Surely there was no magnetism in those grim memories. Equally, there could be no attraction in retreading those awful steps. Yet, despite everything, there was a fascinating interest, and a strange curiosity, to return.

The 'Daily Mail' of July 31st, 1985, re-awakened those thoughts. There was a short insert, mentioning that the Government, through the Ministry of Defence, were sponsoring an Official Pilgrimage to the Far East for widows, veterans, and former prisoners of war, from that campaign. Applications were invited through the Royal British Legion.

At the end of August, I had a letter from the Ministry of Defence. It said: "I am delighted to hear through the offices of the Royal British Legion that you have been selected to attend the Far East Pilgrimage to Singapore."

As I drove in past the barrier check-point to RAF Brize Norton, I wondered whether there might possibly be any of my former companions

FEPOW Reunion 8th November, 1952.
Parsons, Orton, Robbins, Watts, Wilson, Stubbs.

now making this almost historic journey back. I searched the faces of other men now arriving, interspersed with those of the many widows, who had had to face on their own the last four years of the war, and the forty years which had passed since. This was a remembrance largely of the 'Forgotten Army', the 14th Army plunged into battle on the other side of the world, short of arms, short of experience, and only now, tardily included in a nation's homage. This was a recollection of the men of the Royal Air Force, and the Colonial Air Forces, who in their Hudsons and Blenheims, their sluggish Buffalos, and their obsolete Vildebeestes challenged the overwhelming numbers of Japanese in their modern planes. This was a commemoration of the men of the Prince of Wales, and Repulse, the destroyer Encounter, and the many, many small ships which tried so unsuccessfully to run the gauntlet from burning Singapore.

The evening briefing of the three parties, to be divided between Burma, Singapore/Malaysia, and Thailand, was an opportunity to find kindred souls. I was one of the three Naval representatives, the others being ex-Royal Marine Maurice Edwards, and ex-Chief Petty Officer Charles Northcott, both of whom survived the sinking of the Prince of Wales. The naval party was completed by three widows of men who perished on that ship, Elizabeth Hall, Mary Paget, and Mrs Kirkpatrick.

Early on the morning of November 5th, with a support staff, led by Colonel Lea, DSO, MBE, we boarded a Tristar of 216 Squadron, RAF, and were soon away, in the bright daylight, en route for Bahrein, Bangkok, and our group's destination, of Singapore.

Then, nearly a whole day into our adventure, we were tracing our course, down the east coast of Malaysia, dropping lower and lower, sweeping across the Johore Straits, and gliding to a halt at the Changi International Airport.

A bevy of officials were waiting at the aircraft steps, as soon as the Tristar had come to rest, and then we were whisked through the reception lounge to be greeted by pretty, dark-skinned maidens, who presented each one of us with a fresh picked orchid.

Coaches transported us along the new coastal road into Singapore City, and up to our luxurious hotel, the Oberoi Imperial.

My bedroom was No. 656, on the sixth floor. It was palatial. I had a bed which would have slept three – there were in fact, three pillows, and of course, this invited some cryptic remarks. I soon made use of the en suite facilities, and then when changing into something more fitting for the air cooled atmosphere, I took stock of the pictures on the wall. How appropriate – 'Fortcanning in 1846' by J. T. Thompson, and 'Fortcanning in 1843' by E. A. Porcher. How different I thought from the Fortcanning I remembered from 1941/2.

Sea of poppies covers Force Z

With anchor floral tribute, the group which paid homage to those who died in HM ships Prince of Wales and Repulse in the South China Sea: From left, Lieut.-Cdr. S. J. Buck, Mr. R. Stubbs, Mrs. Buck, Mr. C. J. Northcott, Colour Sgt. A. Webb, Mr. M. F. G. Edwards, Mrs. E. Hall, Mrs. L. Paget, Mrs. Ainslie, Lieut.-Cdr. J. D. St. J. Ainslie.

A MOVING service in memory of those who died in HM ships Prince of Wales and Repulse in the South China Sea was an especially poignant part of the recent Far East pilgrimage by a group of 230 war widows and veterans, including former prisoners of war.

The vessels, which formed "Force Z", were sent to the bottom by the Japanese in 1941.

Among those at sea to pay tribute as wreaths and poppies were cast on to the water were the widows of two of the Prince of Wales men, two survivors from the ship, and a survivor from an escort vessel.

HMS Encounter

They were: Mrs. Elizabeth Hall, of Totnes, widow of ERA G. E. J. Hall; Mrs. Lillian Paget, of Teignmouth, widow of PO F. C. Paget; ex-PO Charles Northcott, of Newton Abbot, and ex-Marine Maurice Edwards, of Newmarket, Prince of Wales survivors; and ex-Signalman (C) Ray Stubbs, of Newbury, from the escort ship HMS Encounter.

With them were Lieut.-Cdr. S. J. Buck (Assistant Defence Adviser Singapore and RNLO Singapore), accompanied by his wife, and Lieut.-Cdr. J. D. St. J. Ainslie (Assistant Defence Adviser Kuala Lumpur), and his wife. Bugler for the ceremony — and at other ceremonies on the pilgrimage — was CSgt. A. Webb, from RM Deal.

Wreaths

From the Royal Malaysian Air Force base at Kuantan the group was flown by Sea King helicopter to a point between the wrecks of the ships, and landed on a Royal Malaysian Navy tank landing craft which had been positioned there.

The act of remembrance included the Naval Prayer, the hymn "Eternal Father" and Laurence Binyon's famous lines "They shall grow not old." Then wreaths were cast on the sea on behalf of the Royal Navy, the Royal Marines, the widows and the Far East Prisoners-of-War Association.

Spread across the sea, too, were 840 poppies in memory of the men who died when the ships were lost off the coast of Malaya on December 10, 1941. As the wreaths drifted astern, CSgt. Webb sounded the Last Post and, after the Silence, Naval Reveille.

CSgt. Webb said: "My friends the survivors and widows have asked me publicly to acknowledge their thanks to Lieut.-Cdrs. Buck and Ainslie and to Cdr. Bala, of the Royal Malaysian Navy."

Changi Jail

Purpose of the pilgrimage of commemoration to the Far East was to allow the paying of homage at the graves of husbands and comrades, and at war sites. The party was divided into groups for a range of visits.

The pilgrimage embraced Burma, Malaysia, Singapore and Thailand, and the visits included Changi Jail, Rangoon Cemetery and Cathedral, the River Kwai, and Httauykyan, Kanchanaburi and Chunkai cemeteries.

The Duke of Kent, president of the Commonwealth War Graves Commission, and Defence Secretary Mr. Michael Heseltine joined the group for the Remembrance Sunday ceremony at Kranji War Memorial and cemetery, Singapore.

The visit of the Far East pilgrims, whose ages ranged between about 60-80, was organised by the Ministry of Defence and the small support staff included people from all Services, including RN, QARNNS and WRNS.

Navy News – January 1986.

230

I wandered across to the heavy net covering to the large window. There only a few hundred feet away was the rise of Fortcanning itself. Verdant and tree covered, contrasting strangely with the towering modern office and hotel blocks which now dominated the skyline.

The evening meal was served in a lavish restaurant on the top floor, offering a panoramic view of the city at dusk, with its twinkling neon lights.

Our party were seated at round tables with ten people to each. The white tablecloths were elegantly laid with gleaming silver cutlery, augmented with bone chopsticks. As if at a signal, twenty or more tall, slim girls, clad in traditional Chinese choongsam dresses came gliding into the room, bearing tureens of clear soup. This proved to be the first course of a many coursed Chinese meal – fish, poultry, meat, egg, curry, naturally rice in many guises, other sea food, and fruit which defied description. All the time the waitresses moved silently and efficiently, topping our glasses of iced water, and later dispensing most welcome coffee.

This stupendous meal was to set the pattern for the days to come.

'Salamat Datang' – the welcome was on everyone's lips. Our hosts, and our guides were to make this poignant journey so memorable for its warmth and hospitality.

The next morning, after an early breakfast, four loaded coaches departed for the Kranji War Memorial. What an impressive, and yet, moving sight. The large stone at the entrance, proclaiming 'Their Name Liveth For Evermore', and then behind, the stone steps, and carefully manicured greensward, leading to the central pillar, and flanking memorial walls, on which were engraved the names of twenty-four thousand men of many races, united in the service of the British Crown, who had given their lives, in Malaya and neighbouring lands and seas. It too was simply inscribed 'They died for all free men'.

As we arrived, we could hear the lament of the bagpipes, as two Ghurka soldiers rehearsed for the Remembrance Ceremony to take place two days later.

The Singapore Armed Forces, and the First Battalion, the Royal New Zealand Infantry Regiment, quietly took their positions at the end of each row of simple white gravestones, which spread over, and beyond the brow of the hill. Only a slight breeze disturbed the quiet, and subdued orders drilled the participating service men.

We of the Pilgrimage party moved through the serried lines of stones. An occasional gasp, or cry, as one of the widows found the last resting place of her husband, or a veteran recognised a familiar name.

I found myself, as always, appalled by the ages carved below the name. 'H. J. Cumming, Ordinary Seaman, RN, HMS Scorpion, Age 21. J. P. H.

Brembridge, Midshipman, HMS Repulse, Age 18.' Oh, the criminal waste of war!

The rehearsal over, we made our way thoughtfully back down the hill, to rejoin our coaches, and travel back to our hotel.

That afternoon, when the main body of the party were to tour the island, to rest, or go shopping, our small naval detachment were to fly via Kuala Lumpur, to Kuantan, preparatory to a service the next day, over the sites of the wrecks of HMS Prince of Wales, and HMS Repulse. The Officer in Charge was Lieut-Commander Stephen Buck, who was Assistant Defence Adviser to the British High Commission in Singapore. He, together with his wife, Rosemary, took the greatest care, and worked unceasingly to make our whole visit so memorable.

That evening Mr & Mrs Buck, Lieut-Commander Gerry Ainslie, Mrs Patsie Ainslie, the two widows, three ex Navy men, and Colour Sergeant Arthur Webb, of the Royal Marines, dined under an attap awning at the Hyatt Hotel, Kuantan, to the gentle lapping of the South China Sea, as the restless waters moved constantly on the beach, only a few feet away. We fed royally, before turning in, to be lulled to sleep by this unceasing noise.

On the morning of November 8th, we were taxied to the military airport at Kuantan, and there we boarded a Sea King helicopter, of the Royal Malaysian Air Force. I remember especially a gentle giant of a member of the air-crew, who saw to our comfort. Particularly was he solicitous over one of the widows, Mrs Paget, who had difficulty in walking, but nevertheless was determined to fly out over the watery grave of the two ships. We were warned that we would land on a Malaysian Naval Auxiliary vessel, but if the sea were choppy, we might have to be winched down. This did not deter the intrepid ladies.

It was a bright day, with fresh breeze, just light clouds scudding across the sea.

"A day just like when we were spotted by the Japanese bombers, and sunk," said Chief Petty Officer Northcott, reliving his memories.

The Malaysian vessel 'K. D. Raja Jarom' was riding in position, some few miles off the coast. We had hoped that from the air, it might be possible to distinguish the wrecks, lying a short distance apart, but we were told that the onset of the monsoon was now disturbing the sea bed, and the two huge ships were not to be seen. We circled the small ship, and the pilot made an impeccable landing.

We were greeted aboard by Commander Bala of the Royal Malay Navy, and taken into the wardroom for refreshments, and to meet the other officers.

The quarterdeck of the ship had been cleared, and there, together with the Christian members of the ship's crew, we assembled for the Service of Remembrance.

The sea, 10 or 12 feet below, was running fast, and there was just a slight hum from Raja Jarom's engines, as they held her steady, in position. We stood bareheaded by the taffrail, the freshening wind plucking at our sparse hair, and jingling the multi-coloured medal ribbons.

Lieut-Commander Gerry Ainslie read a short prayer for deliverance from the dangers of the sea, and the violence of the enemy. This was followed by the hymn 'Eternal Father, strong to save'. We were only a party of a dozen or so, including the handful of Malays, but the sound of those voices over the sea seemed to echo and flow, quite undisturbed by anything but nature's brushing of the waves.

Marine Maurice Edwards recited Binyon's famous lines 'They shall not grow old', and then each one of us committed a wreath to the sea. From the Royal Navy, a huge anchor of red carnations, from the two widows, rings of poppies, and from the National Federation of Far Eastern Prisoner of War Clubs and Associations, and from the Royal Marines, two further wreaths of red. Maurice Edwards sprinkled into the water 840 poppies, one to represent each man who died when the two ships were sunk on that sad December day, 44 years before. They were hurried away into the distance, as Royal Marine Sergeant Webb sounded the Last Post.

We were left with our private thoughts, of friends and colleagues in the services, those who perished at sea, those we left in the jungle, and those who had no known grave.

Reveille blew crisp and clear, tensions were relaxed, tears were dried, throats were cleared. We moved silently back to the helicopter. It was a long time after, but we had remembered those men of far off days.

We returned to the Hyatt Hotel to relax until it was time to fly back to Singapore. I hadn't a pair of swimming trunks with me, but Lt-Com Ainslie lent me his. I had a marvellous swim in the South China Sea. I never aspired to carry a Field Marshal's baton, but at least, I had worn a Commander's trunks!

During our absence up country, other parties had been to Changi Prison, to the Residence of the British High Commissioner, and to Labuan. I had conjured hopes of perhaps getting to Palembang, but although this never came to fruition, I feel most privileged to have taken part in that modest ceremony off Kuantan.

Rosemary Buck had kindly offered to take us to what remained of the former Naval Base on the Johore Straits the next afternoon, and I was determined to do a little private exploration on my own in the morning.

I climbed to the top of Fortcanning Hill. Everything I remembered had gone. Not a brick remained of the barracks, signal tower, or 'Battle-box'. There was no trace of the road past the small swimming pool (officers, for the use of). It was now a public park, with a shelter. The view of Keppel

Harbour was hidden by the tall, new buildings. I descended to Collyers Quay, and Change Alley. Here I should find a few souvenirs to take home.

I purchased two silk nightdresses for my wife, and I collected several brooches, orchids plated with gold, some toys for the grandchildren, and a packet of chopsticks, as a little souvenir.

I just had time to route my way back past St Andrew's Cathedral. I had wanted to see the memorial to the Australian nurses, who had been brutally put to death on Bancka Island. Eventually, I found it, and was busy adjusting my camera, when a voice behind me said

"Too dark."

Just two words, but they were from a Japanese.

"Can you read what it says?" I said.

He squinted through his thick glasses.

I read it to him.

IN HONOURED MEMORY OF FORTY ONE AUSTRALIAN ARMY NURSES WHO LOST THEIR LIVES IN THE CAUSE OF HUMANITY. MALAYA, BANCKA ISLAND AND SUMATRA – FEBRUARY, 1942.

HRH Duke of Kent speaking to the author at Kranji War Memorial, November, 1985.

"They were murdered by the Japanese," I said simply.
"Ah so." That is all. It didn't mean much to him.

After a cold lunch, we had a short time before Rosemary Buck was to collect us, and drive us north to the Johore Straits. On the way, we passed by Singapore's Little India preparing for the Hindu Deepavali, or Festival of Lights. I was most impressed by the cleanliness everywhere, but then I learned that even dropping a cigarette butt or paper wrapper could result in a fine of up to 500 dollars. There were other laws and habits upheld by this multi-racial, and apparently harmonious, society, which were to be applauded. Possession of drugs could result in the death sentence, apart from controlled racehorse betting, gambling is illegal; jaywalking across the wide highways can result in a fine; long hair on males is regarded unfavourably; smoking is prohibited in many public places, and tipping is discouraged.

The multi-million pound naval base was unrecognisable. It was just a memory of Empire. The Battle for Malaya, and Singapore, which had had such a fundamental effect on the views of the peoples of the East, and in fact, the whole world, and had ended the days of the Battleship.

The next day was Remembrance Sunday. This was the climax of our visit. His Royal Highness the Duke of Kent, the Right Hon. Michael

Heseltine, then Secretary of State for Defence, and Field Marshal Sir Edwin Bramall, Chief of Defence Staff of Great Britain, were among the many honoured guests.

The Service of Remembrance was commenced by Major (Retd) Derrick Coupland, President of the Singapore Ex-Services Association. Seven religions were represented (Muslim, Buddhist, Christian, Hindu, Jewish, Sikh and Zoroastrian), and a prayer for the fallen was said by the British High Commissioner, His Excellency Sir Hamilton Whyte.

To say that the service was impressive, at the early hour of 7.30 in the morning, would be a gross understatement. The whole atmosphere, the colourful red poppies, contrasting with the green hillside, the service uniforms, intermingled with the many hundred civilian dresses and suits, the still, clear of nature's morning, blended with the bugles and bagpipes of the Honour Guard.

After the ceremony, the principals passed among us, and I was pleased to have a word with HRH. He had clearly spotted my Pacific Campaign medal, and asked me about my service in the Royal Navy. He wanted to know whether my imprisonment had affected my subsequent health, and about my family back home.

I was surprised to learn on my return home that many people had spotted me on television, as the cameras panned across the scene.

Raffles Hotel is, of course, very well known. This was to be the venue for our lunch, and the Guest of Honour was HRH The Duke of Kent. A lavish meal was provided by the generosity of many individuals and companies, and afterwards, following the toasts, we were entertained to a Singapore Spectacular by a Malay Dance Troupe, a Maori Cultural Group, and some young Chinese musicians.

As if that was not enough, in the evening we had a Dinner Cruise on an authentic Chinese Junk. We traversed Keppel Harbour, and anchored some few miles out in the twilight, when a very aromatic, Chinese buffet was served. I couldn't help thinking then, of Friday, February 13th, 1942, when from almost the same point, we had watched the flames and smoke of Singapore, from HMS Tapah, stationed on the edge of the minefield, to guide the small shiploads of evacuees, fleeing from the wrath of the Japanese.

On the morrow, we were to be gone, to land back at Brize Norton, early in the dawn, to a crisp, white November morning.

An unforgettable journey. To many people, thank you.

At Changi Airport, Stephen and Rosemary Buck, shepherded us through the preliminaries.

At the final 'gate', Rosemary handed to each of the seven of our party (3 widows, 3 ex prisoners of war, and the Royal Marine Sergeant) a small carrier bag. Inside was a photograph album, its cover decorated with poppies, together with a pack of about two dozen photographs, taken during our stay. It was an unexpected and magnanimous gesture.

So, my final memory of Singapore was one of kindness, and hospitality. I was one of the lucky ones.

So many individuals, associations, companies, services and departments had combined their efforts to make this Pilgrimage worthy of all those who shared some of their lifetime in that Eastern corner of the world.

Postscript

The enduring argument over whether or not it was right to drop the Atom Bomb on Hiroshima and Nagasaki still goes on. I feel however that had the Allies decided not to explode those devastating weapons, these words

Survivors from Cruiser HMS Exeter, and Destroyer HMS Encounter, taken at Nagasaki, Japan after the Japanese surrender.

237

would never have been written. Such was our situation in Palembang, that had the war in the East lasted more than a very few more weeks, then only a handful of men would have survived in Sungei Geron POW camp. Only the dramatic ending of hostilities, which came about purely because of the use of the Atom Bomb, saved us. In my opinion it also saved many thousands of other Allied and Japanese lives, since as Winston Churchill stated, the Japanese military clique was determined to defend Japan to the death rather than accept defeat. As it was, on August 10th the Japanese Government agreed to an ultimatum, and the terms of their surrender were accepted on 14th of the same month.

The second point I would like to make is this.

Not infrequently, our Japanese captors made the point that the war would last for a hundred years. I don't know the origin of this, but it was a statement not restricted to Palembang. I have heard it repeated by other FEPOWs, and it has been reported in other instances.

We know that in the war of arms, the Japanese nation were quite conclusively beaten. Now, however, nearly five decades later, with the 'war' less than halfway through, we in the West seem ready to accept second place to them in the world of commerce. We welcome their expansion into our industrial markets, we acquiesce to their bland statements of trade equality.

To our European sensibilities, their courtesies, their smiles, their promises, all seem to be believed, without question.

One of the golden rules we learned within the confines of the barbed wire was always to be wary, always to be on guard, and never, ever to turn our backs.

We remember that when the Japanese swept down through Malaya, and into Singapore, they came with promises to the Malays and the Chinese. When they invaded the Dutch East Indies, and beyond, they spread wondrous stories about Asia for the Asiatics. They spoke of the saviours of the coloured races from the yoke of the white man. They told the gospel of the Greater South-East Asia Co-Prosperity Scheme.

In a few short years, the Chinese, the Malays, the Burmese, the Indonesians, and all the indigenous peoples of the countries which were overrun, learned differently.

The late Bishop of Birmingham, the Right Reverend D. John Leonard Wilson, KCMG, DD, DSC, MA (formerly Bishop of Singapore) who was also a captive of the Japanese, once said that we should forgive, but not forget. In remembering we should learn from our experiences, and be careful of 'face' values.

Page 128 (Sungei Geron)

... it was a strange looking array of men who mounted the lorries that day. We needed our hands to load and climb on to the vehicle, and so, from every belt or rope waistband hung pots and pans, crude cloth bags, clogs, hats, drinking tins, and a dozen and one other articles. Everything was precious, and nothing was ever discarded...

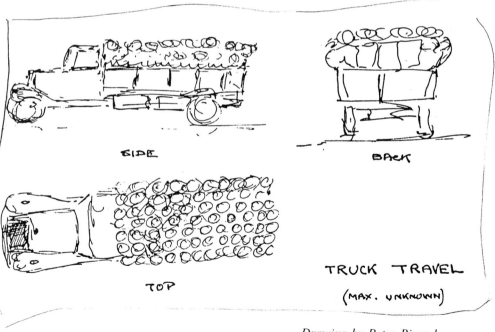

SIDE

BACK

TOP

TRUCK TRAVEL

(MAX. UNKNOWN)

Drawing by Peter Bivand.

Appendix I

Schedule of HM Naval Ships and Auxiliaries in Evacuation of Singapore, February, 1942, onwards.

Name	Commanding Officer	Last News
Aircraft Tender No. 941		Swamped and sunk
Andrew		No information
Anking		Arrived Batavia
Blumut	Cdr F. Livingstone	Captured, Muntok
Bagan		Scuttled, Palembang
Ban Hong Liong	Lt Butler	No information
Bulan	Cdr G. Bayley	Reached Batavia
Circe	Lt Bruce	Reached Batavia
Cecilia	Brig Paris	Not known
Dragonfly, HMS	Lt Iley	Bombed Sebayer Strait
Dymas	Lt R. Banks	Captured, Muntok
Daisy		Reached Djambi River
Eureka 'O'		Beached, Durian Strait
Elizabeth	Lt Beckwith	Sunk, gunfire, Bancka
Excise	Cdr H. Moorhead	Captured, Muntok
Fuh Wo	Lt N. Cook	Reached Batavia
Fanling, ML	Lt Upton	Sunk by gunfire, Bancka
Florence Nightingale	Capt Kirkwood	Damaged, beached, Sinkep
Grasshopper, HMS	Cdr Hoffman	Bombed, Sebayer Strait
Giang Bee	Lt H. Lanchester	Sunk by gunfire, Berhala
Hungjao	Lt R. Henman	No information
Hong Fatt	Lt Bull (AIF)	Captured, Muntok
Heather	Cdr E. St Aubyn	Not known
Hwa Tong	Lt Brown	Sunk, Palembang River
Jarak	Lt Hooper	Damaged, scuttled, Singkep
Jerantut	Lt G. Cooper	Scuttled, Palembang River
Kuala	Lt F. Caithness	Sunk off Singkep Island
Kung Wo	Lt Com E. Thompson	Sunk off Singkep Island
Kulit		No information
Klias	Lt H. Smyth	Scuttled in Palembang River
Li Wo	Lt T. Wilkinson (Posthumous VC)	Sunk by gunfire, Bancka Strait
Launch 36 (RAF)	Cdr P. Reid	Captured, Muntok
Lipis	Lt Steele	Bombed and sunk, Singapore
Launch 105 (RAF)		Sunk, Malan Tigan Island

Motor Launch 310	Lt H. Bull	Aground on Pulau Kaibang (Air Vice Marshall Pulford, and Rear Admiral Spooner)
Motor Launch 311	Lt W. Christmas	Sunk by gunfire off Muntok
Motor Launch 432	Lt L. Herd	Captured off Muntok
Motor Launch 433	Lt Com H. Campey	Sunk by gunfire, Bancka Strait
Motor Launch 1062	Lt MacMillan	Sunk by gunire, Bancka Strait
Mata Hari	Lt A. Carson	Captured, Muntok
Mary Rose	Capt S. Mulok	Captured, Muntok

THE WHITE ENSIGN REPLACED BY THE JAP FLAG.
11 AM FEB.18TH 42. OFF MUNTOK.
Peter Bivand.

Malacca	Lt J. Morphat	Scuttled? No more news
Medusa	Lt Brown	Reached Batavia
Minesweeper 54	Lt Butcher	Reached Batavia
Pahlawan, ML	Lt P. Cork	Captured Muntok
Pulo Soegi	Lt Martin	Sunk by Gunfire, Muntok
Pengail	Lt N. Bell	No information
Ping Wo	Lt J. Fant	No information
Pinnace No. 503		Captured, Bancka
Pinnace No. 54		Sunk by gunfire, Bancka
Panglina	Lt H. Riches	Reached Batavia
Pinnace No. 56		Captured, Bancka
Rosemary	Lt D. Fiennes	Captured, Muntok
Scorpion, HMS	Lt Com C. Ashworth	Sunk by gunfire, Berhala
Siang Wo	Lt A. Woodley	Bombed and beached Muntok
Shu Kwang	Cdr Thompson	Bombed and sunk, Berhala
Seaplane Tender No. 257		Captured, Bancka
Seaplane Tender No. 258		Captured, Bancka
SS Redang	S. Rasmussen	Sunk by gunfire, Berhala
SS Relau	Capt Chamberlain	Captured, Muntok
SS Rentau	Capt Baddeley	Captured, Muntok
Sin Keng Seng	Capt Smith	Not known
Sin Aik Lee	Lt J. Brander	Sunk leading Batavia
Scott Harley		Arrived Batavia
Seaplane Tender No. 262		Captured Muntok
Seaplane Tender No. 328		Damaged and scuttled, Moesi
St Breock (Tug)	Lt A. Clarke	Sunk, Sebayer Strait
Tanjong Pinang	Lt B. Shaw	Sunk by gunfire, Pulo Obar
Tapah	Lt J. Hancock	Captured, Bancka
Tien Kwang	Lt Briggs	Bombed, Pompom Island
Trang	Lt H. Rigden	Aground, Scuttled
Tingarro	Lt Whitworth	No information
Vyner Brooke	Lt R. Borton	Sunk, Bancka Strait
Wo Kwang	Lt Robinson	Reached Batavia
War Sirdar		Aground near Batavia
White Swan (FE5)		Reached Batavia
Yin Ping	Lt P. Wilkinson	Sunk by gunfire, Bancka
Yacht C.14		No information
Yacht FE6	Fl Lt Anderson	Left Muntok for Batavia
FE4 (ex Rompin)	Lt Com Spaull	Captured Muntok
Refueller 1186		Captured Muntok

There were certainly others including water boats, small sailing craft, the Sultan of Johore's yacht, and miscellaneous unarmed craft.

Many of them which reached Batavia, or other parts of Java, were later sunk.

I have indeed seen a list, which names a further 85 vessels, in addition to the 81 listed above.

(See also Appendix II – Appendix III).

Appendix II

"The Final Action of 'HMS Li Wo' near Banka Island."

Report by Chief Petty Officer Charlie H. Rogers, D/JX 125387.

After returning from my last job in Singapore, Johore Straits Patrol, I was detailed to join HMS 'Li Wo', a river boat of 1000 tons, and speed of 15 knots. It had one 4" gun forward, two twin Lewis guns, and one Halman Projector, and ASDIC installation procedure.

My joining orders were to report to Orange Hotel, at 1500 hours, February 13th, 1942. The Japanese were occupying Singapore very quickly, and the hotel was under fire from trench mortars. On reporting I was detailed to take a party of men from about eight different branches to join the Li Wo. Having loaded the lorries with provisions, we proceeded to Keppel Harbour, where the ship was anchored about 1 mile off shore.

Once on board, the First Lieutenant, Lt Stanton, gave me my orders, which were to detail off gun crews, lookouts, and men for the engine and boiler rooms. About midnight we found we were no longer able to communicate with shore, but were advised by another ship to move off. This we attempted, but the Commanding Officer, Lt Wilkinson, found it extremely difficult owing to the lack of marker buoys, and decided to anchor until morning. At dawn, the gun crews were closed up, and the ship got under way.

During the afternoon of the 14th, we were bombed, but luckily no hits were scored. At about 1900 hours, we anchored in a small bay, on one of the islands. The next morning, we were bombed again, but escaped being hit. The planes were very low, which gave us a chance to retaliate with machine gun fire. The Captain then decided he would make a dash through 'bomb alley', the Bancka Straits. Whilst proceeding to this area, we sighted a convoy of about thirty ships, on the horizon, off our starboard bow, heading in the direction of Bancka Island, but were unable to identify them, until we closed to about 16,000 yards. Suddenly, on the horizon, dead ahead, we sighted the tops of three funnels, which turned out to be a Jap cruiser, carrying 6" guns. We also sighted off our port bow a Jap destroyer, heading the convoy, which was in sections of four and six ships. The Captain was also certain that its mission was to support the invasion of Singapore.

Word very rapidly passed around the ship that we were going to go into action, and that the leading ship, in the nearest section, would be our first target. Battle ensigns were hoisted, one on Gaff and one at Masthead, as we closed rapidly with the 4" gun ready to fire. With no signs of enemy fire, we closed to 2000 yards, when the order to open fire was given. The first salvo fell short, the second crossed the bow, and the third scored a direct hit, just under the bridge. She appeared to be on fire, and turned to port. The other ships turned to starboard, and commenced firing at us with small calibre guns.

The damaged ship was now approaching the Li Wo, still firing, so the CO decided to ram her. We hit her at top speed amidships, and became interlocked, our bows being buckled back – we were now really at close quarters. A machine gun duel took place, which was fast and furious, with many men being killed, or wounded. The Li Wo gunners eventually wiped out two guns, which caused the Japs to abandon ship, which by this time was well on fire.

Whilst all this was happening, the Jap cruiser had circled around behind us, and was heading straight for us at high speed. We eventually became disentangled from the crippled Jap ship, and set course away from the cruiser. The cruiser opened fire, and we noticed that the enemy destroyer that had been heading for us on the opposite side was turning away. No doubt she knew that we were at the mercy of the cruiser as we were outgunned and out ranged.

We zigzagged as the salvos fell. We had a poor opinion of the Jap gunners as her salvos of 6" shells were falling wide, sometimes 300 yards or more off target. However, gradually they came nearer and nearer, and shrapnel was now hitting us, causing many men to be killed or wounded. I personally was hit with three pieces of shrapnel in the leg, but not seriously wounded. After about the ninth salvo, we were told to abandon ship, so all who were able to jumped overboard. Very soon afterwards, the cordite locker at the rear of the gun, and amidships, was hit. The last sight I had of the Li Wo, as she started on her last voyage to the bottom of the ocean, was something I shall never forget. Her ensigns were still flying, and the Captain was standing on the bridge, and although listing to port, she was still underway. Then suddenly, she disappeared – the Li Wo was no more. For this action, Lieut Wilkinson was awarded the posthumous Victoria Cross.

HMS Li Wo had fought her last action, and was now at rest on the bottom of the ocean. The few remaining men who had escaped were at the mercy of the sea. There was no land in sight. Eventually in the distance, a lifeboat was sighted, bobbing up and down in the swell. Leading Seaman Thompson and myself struck out towards it, but just as we were approaching, we noticed a ship from the convoy coming towards us. We swam away as fast as possible, and on glancing back, saw the ship ram the lifeboat. Around this area, there were about thirty men struggling for their lives, little realising that the worst part was yet to come. The Japs were not content to leave us to our fate, but circled around, and opened up a murderous attack with machine guns, hand grenades, coal and wood. It was just plain cold blooded murder. Amidst the hell, men could be heard crying out for mercy, but still the Japs continued their 'sport'. I lay on my back, with my arms outstretched and luckily no more shots came in my direction.

After what seemed like an eternity, the ship moved off, leaving the ones that had cheated death again, once more to their fate. Those that were able to, made towards the lifeboat, which by now was about half submerged – there were only eight survivors. Lieut Stanton had a bullet hole through the back of his head, another officer was wounded in the stomach, and had part of his hand shot away. Petty Officer Huntley had his foot blown off, and was in a very bad condition. We helped each other into the lifeboat, which was now submerged to the gunwhale, and tried to make the best of a bad situation. There were no oars, food or medical supplies – all we could do was to let the boat drift. As we drifted, we saw the ship that we had crippled – it was also drifting, and still on fire. We spent a very cold night, and as dawn broke, one of the officers, whom I had been holding in my arms, died from his severe shrapnel wounds. I informed Lt Stanton, who helped me to take off his life-belt, and put him over the side, where he slowly sank below the surface.

After about 2 days, we eventually saw our first sign of land, about 16 miles away. We were all in rather bad shape, but ignoring the sharks which had been swimming around us continuously, and yet never attacked us once, we attempted to tow the boat towards the shore, but all to no avail.

A Jap destroyer came and had a sniff at us, and we wondered if our earlier experiences would be repeated. However, they only gave us a cursory glance, and sailed away, leaving us to our fate, but we were not going to be beaten.

The boat was now getting extremely waterlogged, and we expected her to go down at any time. Lt Stanton decided to try to get to the Jap ship, which was now about 2 miles away, and so, along with the gunnery officer, they started to swim, but the tides were against them, and they were lucky enough to be picked up during the night.

The almost totally submerged boat now contained myself, Leading Seaman Wilding, Leading Seaman Spencer, Petty Officer Huntley, a Malay called Tel, and an unknown soldier. PO Huntley died as a result of his wounds, and the soldier was lost overboard. Leading Seaman Spencer set off to swim ashore, but was unsuccessful, and was picked up extremely exhausted.

Only three of us were now left – myself, Ldg Seaman Wilding, and the Malayan, so we decided to let the boat drift to wherever the tide would take her. As luck would have it, another partly submerged boat drifted towards us, just before dark. We swam towards it and found that it was a naval whaler, split down the centre, but preferable, because it had oars and sail. We boarded her, rigged her for sailing, and had just picked out a sight of land to sail for when we heard yells, and shouts. They came from two rafts we hadn't previously seen. On one raft there were three men, and on the other, four. They were also survivors from the Li Wo, and we were glad to find they had a tin of biscuits with them. I could only let a few on board the whaler, and then we took the rafts in tow. We were helped by a strong wind which sprang up, but the boat was submerged up to the gunwhale, so we were actually sitting in water all the time.

During the night, a Jap patrol boat approached, and shone her searchlight on us, but because we had dropped over the lee side, they did not detect us.

My aim was to try to reach the land ahead, which I knew to be Sumatra, but the tides were so strong, that we could only drift with them. At about 2 am we sighted land straight ahead, so I put six men on the oars, and we started rowing for our lives. We were still rowing 4 hours later, but I knew we were getting nearer to the shore. We went ashore several hours later, on Bancka Island, along with a Jap invasion party, who seemed to ignore us until later, when we were taken prisoner.

After the war, the Daily Telegraph report of the action states:

"Lt Wilkinson told his crew, that rather than try to escape, he had decided to engage the convoy, and fight to the last. After little over an hour, HMS Li Wo had been critically damaged and was sinking. Lt Wilkinson then decided to ram his principal target, the large transport. HMS Li Wo's gallant fight ended when, her shells spent, and under heavy fire from the enemy cruiser, Lt Wilkinson finally ordered 'abandon ship'. He himself went down with her. There were only about ten survivors, who were made prisoners."

VC   Lieut Thomas Wilkinson
CGM   Petty Officer Arthur Thompson
DSM   A B Albert Spendlove
DSO   Sub-Lt Ronald Stanton, RNR
DSM   Ldg Seaman Victor Spencer

Mentioned in Dispatches
Lt Edgar Derbridge,
Sub. Lt J. Petherbridge, } All killed
A B Desmond Palmer

CPO Charles Rogers,
Ldg Seaman William Wilding,
A B John Smith.

Appendix III

Slow Boat to Bancka

An abridged transcript of a handwritten account by LAC Alan Anstead of the journey in PB258 from Singapore to Bancka Island in February, 1942.

PB258 doesn't convey very much, but to just a few of us Air/Sea Rescue Service marine types it does recall one never to be forgotten journey from Singapore to Bancka Island, Netherlands East Indies, in a 40' seaplane tender. . .

Early Wednesday morning, February 11th 1942, I received instructions to proceed from our temporary base to Kallang pier, Singapore, and join other A/S R units, and stand by to help evacuate certain personnel from AHQ. . .

Came the dawn, Thursday, February 12th, the AHQ 'bods' arrived, and at last we got under way. Once past the breakwater, we could see Pulu Bukum in the distance, belching flame and black smoke – it was one of the small islands that had been developed for oil storage, and had been set on fire when the British evacuated – it was an awe inspiring sight.

Having groped through the narrow channel between Sambu and Bintan, we eventually left Sambu behind us, and here made contact with our CO and joined up with the remainder of the boats. The convoy now comprised two seaplane tenders, two pinnaces and a small service dinghy – having formed up some sort of line, we set course south west for the shores of Sumatra.

We travelled all this night, and reached the mouth of a river about noon on Friday, February 13th – here we decided to take cover as the Jap fighter and bomber planes were extremely active, and we didn't exactly wish for more trouble.

Our plan was to move under cover of darkness as the wake from our boats made us so obvious but that night it failed to mature, as when at dusk we were about to get under way, the two pinnaces found themselves aground in the silt, so they were unable to proceed.

At sunrise we gathered ourselves together and formed into convoy order again, P53 taking the lead, P54, 257, 258 following – Bancka Straits next stop. This was not a very comfortable journey for us as our craft was far from complete and lacked wheelhouse glazing and other refinements so we had no protection from the elements up forward, our engines were giving considerable trouble as the diesel oil we had taken aboard at

Singapore was very dirty, and we hadn't time to filter it – as a result our engines were continually choking as the fuel filters and injectors became blocked. Steering the craft was also difficult at this point as we had two huge drums of fuel oil stored, and this weight combined with the heavy swell astern caused us to take heavy plunges into the wave troughs which sometimes might easily have ended in disaster – there were times when we turned complete – circling with our bows completely submerged and our stern well out of the water – it was almost impossible to hold the craft on a steady course once the weather had caught our flat transom – at this time we had only one engine operational – for many miles during this day's trip we were running on one engine – first the port, and then the starboard engine, whilst the fuel systems were being cleaned. One or two of the lads spent most of the day and the ensuing night continuously cleaning fuel filters, injectors and pipes. We made this nerve racking journey often well in the rear of the other boats. We had no charts aboard, so would have been in a fine pickle if we had lost them – but we did know which way it was to Sumatra – anywhere South would eventually find Sumatra or Java, so we weren't unduly worried.

The evening of Saturday, 14th, found us still plodding along, and all eyes and ears cocked for Jap aircraft, and half hoping we had left them behind us. Just before dark we sighted a small gunboat on the horizon. What could it be? RN, Dutch Navy, or Jap? She didn't challenge us, so we kept our fingers crossed. She was only a small craft of about 80 feet or so, and looked as if she was at anchor. Eventually 53 ran up her RAF ensign – 54 and 258 followed suit – we couldn't do likewise as like most things, we were deficient. She saw the signals and ran up a White Ensign – quite a relief for us – we thought that at last we were among friends. We gave our engines the gun – we did have both running together sometimes, but not often. Maybe we'd get some gen from her? Our radio was U/S and had never worked, so was of no use. Sparks said it was like most of our equipment – deficient. Unfortunately the news we learned was not encouraging – it seemed the Japs had landed paratroops at Palembang in Sumatra.

After bidding our Navy and Army friends 'goodbye', and 'good luck' – she was loaded to capacity with RAC troops who had been evacuated from Singapore at the last moment – our little convoy moved slowly and cautiously southwards down the Bancka Straits. It was very shallow here and abounding with sandbanks – we didn't want that running aground business all over again. We dropped our anchors for a while whilst the CO held a conference with the little boat skippers to decide our future movements. We were very close inshore to Sumatra now and could clearly see the mangrove swamps sweeping right down to the water's edge.

Just as the sun was about to set on the horizon westward, we weighed our anchor and set course North. We were now between the northernmost part of Bancka Island, and Sumatra. We clearly couldn't proceed south, as the Japs were well and truly blocking our way – there was only one course to be taken – we must try and nip around the other side of the Island, and make a dash for Java. We set off in great haste – the fitter had serviced both our engines, whilst we were at anchor so now we had two serviceable engines – for a while anyway. With both engines 'full ahead' off we set. It felt good to have power at hand after so much trouble. The two smaller boats had been ordered to keep close, and follow the pinnaces. 257 paired up with 53, and we stuck to 54, and all went well for a while. We were making quite good speed. It was dark now and the flashing light from the lighthouse on Bancka Head (Muntok) was visible on our starboard hand. The Dutch had left their navigation lights on in these parts to help the evacuation.

The first thing to upset us was the sight of a steely blue searchlight, sweeping the seas well astern of us – it eventually picked up our naval friend, the patrol vessel – a few shots were exchanged, and then regretfully, we saw her burst into flames – she had been hit by incendiary fire.

The searchlight was still sweeping the seas, and more gunfire flashes split the darkness. Soon it was to be our turn. The same steely blue searchlight had found us. A few warning shots from a machine gun, or the like, whizzed uncomfortably close. We didn't wait for more, so we scattered. 54 shot off to port, and we put hard over to starboard, and gave our engines everything we had. We dodged them after a while, and kept well on the move – fortunately our engines were both behaving themselves extremely well for a change. Eventually, after much listening and scanning of the almost pitch black night, we found P54, and again took up our position aft, and attempted to continue our journey. Unfortunately, soon afterwards, both our engines conked. After much shouting to attract attention, 54 took us in tow – those ruddy engines!! Our trusty fitter got weaving as soon as we were made fast, and eventually got them operational about an hour before dawn – we didn't know at the time how fortunate that was, as hardly had he reported them both OK, when to our dismay, and I might add, horror, up popped that steely blue light again. This time it was us, and they'd caught us both fair and square, in the beam. We couldn't see what she was at the time, except that it was a darn sight too big for us. She was not very far astern right on our port quarter – it was most uncomfortable being floodlit at such an early hour.

We waited for a few moments, not knowing quite what to do – it seemed years, and that shape astern seemed to be growing larger every minute. 54 moved first – she ran up her RAF ensign – it looked very colourful in that light, but that was to be the last we should see of it, as no sooner had it reached the top of the staff, when there came a stream of pink tracer shells at great speed in our direction – they whizzed past my wheelhouse – missing me by inches and buried themselves in the stern of 54 – that was finis for her – we were on tow at the time, but our engines were now serviceable, thank God! We cut the tow rope, started up and went along the now sinking 54, keeping on the lee side, just in case they decided to have a pot at us too. We took off all those remaining aboard. Most of the lads were old pals – some were very badly injured, and others had been blown overboard by the explosion. The lucky ones didn't even get their feet wet, and just jumped aboard our craft – we were more than busy now, and I must confess we forgot all about the Jap vessel in our efforts to get the injured aboard, and make them comfortable. We learned that one of the lads had been killed outright – the skipper was also past our help. We would also have to search the water for others. By this time it was light, and we could see what we were doing – 54's engine room bulkhead had held and she was still afloat – her stern well under, and her bows reaching for the sky. We could also see what had hit her, and hunted us during the night – four destroyers and a four funnelled cruiser – rather overwhelming odds for such small craft as ours.

The cruiser was now ordering us by flashlamp to proceed to Muntok. 'Proceed Muntok'. 'Proceed Muntok' in morse plain language – rather galling, but what could we do – by this time our little boat was heavily overloaded, we already had seven crew and had taken aboard these eleven survivors, and were still searching for more. Later, we spotted a raft to the north of us, so went to investigate, and found four survivors on a raft – they were survivors of the Li Wo – two officers and two seamen – they were in a rather bad state. One of the officers had been shot at with machine guns whilst in the water, and had managed to stop one, which just parted his hair for him – a lucky escape. We managed to fix them up with something to eat and drink, but they were so parched with thirst that they had great difficulty in swallowing anything – I believe these lads were almost the sole survivors from that gallant little ship, the Li Wo. We took their raft in tow, as we were being continuously buzzed by Jap reccy float planes, and it may have come in handy – one never could tell – we made every one as comfortable as we could, and set course for the lighthouse on the northern tip of the island.

We were overloaded for this type of craft, twenty-four in all, and quite a few lying around on makeshift stretchers – two on the engine covers, two in the cabin, and two on the cabin top – the boat was almost unmanageable, so we decided to put the able bodied ashore to make their own way. The raft was used for this purpose, and the breakers carried it towards the shore, laden with bods – some swam alongside. Having seen them safely ashore, about seven of us remained with the injured, and set course for Muntok and come what may. During our journey, we started ditching anything we thought might be of use to the enemy – what arms and ammunition we had, tools etc.

After a while we found the harbour. What a sight greeted us – landing barges, troop carriers, motor gun boats, and the like – quite a hornet's nest. They were all flying the now familiar 'poached egg' – how we grew to hate that flag.

Once alongside the pier we met our first Japanese soldier – a ragged, short arsed, little bloke, grinning like a Cheshire cat – what a horrible sight. We landed our dead and wounded.

From hence onwards we were prisoners of the Japanese, and that's another story.

Appendix IV

The Last Hours of HMS Encounter

This narrative would not be complete without an account of the final days of HMS Encounter, related to me by survivors, after the ending of hostilities, and also as recorded by both British and Japanese authorities.

After I had left the ship at Singapore in December, 1941, she continued to operate principally on convoying duties in the Java Sea, in company with ships of the ABDA Command (American, British, Dutch and Australian forces).

When Singapore became untenable as a naval base, the Eastern Fleet, such as it was, retreated to Java, and operated from Batavia and Sourabaya.

The mounting toll of losses in the Atlantic, and the Mediterranean, had meant that the British Eastern Fleet was parlously short of strength, and the early sinking of the Prince of Wales and Repulse, off Malaya, accompanied by the grounding of the aircraft carrier, Indomitable, during her working up trials in the West Indies, prior to joining the Fleet, denuded that squadron of the support of capital ships, and air cover. In fact, this Force Z, as it was to be known, very largely was comprised of older vessels, which could be spared from other areas of action, supplemented by equally dated cruisers and destroyers of the Royal Netherlands East Indies Navy, and a small representative force from both the Australian and American Navies.

In subsequent attacks on the Japanese invasion fleet, heavily protected by naval ships, Force Z suffered grievous losses. Regretfully, while the strikes achieved significant successes, the overall inquest on these actions sums them up as being ill-planned, futile, and tragically wasteful.

By February 24th, the Allied naval forces had been savagely reduced, and on that day, Dutch Admiral Helfrich ordered the cruiser Exeter, Australian cruiser Perth, and destroyers Electra, Jupiter, and Encounter from Tanjong Priok (the port of Batavia) to Sourabaya, to join the Dutch ships under Admiral Doorman.

On the afternoon of February 27th, the combined ABDA group led by cruisers De Ruyter (Dutch), Exeter (British), Houston (American), Perth (Australian) and Java (Dutch), sailed with destroyer escort (including Encounter) to intercept a convoy of invasion transports off Java, accompanied by a heavy concentration of Japanese cruisers and destroyers.

Within a short space of time, the two opposing fleets were in action, the 8" guns of the enemy considerably outranging all but the 8" guns on

Houston, and Exeter (which had only four 8" guns still serviceable).

The other Allied 6" cruisers, and the destroyers, with 4.7" armament had to suffer being Aunt Sallies until they were within range.

At an early stage, both the Houston and Exeter suffered minor damage, and several other ships, including the De Ruyter were straddled. The British destroyers, which had been screening the cruisers, came in for heavy fire at a range of about 18,000 yards.

Within an hour, the range had closed to about 8000 yards, and the Japanese also launched a concerted torpedo attack, coupled with shelling from the heavy cruisers. Soon after 1700 hours, Exeter sustained crucial damage to her boiler room, which reduced her speed to about 5 or 6 knots.

Some damage had been inflicted on at least two enemy cruisers and one destroyer, but the heavy fire from the enemy resulted in a direct hit on the Dutch destroyer Kortenaer, which exploded and sank immediately.

Electra, Encounter and Jupiter were ordered to make a smoke screen around Exeter, and then to launch a counter attack. As she left the protective smoke, Electra, in the van, came under concentrated fire, and was sunk.

Encounter loosed a salvo, and retreated into the smoke with Jupiter.

The author of 'A Battle History of the Imperial Japanese Navy' comments on the bravery shown by the British destroyers in countercharging a superior force of two light cruisers, and fourteen destroyers, which was in the best traditions of the British Navy.

The American destroyers left the action soon after nightfall, being low on fuel, and their torpedoes being expended.

The crippled Exeter headed for Sourabaya, with the Dutch destroyer Witte de With escorting her, while Encounter, reduced in speed, was detached to pick up the survivors of the Kortenaer, and then make for Sourabaya to refuel.

The four remaining Allied cruisers, devoid of destroyer protection, still attempted to sail north in search of the invasion convoy, but shortly before midnight, both De Ruyter, and Java, were torpedoed and sunk. The Perth and Houston were left no alternative but to head back to Batavia.

The outcome of these various actions was that from a comparative numerical force, the strength of the alliance was now the damaged cruiser Exeter, Perth and Houston, the destroyer Encounter, the American destroyer Pope, and four others.

The conclusion was inescapable. The four old American destroyers were despatched, via the Bali Strait, to Australia. They were the only four ships to escape from the Java Sea. Perth and Houston were directed to the Sunda Strait, but alas, were intercepted by a superior force, and both were sunk, with considerable loss of life.

Exeter buried her dead, refuelled, and received some emergency repairs, so that she could manage to steam at just over 20 knots. On the night of February 28th, she was instructed to sail for Colombo via Sunda Strait, escorted by Encounter and Pope. No torpedoes had been available at Sourabaya to replenish the destroyers.

Thus, the remnants of Force Z, these three ships – a damaged cruiser, and two elderly destroyers, minus their main armament, ran the gauntlet towards the Indian Ocean.

When dawn broke on that lovely Sunday morning, March 1st, all hands were at 'Action Stations'. In due course, when an enemy plane appeared, they knew that their attempt to escape by stealth would be thwarted.

At about 8 o'clock in the morning, top masts were spotted in the distance, and course was altered to take avoiding action, but an hour later, two large cruisers were sighted to the southward, and soon after, a big destroyer could be seen dead ahead, with two more cruisers a little further off. Again the destroyers resorted to smoke, to shield the Exeter, but this ploy was ineffectual because of Jap spotting aircraft now overhead.

The enemy fire was directed on Exeter, which again sustained heavy damage, and was slowed to only a few knots. The main engines had virtually stopped, the steering failed, and the gun turrets, lacking power, stood motionless. One enemy destroyer was sunk, but the odds were too great. Exeter was hit again, and being mortally impaired, with ammunition almost spent, her Captain Gordon ordered Encounter and Pope to leave her to her fate. Repeated torpedo hits were scored on the almost static ship.

Lt Cdr E. V. St J. Morgan, on Encounter, stood by, circling with smoke, until the situation was hopeless, and she herself then became the object of attention. A near miss damaged the lubrication system. The engines stopped. The noise and bustle became subdued, as the throbbing engines ceased. The ammunition was expended. The Japs continued shelling. There was nothing for it, but to abandon ship. The sea cocks, and watertight doors were opened, the boats lowered, and the Carley floats slipped away.

The last wireless signal from H 10 was

"AM HEAVILY ENGAGED BY SIX CRUISERS, AND
FOUR DESTROYERS. OUT OF ACTION".

The official Japanese naval account names four cruisers (Nachi, Haguro, Myoko, and Ashigura) and four destroyers (Yamakaze, Kawakaze, Akebono, and Ikazuchi).

From the sea, the survivors in the water could see Exeter blazing from stem to stern, as she settled and sank at about 1115, then a few minutes later, Encounter, her battle ensign still flying, rolled over and went down.

Three aircraft came over, and fired on the survivors in the water, until a signal from a cruiser sent them away, presumably after USS Pope.

Pope had headed for a rain squall, with every ounce of steam she could raise, but she was pursued by Jap planes, and after repeated dive bombing attacks, was sunk an hour later. The last Allied warship in the Java Sea had met its doom.

In the action, it was reported that seven ratings from Encounter had died. Among these were two of the Encounter 'characters'. 'Tiger' was a little Cockney humorist from Deptford. He was almost albino, and flushed pink at the least exposure to the sun – perhaps his demise was a blessing, for surely he never would have survived the tropical sun in a POW camp.

The other was the Scottish NAAFI manager, of the store cupboard, which boasted the name of 'canteen' on board.

It was almost 24 hours later before a Japanese destroyer picked up the men from out of the shark infested water, many wounded, and others suffering from immersion in fuel oil. They were taken into captivity in the Celebes, where a further thirty seven of the crew died. They had no contact with the outside world again until after the war was ended.

The monkey, Jenny, and the kitten, Smuts, had been saved from drowning. I am told the Japs kept Jenny, but threw Smuts back into the water. Perhaps from what I saw later of Jap treatment of animals, Smuts was the more fortunate.

Four years later, I was glad to revive some of my good friendships – Robert (Jock) Steel, Sid Lillywhite, Doc Hughes, and others. They had indeed been brothers in arms.

Appendix V

The reader might find the following list of some of the books that were in circulation to be of interest:

Typhoon	Conrad
Invisible Man	H. G. Wells
Theatre	W. Somerset Maugham
Four Feathers	A. E. W. Mason
And Now Goodbye	James Hilton
O Absalom	Howard Spring
Oil	Upton Sinclair
My Best Spy Story	Miscellaneous
The Refugees	Conan Doyle
Sincerity	Warwick Deeping
Century of Sea Stories	Miscellaneous
Captain Scott	S. Gwynn
Nicholas Nickleby	Charles Dickens
Haven	Taffrail
Golden Spaniard	Denis Wheatley
Jamaica Inn	Daphne Du Maurier
Grand Hotel	Vicki Baum
Century of Humour	Miscellaneous
Carrying On	Ian Hay
Traitor's Gate	Edgar Wallace
The Stars Look Down	A. J. Cronin
Greenmantle	John Buchan
Barren Metal	Naomi Jacobs
South Riding	Winifred Holtby
I was Graf Spee's Prisoner	Capt Dove
Count Luckner	Lowell Thomas
Water Gypsies	A. P. Herbert
East Wind, West Wind	Pearl Buck
The Earth in the Lord's	Taylor Caldwell
The Story of San Michele	Axel Munthe
Dodsworth	Sinclair Lewis
Three Men in a Boat	Jerome K. Jerome
Thirty Nine Steps	John Buchan
Great Unsolved Crimes	Miscellaneous
Dynasty of Death	Taylor Caldwell
The Rains Came	Louis Bromfield

Adventure	Jack London
The Citadel	A. J. Cronin
Lord of Arabia	Ibn Saud
Scarlet Pimpernel	Baroness Orczy
Roads of Destiny	O. Henry
Wind in the Willows	Kenneth Graham
This Above All	Eric Knight
Main Street	Sinclair Lewis
European Painting and Sculpture	Eric Newton

SOME CAMP HUMOUR

ARNOTT'S ARMY BISCUITS

We don't want bacon, kidney, eggs
We don't want any grill,
We don't want beans on toast because
They'd only make us ill.

Cold pickled pork would make us belch,
And so would brawn or brisket,
But send us please occasionally
A rough old ARNOTT'S Biscuit.

IF

If you can keep your temper when you get back from the docks,
All wet with sweat and on your flaming knees,
And you dash into the bathhouse, and turn on all the cocks,
And all you get are drips, like off the trees.

When you look into the rain tubs, and they're like a badger's . . .
So you shake them, and they turn to lumps of rust,
And you dash up to the water tap, and tread on lumps of glass,
And step on someone's soap, and bang your crust.

If you can wake up smiling, when the morning gilds the skies
And the rats have gone to hiding for the day,
Then you dream that you're in Blighty, and you sharply realise
That some fool's shouting 'Get up and meet the day'.

If you can keep from cursing, when you're out there in the grounds,

259

With oil and rice, and kong and beans to fry,
And just as your fire gets cracking, and you hear some rumbling sounds,
And old Peter turns the taps on in the sky.

If you can keep your temper when – oh well,
YOU AIN'T BLUE PENCIL OOMAN!!

POWs ALPHABET

A	stands for Ananas – Pineapple to you	
B	is for Benjo, or maybe for Brew	(Benjo – toilet)
C	is for Corned Beef, more precious than gold	
D	is for Dhobi, do often we're told	(Dhobi – washing)
E	stands for Empire, of which we were rooked	
F	is for Field, where big eats are cooked	
G	is for Gashbin, and naturally Grub	(Gashbin – rubbish bin)
H	is for Home, and the old local pub	
I	stands for Island – we're on the wrong one	
J	is for Jaunty – God give me a gun	(Jaunty – naval police)
K	is for Kashkan, we've got quite a few	(Kashkan – Jap officer)
L	is for Lousy, and this includes you	
M	stands for Money, and roll on that pay	
N	is for Nippon, who ain't come to stay	
O	is for Organ, Wurlitzer, not sex	
P	is for Pisang, and physical wrecks	(Pisang – banana)
Q	stands for Queer, there's some of those too	
R	is for Rations from out of the blue	
S	stands for Sick Bay, where fairy feet flip	
T	is for Tenko to see you don't skip	(Tenko – count, roll call)
U	is for Ubi, bloomin' fine tack	(Ubi – tropical potato)
V	is for Vitamins – refer to the quack	
W	stands for Water – soup to the cooks	
X	is for Christmas, read of in some books	
Y	is for Yasume, so light that dog-end	(Yasume – stand easy,
Z	is the finish, so that is the end.	rest)

Appendix VI

War Crimes Trials

The trials of twenty four Japanese and Korean guards from Palembang took place during July, August and September, 1946. They were held in Singapore before Lt Col F. A. Forsythe, MC, Major J. C. McMarth, and Major A. Dumont.

Following experience gained at the end of the European war, the Allied Forces prohibited the movement of Japanese troops, and there was apparently no difficulty in bringing our guards to trial.

However, what does become abundantly clear on reading the verbatim reports of the trials, is of the problem of producing evidence, mainly because many witnesses had by that time been sent home to the United Kingdom, and secondly, the dearth of written record at the time the offences took place. This was quite impossible because of the lack of facilities to document these happenings, and the inherent danger in keeping such records. Then again, when incidents of ill-treatment, torture, or humiliation took place, the victim was hardly in a fit state to identify his assailant(s), or to then make a positive mental and accurate timing. Some of the worst beatings, of course, occurred in secluded circumstances, and the very, very bad ones in the secrecy of Kempei Tai HQ. We never did know the precise circumstances of the death of Aircraftsman Saunders, dragged away after striking a guard, and never seen alive again.

It seems also from the trial reports that there was a reluctance to connect the death of a prisoner with bashings only a short while before, since the cause of death might also include starvation, or one of the many tropical diseases.

For these reasons, it would be presumptuous of me to do other than to try and precis the reports kept by the Public Record Office, together with extracts from the Singapore newspapers at the time.

The Prosecutor was Major F. E. Mostyn, and Defence Counsel, Mr Y. Araki.

In general it was claimed that all responsible for the well-being of prisoners of war, were in violation of the laws and usages of war, and together concerned as parties to the ill-treatment of the said prisoners, resulting in the deaths of many, and in physical and mental sufferings to many others.

The charges refer to POW Camps of Chung Hwa, Mulo School, and Sungei Geron.

The ill-treatment, according to the prosecution, included mass beatings, general humiliation and degradation. There were many instances of men working until the very day they died. Prisoners were not given adequate clothing to protect them from the sun, and were forced to live in disgraceful conditions.

Prisoners' rations, particularly fresh vegetables, were allowed to rot deliberately, and then issued when inedible. The rice ration in May, 1945, was Heavy Duty 400 grams, Light Duty 200 grams, Sick 150 grams. Doctors said a man could not live on 150 grams of rice. No meat was received at Sungei Geron from May 1944 until after the Japanese surrender in August, 1945, except on three Jap holidays, when one pig was supplied for 1200 men.

In October, 1944, the food supplied to Sungei Geron was inedible tapioca root. Because of the starvation diet, prisoners were forced to eat snakes, lizards and insects. Dogs were cooked, and men were reduced to eating blue bottle larvae from out of the latrines.

POW Ration Officers were forced to receive and sign as correct, bags of rice, purporting to contain 100 kilograms, which in fact contained only 80 kilograms, and then sometimes warehouse sweepings including cement dust and rats' dirts.

Sgt Ito, in charge of rations stores, gave drunken parties, and lived far beyond a sergeant's means. He had two mistresses in Palembang, and had been handing in meat and fish to comfort houses. Lieut Yamakawa fed prisoners' ration vegetables and maize to his personal livestock.

Red Cross supplies, and medicines, were stolen by the guards.

Prisoners were made to work long hours in extremely high temperatures, and tropical rains. They had to work on constructing anti-aircraft gun emplacements, and searchlight positions, and to extend an airfield, contrary to conventions, and to repair lorries and instruments in the same category.

As punishment, men were made to stand for hours in the sun, often with tools held above their heads. A barbed wire cage was used as a cell. It was approximately 5' × 7'. At one time there were several in it. One man was confined for 60 days for stealing tapioca – he was allowed to wash once in 10 days.

For a time it was decreed that all orders were to be given in Japanese. This led to misunderstandings, and beatings.

Following an air raid alert, men were permitted to build trenches in their own time, but men who used the trenches during an air raid warning in August, 1944, were beaten up. After that, men were confined to the flimsy huts.

Men were paid 10 cents per day (NCOs slightly higher) for a full day's labour, in 1942. An egg cost 1½ guilders, so that it took 15 days work to buy an egg. Rampant inflation soon made money worthless.

There were examples of torture, with bamboo sticks between the fingers, caning, deprivation of drinking water, and the like.

Photograph of Palembang guards, taken at War Crimes trials in Singapore, during July and August, 1946.

No.	Name	Rank, and Nickname	Sentence 6/9/46	Appeal 13/11/46
1.	Hachisuka Kumitura	Captain Camp Commander	Death	Hanging 25/2/47
2.	Yamakawa Yasuji	Lieutenant Rations Officer	Death	Hanging 25/2/47
3.	Nakai Kosuka	Lieutenant Doctor	Death	15 years
4.	Ito Katsusaburo	Sergeant 'Squeaker'	Death	Hanging 22/11/46

5.	Onishi Shigezo	Sergeant 'Wolf'	Death	Hanging 22/11/46
6.	Kurata Takeo	Sergeant	Death	15 years
7.	Shirakawa Rakustiaku	'Pig Eyes'	18 years	10 years
8.	Takayama Haremitsu		20 years	10 years
9.	Matsumoto Hara yoshi	'Oil baron'	Life	15 years
10.	Kobayashi Torao	'Tor' or 'King Kong'	Death	Hanging 22/11/46
11.	Ishihara Tatsuo	'Bungo'	20 years	20 years
12.	Rayama Tokuishi	'Buff Head'	Life	Life
13.	Ohara Seiichiro	'Gladys'	Death	Life
14.	Kaneyama Shorei	'Black Mamba'	Death	Life
15.	Kaneshiro Kiei		12 years	10 years
16.	Watari Jiro	'Crank Handle'	20 years	10 years
17.	Kimura Tasei	'Pineapple'	20 years	10 years
18.	Kurekawa Zentaku	'Leggings'	Life	10 years
19.	Yasuda Yoshi		10 years	10 years
20.	Tomada Shakujin		3 years	3 years
21.	Okano Sakae		15 years	10 years
22.	Miyama		Acquitted	
23.	Kanemoto Yoshio	'Cats Eyes'	15 years	10 years
24.	Kuwa		Acquitted	

No. 1 – Capt. Hachisuka said camps of which he was Commandant were administered by the 25th Army in Sumatra, and he could not depart from Regulations. He said he had throughout pursued a humane policy towards POWs. Ration scales were fixed, and before the final cut in May 1945, he had no complaints about food. He said death rate was not known to him, and sick had never been made to work.

No. 2 – Yamakawa – (Rations Officer) claimed that all food was supplied by Palembang Supply Department, and he made up any deficiency in short weight sacks from his own reserve.

No. 3 – Lieut Nakai – (Doctor) said medical supplies were at no time sufficient, even for the Japanese. POWs were to receive one third of the Imperial Japanese Army scale.

No. 4 – Sergeant Ito – (subordinate of No. 2) denied misappropriating food by illegal sales, and in particular by gifts to comfort girls. He did not buy POW belongings at absurd prices. He denied beatings. He maintained that all POWs were adequately supplied with blankets, clothes and mosquito nets.

No. 5 – Onishi – (In charge of guards) admitted making wire cage on orders of Takahashi. Claimed never to have beaten POWs.

No. 6 – Kurata – (Sergeant in charge of vehicles), claimed never to have beaten POWs, or incited others to do so.

No. 7 – Shirakawa	
No. 8 – Takayama	All guards, said 1 and 2 had instructed them to
No. 9 – Matsumoto	beat POWs, but denied ill treatment
No. 10 – Kobayashi	
No. 11 – Ishihara	All guard commanders, admitted striking
No. 12 – Rayama	POWs, but did so to save them from more
No. 13 – Ohara	severe punishment, had they been reported. Denied watching beatings, without interfering.
No. 14 – Kaneyama	Denied being taken off duty as a result of complaints by Cdr Reid.
No. 15 – Kaneshiro	
No. 16 – Watari	
No. 17 – Kimura	
No. 18 – Kurekawa	All denied beatings.
No. 19 – Yasuda	They maintained that witnesses were lying.
No. 20 – Tomada	
No. 21 – Okano	
No. 22 – Kanemoto	

Lieut Takahashi (Japanese Second-in-Command to Capt Hashisuka) was killed in the Nationalist uprising in Indonesia. There is little doubt that had he survived, he would have been sentenced to death.

On behalf of the accused, various Regulations for the Treatment of Prisoners of War, were recited.

Article 2 provided that POWs were to be treated humanely, and were never to be ill-treated or insulted.

Article 4 decreed that POWs were to be controlled according to Japanese Army discipline, and except on those occasions, they were not to be put in any bodily restrictions causelessly.

Article 6 declared that if prisoners were disobedient, they may be confined, or bound, or put under any other necessary punishment. If POWs attempt to escape, military force may be used, and when necessary, they may be injured, or killed.

Major General Saito, the Chief of Malayan POW camps, stated that the Emperor had asked him "Are you taking good care of the POWs?". Thus, we Japanese were to take good care of the POWs, and that was our Emperor's will.

Capt Hachisuka said that he had given the POWs advice 'not to become weak and exhausted and to keep up their health'. He said that he lectured his guards once a month. At these lectures he told them not to drink too much and misbehave.

4, 5 and 6. Pleaded that they had definite orders from 1 to beat prisoners, which they could not disobey.

10, 13 and 14. Claimed to be Koreans, misled by Jap militarism, and pleaded superior orders. The accused were well identified by prosecution witnesses. The evidence showed ill-treatment meted out to POWs over a period of years, with savage ill-treatment in the mass, on several occasions. Guilt fully justified.

3. Representations were received from Dr J. G. Reed that Doctor Nakai was at no time guilty of acts of violence or brutality. He listened to complaints, but did nothing. He had a timid disposition, was wholly incompetent and ineffective, and evaded responsibilities wherever in conflict with Hachisuka. There was overwhelming evidence of frightful conditions in the POW hospital huts. There was a lack of blankets, drugs, medicines and equipment. Filth and squalor prevailed.

6. Forced sick POWs to do heavy manual work. Found guilty of three charges of ill-treatment, in one resulting in death, and in the other two of contributing to death. Evidence to show callous and brutal treatment. Hanging commuted to 15 years.

7 and 8. Continually beat POWs savagely, and were among worst in camp, but evidence indicates that they were incited to do so by Onishi. Sentences reduced to 10 years each.

9. This guard terrified the POWs. Of a low type. Beat men up in hospital. Forced men to sell scanty possessions at his price. Stole M and B tablets from Dr Reed. Record bad, but mitigate to 15 years.

10. Had been found guilty on four charges of ill-treatment. Beatings and savagery were such as to drive men to the grave. There is no evidence that he actually killed any POW outright, but there is evidence that he beat a man (Brophy) so badly that he went into decline, and died two months later. He beat men in three camps with brutal ferocity. King Kong is indication of how POWs regarded him. Sentence of Hanging confirmed.

11, 12 and 13. All Commanders of Korean guards, and could have stopped the brutal treatment. Far from doing so, they encouraged it, and themselves took an active part. Not much to choose between all three. Ohara (13) sentence commuted to Life.

14. Sadistic guard second only to Kobayashi in ferocity. It is said that beating he gave Private Fletcher resulted in his death, but this not fully proved. This case can be distinguished from Kobayashi. Commuted to Life.

15. Having regard to general incitement and brutality, two years of his

sentence remitted. Brings him in line with 7 and 8.

16. This man was a savage brute, but difficult to distinguish from others. 10 years would be adequate.

17. Ten years would be equitable.

18. Particularly brutal guard. On one occasion made a savage attack on British and Dutch, leaving eight men unconscious, and gave one man the cruellest individual beating witnessed. twenty years is excessive – suggest 10 years adequate.

19. No comments.

20. No comments.

21. Ten years ample.

23. Brutal type of man, but not proven to have taken part in any of the major incidents. Ten years adequate.

Colonel Officiating DJAG,
Allied Land Forces, South East Asia.

Closing Address by Defence Counsel

Defence Counsel wishes to express their extreme regret for the deaths of so many prisoners of war, whatever the actual causes may have been. For when the arduous conditions and difficult circumstances of those times are calmly weighed and considered in detail, it must be seen that the accused personnel arraigned before this Court, deserve on numerous accounts to be excused in that a criminal misdemeanour was never intended.

It has been made clear through the evidence given by defence witnesses that the fundamental policy of the Japanese Government towards the POW was that

1. POWs were not to be indulged or spoilt, but were to be treated correctly and fairly.

2. POWs were to be used for labour and production work for the Japanese Empire.

3. POWs were to be treated humanely, and international laws and regulations were to be applied.

By this it can be seen that there was never any intention, even remote, of making the feeding, or medical treatment, of POWs bad, or to reduce the physical condition of POWs purposely.

Reasons such as naval blockade were given for shortage of food and medical supplies.

It is claimed that each accused did not want to see POWs die or ill-treated, but also did not act viciously in waiting for the death, or causing ill-treatment of POWs.

They ran the camp faithfully and diligently, following the commands of their superiors.

We can nowhere find their will to commit to criminal offence.

It we take the unhealthy tropical climate, and sudden change in their mode of life into account, the death rates, 20 per 1000 in 1944, and 24 per 1000 in 1945, are just a reasonable rate of death, from which we may infer that the hygienic conditions were sufficiently good.

Various individual actions are recorded.

It is very regrettable that some guards slapped POWs once or twice – it was never done with malice. It was done to maintain discipline.

In conclusion, let us say in the hearing of this Honourable Court, that the tide having turned against the Japanese in the fortunes of war rapidly changing adversely, this gallant nation, now fighting alone against the world, it was natural that individual Japanese in parts of the widespread battle front should feel themselves 'up against things', and taking themselves severely to task, should discipline themselves with Spartan severity, and live as those who never expected to see their houses or loved ones again.

Is there any surprise therefore if we find them scornful of the milder ways of peace, and impatient with seeing sentiment. They may have been incensed that the prisoners of war in their midst should appear bright, blithe and blase (with secret radio news of daily victories to boost their morale), while they were fighting a losing battle, with their backs to the wall. They were angry, disappointed men, and there is little wonder that they often failed to treat the POWs as men could treat their friends.

Yet, they did feed, clothe, and protect, as to the very end, when all was lost for them, as many living, and rejoicing, POWs can testify – even here today, and in Singapore.

Let me, therefore, humbly beg this Court to take the sworn statements of the Officers accused.

They did actually show much kindness, and were definitely helpful, when there was no special call, by race, or cast, to do so.

T. ARAKI
Judge of the Nagoya District Court

Closing Address by Prosecuting Officer

Forty witnesses have given evidence, thirty three of these were actually prisoners, and five were Korean guards.

Evidence has not been lacking to show the cessation of privilege, the removal of rights, and the gradual degradation and indifference to the condition of the prisoners.

It is before the Court that air raid trenches available were forbidden to the POWs, herded like animals in their huts during raids, that POWs were engaged in work relating directly to the Japanese war effort.

POWs were also used for dangerous and unhealthy work, working hours were arduously long, without proper provision made for adequate rest.

It is on record that the first accused, far from instructing his subordinates regarding the rules relating to the treatment of prisoners, told them to beat prisoners.

The Commander suggested that Japanese themselves were dying, and there was nothing to be done about the POWs at all. In fact, the evidence shows that so far as these camps were concerned, not one Japanese died, as against nearly 400 prisoners.

The evidence tells of innumerable beatings. Some of these have been described, but many now will never be known.

Evidence has shown that there was plenty of food in Palembang, and that in August, 1945, when the war was over, so much food and stores generally poured into the camp, that the Rations Officer could not easily handle it. Cigarettes, bully beef, and other Red Cross articles were stolen.

There were few blankets, no sheets, mattresses, mosquito nets, or protective coverings.

The laws and usages of war require the provision of clothing, underwear and footwear.

If I see a man walking around with a piece of dirty, filthy rag tied to his loins, which is not really sufficient to cover his private parts, I should say he has no clothes.

Officers were beaten for not bowing. Guards entered huts during rest hours, and forced men to their feet, and beat those slower, with butt ends of rifles.

There is a great deal of evidence of beatings.

Details of the food allowances were given in full.

If you are satisfied beyond a reasonable doubt that the evidence in the case has established the guilt of all, or any, of the accused, then it is your duty to convict any one, or all of them.

F. E. Mostyn, Major, Prosecuting Office September 4th, 1946

Plea in Mitigation

The idea of punishing war criminals is to prevent future wars, and the disastrous casualties of war.

The aim is to bring peace and happiness in this world by making future war crimes impossible.

The Japanese, especially professional soldiers, were not taught that even war has its morals, and I believe that this lack of education was the main cause for the numerous war crimes committed.

The people have now realised their mistake.

We do believe that some of the war criminals, not many, but some of the more vicious, certainly should be sentenced to death. But on the other hand, those who do not fall into this category should be saved.

Christ said, "Love your enemies, and bless them that curse you."

What the Koreans did, they did because they had been educated under a system not of their choosing.

As members of the Japanese Army they were bound by orders, and could not go against them.

They were repeatedly told by Hachisuka and Yamakawa to beat the prisoners if they did not behave the way they were told to, and were bound by their masters' orders, and knew no other way.

One does not make a child responsible for its sometimes cruel, because childish, actions.

The fairness of British trials is known to all.

We submit the extenuating circumstances for the accused.

These are given for Doctor Nakai – extend its sympathy.

> Sergeant Ito – may the Court have mercy.
> Sergeant Onishi – he was sorry for the POWs, and put flowers on their graves.
> Sergeant Kurata – he was subject to superiors.
> Guard Kobayashi – he is not such a bad man, and we plead for his life.

As for the remaining accused, we beg the Court to give its most lenient judgement.

STATISTICS GIVEN DURING TRIAL

Camp Strength, May 1st, 1945	British	Dutch	TOTAL
	723	482	1205
Draft to Singapore, May 26th	144	118	262
Camp after Draft	636	523	1159
September 15th	532	367	899

Deaths during 1945

	British	Dutch	TOTAL
January	3	0	3
February	1	5	6
March	2	3	5
April	0	1	1
May	4	13	17
June	16	25	41
July	42	57	99
August	43	66	109
September (1/20)	7	3	10

In May 1945, a draft of 'Light Duty' men were sent to Singapore. Thus the rapidly escalating casualties were among the 'Heavy Duty', or so called fit men.

Appendix VII

EVENING ADVERTISER, SATURDAY, NOVEMBER 8, 1986

● Charlie Rogers then...

... and now

I'm a very lucky man

WHEN it comes to cheating death, Charlie Rogers knows more about it than most people.

As a Chief Petty Officer in the Navy during the war, he was sunk three times by Japanese ships.

And after the third time, he was captured by the enemy and spent a harrowing three years as a POW.

That third ship was the Li-Wo, a converted Chinese river boat with 150 men on board that accidentally stumbled across a 30-strong convoy of Japanese ships going to support their invasion of Singapore.

Totally outnumbered and outgunned, the Li-Wo nevertheless attacked and hit and rammed one of the convoy before being hit several times herself.

Even in the water, the danger was not over. The crews of the Japanese ships gleefully sprayed the floating Allied survivors with machine guns and only by pretending to be dead did Charlie avoid being hit.

Seven of them survived the sinking and these were captured a few days later when they reached land at Bangka Island in the Java Sea. The Japanese and sharks finished off the rest who survived the sinking.

For the next three years, Charlie — who now lives in Church Walk South, Rodbourne Cheney, Swindon — was a medical orderly in the prison camp that had over 450 inmates when he arrived in February 1942.

With virtually no medicines, a shortage of food and appalling conditions, very little could be done for the dozens who became ill.

"I just used to sit with them for the few hours before they died and keep the flies off — they always came buzzing in when someone was about to die," recalled Charlie.

Only 100 men were left when Charlie was sent home in September 1945. Disease and frequent beatings from their captors took care of the other 350.

Food was meagre and boring. "We ate nothing but rice for three-and-a-half years," said Charlie, who went from over 13 stone to around eight.

He served in the Navy for 25 years and was the last in a long line of Rogers to do so — Charlie's great-great-grandfather served on HMS Victory at the Battle of Trafalgar.

'We ate nothing but rice'

Appendix VIII

Courier and Advertiser, Saturday 2 November 1985   9

A-Bomb anniversary's special memories for Tarbert man

THIS YEAR'S anniversary of the dropping of the atomic bomb in Hiroshima, Japan during the second world war brought back memories for one local man who was a prisoner of war for over three years in a Japanese death camp.

Headlines in the national paper, "The Bulletin and Scots Pictorial" on Tuesday, October the 9th, 1945, read "Scottish P.O.W. is first to land," that man was 27 year old John MacMillan, Argyll House, Tarbert, who was the first prisoner of war from Singapore to step ashore at Liverpool.

Mr. MacMillan was a survivor of H.M.S. Prince of Wales which was sunk along with H.M.S. Repulse by Japanese aircraft off Singapore in 1942 in one of the worst naval disasters of the war.

After spending some time in the Queen Alexander Hospital, Singapore, he was one of the last of the evacuees before the fall to the Japanese.

But the boat he was on was captured by the Japanese and he was taken to Mentok Prison Camp, and then to Palembang, Sumatra.

"The dropping of the Hiroshima bomb in Japan saved our lives," Mr. MacMillan said, "for conditions inside the prison were deteriorating badly and as many as twenty men were dying each day."

The prison camp atrocities will remain fixed in the minds of those that survived the ordeal. Mr. MacMillan remembers having to boil maggots and then eat them because they were all so hungry.

John MacMillan, pictured in wartime

It was over two years before any prisoner was allowed to send home a postcard and even then they had to write set phrases such as I am being treated very well.

When they took our cards they proceeded to burn them in front of us to try and break our spirit."

The next plane which was able to carry our mail home crashed in Ireland but someone found the burnt remains of a few letters including a card sent to my mother and it was posted on. That was a chance in a million," he said.

The Monowai, a 10,000 ton New Zealand liner was the first of 16 ships which arrived in the Mersey with repatriates from the Middle East.

Mr. MacMillan remembers the landing well. The sirens of every ship roared out a welcome and river steamers circled the cheering happy homecomers. Relatives of the returning men had a grandstand view from the landing stage while thousands of Mersey side people gathered at the dock gates and lined the streets to the centre of the city to cheer.

The King sent a special message, and a printed copy of the message was sent to each man.

"The Bulletin and Scots Pictorial" wrote: "From the landing stage the men looked sunburned and healthy but closer in spection produced evidence of the ordeals they had undergone. Faces were gaunt, eyes were staring and many had an unhealthy palor."

Mr. John MacMillan

Appendix IX

Wynberg sculptress Jean Doyle's concept of what her statue of Able Seaman Just Nuisance could look like if mounted on a boulder, to be sited on Jubilee Square, Simon's Town.

Boulder chosen for Nuisance

Chief Reporter

A "MAGNIFICENT" granite boulder off Runciman Drive, Simon's Town, has been selected for possible use as a base for the life-size statue to be erected on Jubilee Square, Simon's Town, of the famous dog-of-war Able Seaman Just Nuisance, being sculpted by Wynberg artist Jean Doyle.

Mrs Doyle, recently declared the winner in a national competition for the best design for the statue, has produced a sketch of her "Nuisance-on-a-boulder" concept, which she feels would be preferable to a more formal type of memorial.

The boulder was chosen by Mrs Doyle and fellow-artist and sculptor Eduard Ladan of Kalk Bay, who said yesterday that it would make "a magnificent mounting for the statue".

Mrs Doyle's idea is to have flowers and other plants at the foot of the boulder, so that the statue will have a natural and attractive setting.

The statue is to be a permanent collection point for much-needed funds for the SPCA and the Animal Welfare Society.

● Donations to the memorial fund have been coming in slowly and only about R2 000 of the target figure of R10 000 has been raised so far.

Further contributions should be sent to: The Just Nuisance Memorial Fund, c/o the Town Clerk, PO Box 31, Simon's Town 7995.

"CAPE TIMES" DECEMBER 1984.

Appendix X

Royal Navy
British Pacific Fleet – Fleet Air Arm

In memory of

----- ● -----

S/Lt (A) J R Burns RNVR (P)	Lt(A) K M Burrenston RNVR (P)
S/Lt (A) D V Roebuck RNVR (O)	S/Lt (A) W E Lintern RNVR (O)
PO (A) I Barker (TAG)	PO (A) W J S McRae (TAG)

Two Crews from

849 TBR Squadron (Avengers) – HMS VICTORIOUS

----- ● -----

Lt (A) E J Baxter RNZNVR

S/L (A) R J Shaw RNVR

Pilots from

1833 Fighter Squadron (Corsairs) – HMS ILLUSTRIOUS

----- ● -----

Lt (A) J K Haberfield RNZNVR

Pilot from

1839 Fighter Squadron (Hellcats) – HMS INDOMITABLE

----- ● -----

Their aircraft were shot down during attacks on oil refineries at Palembang, Sumatra in January 1945. They were imprisoned at Changi Gaol, Singapore and executed by their Japanese captors at the war's end in August 1945.

"NONE OF US SHOULD FORGET"

Following the raids on Palembang in January 1945, nine Fleet Air Arm aviators were captured by the Japanese. They were taken to the Kempei Tai prison at Outram Road, Singapore, where they were kept in solitary confinement, and were beaten, tortured and starved. Several days after the cessation of hostilities on 15 August 1945, they were beheaded on a beach near Changi, and their weighted remains taken out to sea and thrown overboard.

The above inscription is that shown on a Memorial Stone at St Bartholomew's Church at RNAS Yeovilton, the Fleet Air Arm Memorial Church. There is a Plaque with identical wording at Changi Prison Chapel.